DAVID HUME

★

WRITINGS ON ECONOMICS

DAVID HUME
Medallion by Tassie
By courtesy of the Scottish National Portrait Gallery

DAVID HUME

★

WRITINGS ON ECONOMICS

Edited with an Introduction
by
EUGENE ROTWEIN

Essay Index Reprint Series

BOOKS FOR LIBRARIES PRESS
FREEPORT, NEW YORK

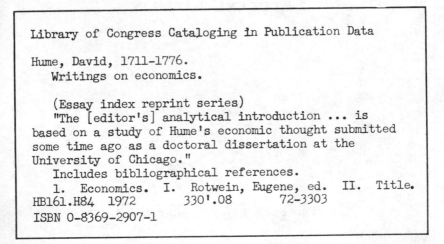

Library of Congress Cataloging in Publication Data

Hume, David, 1711-1776.
    Writings on economics.

    (Essay index reprint series)
    "The [editor's] analytical introduction ... is
based on a study of Hume's economic thought submitted
some time ago as a doctoral dissertation at the
University of Chicago."
    Includes bibliographical references.
    1. Economics. I. Rotwein, Eugene, ed. II. Title.
HB161.H84 1972   330'.08   72-3303
ISBN 0-8369-2907-1

CONTENTS

PREFACE

DAVID HUME belonged to the same generation as that of his friend and fellow-countryman Adam Smith. He was twelve years Smith's senior. Though in many ways the interests of the two were similar, Hume's economic writings, unlike Smith's, comprise a relatively small portion of his published works. They consist of nine of twelve essays in *Political Discourses*, an octavo volume of just over 300 pages, first published in 1752, and a rather small number of passages in Hume's extant private letters to such correspondents as Smith, Montesquieu, Turgot and Oswald. They are here brought together for the first time in a single volume.

Those portions of the letters which have been reproduced contain such relevant material from both sides of Hume's correspondence as appears to be significant. This accounts for most of the relevant correspondence now apparently extant ; other correspondence of a comparatively minor importance or fragmentary nature is noted at pertinent places. This is, I think, the first time that both sides of Hume's correspondence on economic questions have been printed together in one sequence. Though less valuable than the essays, it contains some interesting debate, and while casting light on the growth of some of Hume's ideas, it helps to amplify the argument of the essays.

A word is required concerning the inclusion of the essay "Of the Populousness of Ancient Nations". On the basis of present disciplinary classifications, especially in their narrower constructions, much of this would fall outside the scope of an "economic essay". I have included it not only because it is germane to the development of economic thought, but also because when published in 1752 it was a milestone in the empirical treatment of

vii

questions about population. As a study involving the extensive use and evaluation of evidence on an important question with numerous related facets, it is a work for which Hume has long been known ; and, in its broader dimensions, I believe that, along with other of the essays, it should prove of interest to students of many of the social sciences.

The analytical introduction which precedes the essays is based on a study of Hume's economic thought submitted some time ago as a doctoral dissertation at the University of Chicago. For very considerable and generous assistance in the preparation of the earlier study, I am indebted to Professors Frank H. Knight and Jacob Viner. I am similarly indebted to Professor Ronald S. Crane, whose suggestive ideas proved very fruitful while I was engaged in framing the broad philosophical pattern of my analysis. I also wish to express my appreciation to Professors Martin Bronfenbrenner and James S. Earley, who read parts of the manuscript and gave freely of their time in discussing it, and to Professor Rondo E. Cameron who reviewed parts of the historical material of the opening chapter. Any errors of fact or interpretation are of course entirely my own.

The greater part of the painstaking work of checking the various editions of Hume's economic essays was done, and very ably, by Mr Taro Yamane, whose assistance was made possible by a grant from the Research Committee of the University of Wisconsin. I also wish to thank this committee for providing a summer grant to aid in the preparation of this volume. Miss Geraldine Hinkel and Mrs Josephine Bradley gave invaluable help in typing various portions of the manuscript.

I should like, most of all, to express my deep gratitude to my wife, Jane, who unselfishly assumed many of the tasks associated with this undertaking.

E. R.

INTRODUCTION

Chapter I

THE BACKGROUND

DAVID HUME was born in Edinburgh in 1711 and died there in 1776, not long after the publication of Adam Smith's *Wealth of Nations*. The essays reprinted in this volume were, with one exception,[1] originally published in 1752 under the title *Political Discourses*. In a period of very considerable intellectual activity Hume was perhaps as acutely aware of the general character and tendencies of his time as any of his greatest contemporaries; and, like other of his writings, his economic essays—though displaying a broad theoretical sweep—sought to clarify the problems of his society and to suggest remedies for their solution. In viewing them two centuries later it is well therefore to recall, if only briefly, some general aspects of the scene upon which they appeared.

Hume wrote virtually on the eve of the "industrial revolution". Still ahead lay the thoroughgoing mechanisation of industry, an extensive factory system, and the full ascendancy of the industrial capitalist. The economic changes which were to come, however, were products of a period of ferment which had begun long before. By Hume's time, much of the transition had already been completed and in the broader sense a significant, if preparatory, phase of the industrial revolution had already run its course. Perhaps most striking in this connexion was the remarkable expansion of trade which had taken place in the preceding centuries. The markets of the Middle Ages, which were by no means insignificant, had developed into an intricate distributive network which

---

[1] "Of the Jealousy of Trade", which appeared in 1758.

already linked widely separated areas of England to one another, to the European continent, the East, and the New World. It appears on the basis of available evidence that between the early part of the seventeenth and the middle of the eighteenth century alone, England's foreign trade had increased roughly seven-fold. The expansion of trade in turn had facilitated other important changes. Encouraged by increasing quantities of capital and by new techniques and products, both of which came in no small measure from abroad, Britain's industry was growing at a rapid rate. Helping to provide the necessary food supply for the growing industrial population, new methods of cultivation had already been introduced on the farm. These had disrupted the traditional open-field system ; and land, drawn increasingly into the orbit of commercial enterprise, had already substantially become a marketable commodity and a profitable investment for the rising monied class.

The character of productive relations was also undergoing change. Not only had the "gild" system, with control of the productive process vested in the artisan, begun to give way to the "putting-out" system—the merchant now owning the materials and marketing the finished product—but there was already considerable evidence of a nascent factory system, and labour forces working within the entrepreneur's plant sometimes ran into the hundreds. Consisting in large measure of both artisans and small farmers—tenants and owners alike who had been forced out by the enclosures—this group was rapidly assuming the characteristics of a "working class", and suffering as it did from periodic enforced idleness (and allegedly given to voluntary idleness as well), it had already become one of the major socio-economic problems of the period.

In the accommodation to this general expansionary process, changes of an important nature had already taken place in England's credit system as well. Book credit and the bill of exchange had been introduced. Although still in embryo, and not very extensive outside London, a modern banking system issuing its own notes had begun to develop. The Bank of England itself had been in existence for over fifty years. Forms of business organisation had likewise been altered as increased capital requirements led to the development of the partnership and the joint stock company. In all, England was in a mature stage of what is commonly termed "merchant capitalism", with far more than faint suggestions of the approaching full industrialisation of her economy already apparent.

As is not uncommon, the pace of economic events had not been uniformly paralleled by changes in the legal and institutional framework of society. The practices of both the feudal order and the mercantilist state which followed reflected the belief that the pursuit of individual interest, unless closely controlled, would conflict with the social interest ; and in Hume's time many of the resulting regulations were still in existence. But, as a result of the growing influence of the entrepreneurial class—which, joined with liberating political and religious forces, found its fullest expression in the revolutions of the seventeenth century—many of the traditional internal regulations had been weakened ; some were rapidly falling into decay, and the trend was unmistakably, if somewhat haltingly, toward increasing individualism and a free-market economy. Wage-fixing, for example, continued, but largely on a local and increasingly erratic basis ; the practice of fixing terms of employment, which interfered with entrepreneurial control of investment, had lapsed altogether ; apprenticeship regulations, which with wage-fixing were the primary obstructions to a free labour-market, had lost their legal sanction, but persisted through the influence of custom ; price-control was no longer extensively employed, although introduced periodically on various necessities such as bread and coal. In this process it was inevitable that the authority of the gilds would shrink, and, though still in existence, by Hume's time they were rapidly becoming vestigial institutions. The major exception to this trend lay in the continuing control of international trade. The mercantilist state, as is well known, had developed an elaborate network of restrictions on foreign trade. It was not until the latter part of the eighteenth century that this regulatory structure began to give way, and not until the first part of the nineteenth—with the abandonment of the Corn Laws— that Britain fully committed herself to the policy of liberalism in her international relations that had so long before taken root at home.

If institutional arrangements had not kept uniformly abreast of economic developments, this, as might be expected, was no less true of the state of thought concerning economic affairs. This is reflected in the prevailing treatments of the ethical aspects of economic pursuits by professional moralists. It is a widely accepted view that, particularly in its Calvinist variant, the Protestant Reformation provided a religious sanction for the growing commercial spirit. This, however, applied to economic activity, not to the indulgence in luxury which, as before, was regarded as sinful and generally as the source of evil. The basis for a more thoroughgoing secular morality had already been laid in various writings of a utilitarian nature. But some of the outstanding British moralists of the period (Shaftesbury and Hutcheson) still frowned on the emphasis on material values. Moreover, one of the most notorious of the utilitarian and materialistic writings of the time was Mandeville's *Fable of the Bees* (1705–29), and the deliberately scandalising vein in which Mandeville wrote may itself be regarded as some indication of the extent to which the writings of an ethical character still reflected the more traditional attitudes toward luxury.

A similar mixed pattern characterised economic analysis and discussions of economic policy. For a long period economic thought had been dominated by the mercantilist writings—a heterogeneous and often conflicting body of ideas authored to a considerable degree by merchants and men of practical affairs. The heterogeneity of the writings has given rise to various interpretations of their major elements. Several have found the key explanatory principle in a particular political orientation and have argued that the most general rationale of mercantilist theory is to be found in a predominating concern with state power or with "state-building"[1] This view has recently been rejected by one writer.[2]

Among the purely economic considerations several elements stand out. As characteristic as any was the belief in the importance of a favourable balance of trade which, in its fullest elaboration, provided a general theoretical basis for prevailing foreign-trade policy. In part this view was premised on the direct influence of a favourable balance on domestic employment and output. This reflected a concern both with the protection of existing industry and with the development of additional productive capacity ; and this latter was also reflected, among other ways, in an interest in such matters as the skill, diligence, and growth of the population.[3] The protectionist objective appeared especially compelling because of a widespread assumption that the economic opportunities of the world were rigidly circumscribed, hence that nations could prosper only at one another's expense.

Perhaps even more pronounced in the literature was the attention given to the direct relationship between the balance of trade and money. The reason for the mer-

---

[1] This is the view taken by Eli Hecksher, among others. Cf. his *Mercantilism* (London 1934), VOL. II, pp. 13 ff.

[2] Cf. J. Viner, "Power versus Plenty as Objectives of Foreign Policy, in the Seventeenth and Eighteenth Century", *World Politics*, I (Oct. 1945), 1–29.

[3] Cf. Hecksher, *op. cit.*, pp. 157 ff., and E. A. J. Johnson, *Predecessors of Adam Smith* (New York 1937), pp. 259 ff.

cantilist emphasis on the acquisition of specie (through a favourable trade balance) has also been a matter of dispute. During the period itself some writers tacitly assumed or, as in the case of Adam Smith, pointedly charged that the mercantilists were generally guilty of identifying money with wealth. In substantially modified form this charge has been repeated by modern critics.[1] Others have rejected it as a position too patently absurd to be held by anyone, though, whatever they may have known apart from their technical discussions, it seems clear that the mercantilists often wrote as though they were making this identification. It is clear, however, that among a substantial number of mercantilists money was not desired in itself but mainly because of its beneficial effects on trade. The literature contains numerous references to the need of money to "drive trade", and in some cases it was recognised, in a departure from the usual stress on specie and the balance of trade, that paper money would serve this purpose equally well.[2] A similar and related monetary emphasis appeared in another connexion. Money was regarded as the determinant of interest rates and the need for an increase in its supply was stressed as a means of lowering production costs and enabling the producer and merchant to compete on more favourable terms with foreigners.

A considerable literature also developed around the issue of the (alleged) idleness of the labouring class. Reflecting an interest in economic psychology, this was another facet of the concern with national productive capacity. On this question there was a very substantial measure of agreement. It was commonly believed that labour—possessed by a chronic indisposition toward work—would forgo leisure only for a relatively fixed

[1] Cf. J. Viner, *Studies in the Theory of International Trade* (New York 1937), pp. 15 ff. On this issue Hecksher is rather equivocal. Cf. *op. cit.*, pp. 185 ff.

[2] The best known proposal of this type is to be found in John Law, *Money and Trade Consider'd : with a Proposal for Supplying the Nation with Money* (London 1720).

income made up of subsistence and the "low" pleasures of "tippling and carousing in the alehouse". Writers of this persuasion argued that the only way to evoke increased effort was through a decrease in real wages, and from this point of view regarded both higher prices and higher excises on items consumed by labour as socially desirable. Apparently inspired by a desire for a cheap and large labour-supply intermixed, if not mainly cloaked, with the nationalistic purpose of enhancing England's economic power and prestige, this view has been aptly characterised as a belief in the "utility of poverty".[1]

The foregoing doctrines are those which were more generally characteristic of the writings before Hume. However, the earlier writings also contained many, if frequently scattered, anticipations of the major features of later doctrine, and a few were already almost wholly in this later tradition. In various of the writings, attention is given the desire for increased consumption (and for the merchant also monetary gain) as an incentive essential to economic activity and its growth and, departing from the more common view, this was seen as applicable to the mass of labour.[2] Though generally their position called for restrictions on international trade, not an insignificant number displayed an appreciation of the free-trade position in the domestic area, and, arguing from the advantages of international specialisation, some applied the doctrine to foreign trade as well.[3] There were also important signs of a departure from the prevailing preoccupation with money. Anticipating the later more common assumption of conditions of full employment, the argument that more money only meant higher prices (the quantity theory) had long before appeared in the literature, if often only in *ad hoc* form. Correlatively, some had argued that interest-rates were determined

---

[1] Cf. E. S. Furniss, *The Position of the Laborer in a System of Nationalism* (Cambridge, Mass., 1920), esp. chaps. 6 and 7.
[2] Cf. Viner, *op. cit.*, pp. 56-7.   [3] *Op. cit.*, pp. 91-108.

by the supply and demand, not for money, but for real capital.[1] The most general rationale of the mercantilist restrictions on international trade had itself been called into question as—linking specie flows to quantity theory considerations or to effects on income and demand— several writers had grasped, with differing degrees of adequacy, the idea of a self-regulating mechanism in the distribution of the world specie supply.[2] It is clear that Hume was writing during a period of marked transition. The "old" economics was slowly giving way to the "new", but, as is to be expected, in an uncertain manner and with the outlines of its future direction not clearly established.

*

These background considerations provide a brief view of some of the relevant general elements in the external setting of Hume's economic essays. Long recognised as a major influence in the transition from mercantilist to classical doctrine, Hume's economic thought has often been examined, and in a variety of ways. This is primarily an internal study. It is mainly concerned with the relations between different parts of Hume's own analysis, and it selects for special attention two of its aspects : the places it accords psychology and historical (or developmental) process. Needless to say, in this respect (as in others) Hume's economic thought exhibits direct relations to the earlier writings. While it is not part of the central purpose of this study to explore these relations in detail, several of these will be mentioned at pertinent points.

In an internal study of Hume's economic thought there is justification for giving primary place to its psychological and historical elements. These two elements persist throughout virtually his entire analysis. They

---

[1] Cf. below, p. lxvii *n*.   [2] Cf. Viner, *op. cit.*, pp. 74–87.

comprise its dominant emphasis, shape its general pattern
and determine the manner in which he developed most of
his major doctrines.

Furthermore, when attention is given to these elements,
a fundamental relationship between Hume's economic
thought and his philosophical thought is exposed. This
relationship throws considerable light on his general
emphasis. Though in dealing with psychology and
historical process Hume developed strains already present
in the economic literature, this relation between his
economic and philosophical thought explains why he
selected these strains for such explicit and full elaboration.
While of widely varying importance in particular writings,
generally speaking these strains of thought had earlier
not received equally extensive and systematic treatment.
Hume's philosophical perspective also sheds light on many
specific dimensions of his analysis. Indeed, it is proper
to regard his philosophical perspective as the most important internal factor shaping his appraisal of the different
aspects of prevailing economic doctrine and his approach
to the various issues of his period.

To stress these relationships also seems appropriate in
view of the treatment commonly accorded to Hume's
economic analysis in the histories of economic doctrine.
For though Hume is widely recognised as one of the great
eighteenth-century "philosopher-economists", the critical
literature, with infrequent exception, has treated his
economic analysis as an isolated compartment of his
thought. This treatment along with the primary attention
given the mechanical aspects of his analysis has obscured
the significance of its psychological and historical dimensions.[1] Before dealing with the substance of the essays it

---

[1] In a general fashion the psychological and historical elements in
Hume's economics are noted by J. K. Ingram, *A History of Political Economy*
(London 1915), esp. pp. 82–4 and J. Bonar, *Philosophy and Political Economy
in their Historical Relations* (London 1893), esp. pp. 105, 111, 121. In his
study of Hume as a "Synthetist" E. A. J. Johnson (cf. *op. cit.*, pp. 161 ff.)
deals with these matters and in various contexts clearly sees the role of

is well, therefore, to consider briefly the general character of Hume's philosophical "system".

Hume's economic writings belong to a large group of essays which first began to appear shortly after he published his maiden work—*A Treatise of Human Nature* (1739)—a work which, although now recognised as his greatest achievement, received little recognition during his own time. Hume himself regarded his *Treatise* as having fallen "dead-born from the press".[1] The first series of this group of essays was entitled *Essays Moral and Political* (1741), and these, together with his later *Political Discourses* and several additions, were subsequently incorporated into a larger volume entitled *Essays Moral, Political, and Literary* (1758).[2] Following the customary usage of his time, the term "moral" was meant to denote all aspects of individual psychology (including ethics proper), while "politics", as a further extension of the "moral" sciences, dealt with all economic as well as political relations or, in Hume's own words, with "men as united in society and dependent on each other". As indicated by the titles, the scope of these essays was very

---

[1] Cf. Hume's brief autobiography, *My Own Life*, in *Letters of David Hume*, ed. J. Y. T. Greig (Oxford 1932), VOL. I, pp. 1–7 and in *Philosophical Works of David Hume*, ed. T. H. Green and T. H. Grose (London 1898), VOL. III, p. 2. (All future citations to this will be referred to as *Phil. Wks.*) Greig notes that the first edition of Hume's *Treatise*, totalling one thousand copies, "satisfied English readers for 80 years". Cf. his *David Hume* (London 1931), p. 106.

[2] Green and Grose provide a thorough discussion of the various editions of Hume's essays. Cf. *Phil. Wks.*, VOL. III.

---

psychology and history in Hume; but he does not relate this to a more general scheme and its significance within Hume's economic thought is not fully developed. A major exception to the more usual treatments of Hume's economics is the work of A. Schatz, *L'Oeuvre économique de David Hume* (Paris 1902)—an excellent analysis which, it appears, has suffered from serious neglect. Though in many respects the points made in this and Schatz's study are similar, the basis for this analysis was completed before Schatz's work was seen. Because there are differences between the two—in scope, perspective and in the emphasis on history as against psychology—it, however, is well worth while consulting Schatz's study as well.

extensive. When Hume undertook to consider economic matters he had already in fact treated various facets of virtually the whole range of the human sciences, and aspects of the humanities as well.

Read without careful reference to the *Treatise*, these essays, however, give but little evidence of any intrinsic dependence upon Hume's philosophy. For example, the essays generally do not contain references to the body of his philosophy proper, and it would seem clear that here, as in other of his post-*Treatise* works, Hume was deliberately writing in "the easy style and manner" of the man of letters.[1] Indeed it has been explicitly held or implied that there is in fact little connexion between the *Treatise* and his essays as a whole. The philosophers themselves have sometimes charged that in undertaking the latter, Hume was entirely abandoning his earlier philosophical interests for the sake of a literary fame which his *Treatise* failed to bring him. And in answering the charge his recent biographer, Greig, is led to adopt a position at the other extreme. For him the true Hume was the Hume of the essays and the *Treatise* "really was a youthful aberration, a sort of accident in David's life".[2] That in the essays Hume, generally speaking, was no longer dealing with the highly technical and abstruse aspects of philosophy is, of course, undeniable. It is also not implausible that Hume's disappointment with the *Treatise* was at least in some part responsible for his turning to the more popular essay form. However, that he was not here entirely forsaking the general intentions with which he wrote the *Treatise* is quite apparent in his own statement on the broader purpose of his philosophy.

Like Locke and Hobbes before him, in undertaking a

---

[1] Cf. for example the opening statements to his *Enquiry Concerning Human Understanding*, in *Hume's Enquiries*, ed. L. A. Selby-Bigge (Oxford 1936), pp. 1 ff. This work itself represented an attempt to simplify Book I of his *Treatise of Human Nature*. (All further references to this *Enquiry* as well as his *Enquiry Concerning the Principles of Morals* will be to this edition.)

[2] Cf. his *David Hume*, p. 166.

study of human nature Hume sought not merely to ascertain the character of the human percipient but also thereby to lay a firmer basis for a study of all aspects of man's experience. This he makes clear in the introductory comments to the *Treatise*, where he opens with a general criticism of prevailing highly rationalistic systems of philosophy. "Principles taken upon trust, consequences lamely deduced from them, want of coherence in the parts, and of evidence in the whole, these are everywhere to be met with in the systems of the most eminent philosophers, and seem to have drawn disgrace upon philosophy itself".[1] His *Treatise*, he announces, will seek to remedy these deficiencies by reconstructing philosophy upon a comprehensive analysis of human nature. This latter, he regards, as the "capital or centre" of all the sciences. "'Tis evident, that all the sciences have a relation, greater or less, to human nature ; and that however wide any of them may seem to run from it, they still return back by one passage or another".[2] As their subject-matter takes form within the human mind, this, he points out, is true even with respect to such sciences as "Mathematics, Natural Philosophy and Natural Religion", and, needless to say, it is especially true in the case of the "moral" sciences, such as logic, morals, politics and criticism. Thus, "In pretending . . . to explain the principles of human nature, we in effect propose a compleat system of the sciences, built on a foundation almost entirely new, and the only one upon which they can stand with any security".[3]

When undertaking the *Treatise*, it is apparent then that Hume had in mind a twofold process. In the first and what may be termed the analytical phase of his inquiry, he would distil from all human experience those qualities and relations which seemed to be common to mankind as a

---

[1] *A Treatise of Human Nature*, ed. L. A. Selby-Bigge (Oxford 1888), p. xvii. (All future citations will be from this edition, which will be referred to as *Treatise*.)   [2] *Op. cit.*, p. xix.   [3] *Op. cit.*, p. xx.

whole, the underlying structure of all human behaviour. This is considered in Books I and II of the *Treatise*, under the headings "Of the Understanding" and "Of the Passions" respectively, and forms the body of his "principles of human nature", or as he sometimes called it, his "science of man". The second part of the process—the synthetic phase—would then consist of the application of these principles to the various realms of experience for the purpose of organising their complicated relations into general uniformities, or what may perhaps be termed "laws of behaviour". These laws, which explain how man behaves in response to specific stimuli, would thus make up the substance of the various branches of the "moral" sciences (which were left largely to the essays) ; and, taken together, the two parts of this system—the principles and laws—would form a single organon, a comprehensive science of human experience. What is most interesting, moreover, is that Hume makes it clear at the outset that he himself intended to employ his principles of human nature as the basis for exploring the field of economics, (i.e. "politics"), among the other "moral sciences" ; and, to accommodate these, he had originally planned to expand the *Treatise*. This is indicated in the frequently overlooked Advertisement prefixed to its first printing. *"If I have the good fortune to meet with success, I shall proceed to the examination of* morals, politics *and* criticism ; *which will compleat this,* Treatise of human nature".[1] It is to be noted, too, that a portion of this original programme was later fulfilled. A third book on ethics proper subsequently was added to the *Treatise*, and, in its treatment of the origin and development of "justice", this also dealt in large part with "politics".

This brief treatment of Hume's philosophical system suffices to indicate the central importance of psychology within his broad science of human experience. There remains to be considered the role of history. As the

---

[1] Italics in original.

age of Voltaire, Gibbon, Robertson, among others, the eighteenth century as a whole was unusually conscious of the importance of the study of man's past, and, although it is now sometimes forgotten, Hume was in this respect one of its most distinguished figures. Both during his own lifetime and for several decades after it was largely for his achievements as an historian that he received recognition. The full fruition of this interest did not come until the last part of his writing career with the completion of the several volumes of his pioneering and highly controversial *History of England* (1757–62). As a philosophical empiricist, however, Hume's interest in history was of long standing. Statements concerning the indispensability of history to human knowledge appear repeatedly in his technical philosophy and elsewhere,[1] and indeed there is evidence in an early work that his historical interest antedated the *Treatise*.[2] But, what is most significant, long before the *History of England* Hume had sought with the aid of his principles of human nature to develop what was essentially a form of scientific history, or, as he sometimes called it, "natural history". As a synonym for "scientific", the term "natural" here denotes the most probable or the "usual", and within his historical contexts it thus refers to those broad historical movements which under the specified conditions could be expected to recur. The sequences of "natural history" contrast then with those of the more conventional variety, including much of Hume's own *History of England*, which are concerned with the specific and the unique events of history.

It has been said that the nucleus of this type of history is to be found in Hume's own principles of human nature. So seen, these histories then are properly to be regarded

[1] Cf. below, p. xxvii and *n*.
[2] The work indicated can be found in E. C. Mossner, "David Hume's 'An Historical Essay on Chivalry and Modern Honour'," in *Modern Philology*, xlv (August 1947), pp. 54–60. Mossner believes it probable that this essay was written between 1725 and 1727 while Hume was still attending college.

as parts of his more general science of human experience. That is, in treating the general aspects of the process of social change—such as changes in "habits, customs and manners"—Hume was attempting to show that they were the normal effects of changing environmental forces operating most basically on the intensity and direction of human passions or, in a word, that they could be reduced to well-defined historical laws of behaviour.[1] Like many other studies of this period—variously called "theoretical", "ideal", or "conjectural" history and the "*histoire raisonée*" of the French [2]—this type of history frequently drew upon inference from general observation for purposes of eliminating the gaps in recorded history or for historical projection; but to a large degree it represented a genuine attempt to reconcile the general speculative sequences with the available historical data, although in many cases this was of course deficient at the time.

Only one history bears the term "natural" in its title —the *Natural History of Religion*. But as one studies Hume's various writings it becomes apparent that histories of this kind or small groups of generalisations approximating to them in differing degree are to be found scattered throughout a wide variety of contexts. This is likewise true of his economics. Apart from the avoidance

---

[1] Though largely of the more conventional type, the *History of England* likewise reflects much of Hume's characteristic emphasis on psychology; moreover, in separate sections at the ends of chapters an attempt is made to summarise changes in "manners, customs and habits" and in their generality these approximate the sequences of his "natural" histories. It is interesting to note that a near contemporary of Hume's stated that Hume's *History of England* "has been aptly styled the 'History of English Passions, by Human Reason'." Anonymous introduction to the *Private Correspondence of David Hume with Several Distinguished Persons between the Years 1761–1776* (London 1820), p. iii.

[2] In this connexion see Dugald Stewart, "An Account of the Life and Writings of Adam Smith", in his edition of the latter's *Essays on Philosophical Subjects* (London 1795), p. xxxiii; F. J. Teggart, *The Theory of History* (New Haven 1925), p. 87; and Gladys Bryson, *Man and Society: The Scottish Inquiry of the Eighteenth Century* (Princeton 1932), pp. 85, 109.

of any technical references to his "science of man", the extent to which the method of natural history plays a role in the economic essays is obscured by the special nature of his context. As Hume was interested in dealing with specific economic problems, his organisation is shaped primarily by the requirements of these. The historical sequences do not appear in a conspicuously systematic form. Moreover, in his discussion of the issues of his time, he was led to introduce considerations which do not reflect this historical perspective. When all its applications are considered, however, it is found that this perspective plays so dominant a role in his analysis, that, if Hume's economic thought is in any sense a "system", it may be said that it is from this that it derives its major principle of organisation.

This is best seen when his economic thought is treated as a composition of laws developed on three levels of analysis. The first is his economic psychology. This is the most basic level, for, as it is concerned with the motives underlying economic activity, it is here that his economics, as one of the "moral sciences", is joined to the "capital or centre" as developed in the *Treatise*. On this level the historical analysis takes the form of what Hume refers to in one place as a natural history of "the rise and progress of commerce".[1] More particularly, in this context of considerations Hume is seeking to frame a generalised account of the then unfolding expansion of economic activity in terms of the effect of certain influences on particular human passions. Here these passions are regarded specifically as "causes of labour".[2]

[1] Cf. below p. xxx. Among earlier discussions of the growth of economic activity to which Hume's treatment exhibits a similarity cf. Daniel Defoe, *A Plan of the English Commerce* (London 1749), chap. 1 ; Nicholas Barbon, *A Discourse of Trade*, ed. J. H. Hollander (London 1609), esp. pp. 13–14, 23–5 ; Dudley North, *Discourses Upon Trade*, ed. J. H. Hollander (London 1691), esp. p. 27. Particular aspects of these are likewise germane to other parts of Hume's analysis. Various of these relations are indicated below.

[2] Cf. below, p. 11.

The next level of analysis concerns the largest part of the material of the essays—Hume's political economy proper, where he deals with specific aspects of market relations. Here the general sequences treated in the "natural history" provide the framework for most of his analysis of the issues of his period. For throughout, either by general reference or by further elaboration, he seeks primarily to show that a correct and fully adequate treatment of these issues requires a careful consideration of the economic implications of this same historical process.[1]

The last, and in a sense the highest, level of his analysis may be termed his economic philosophy. This takes the form of a comprehensive moral evaluation of a commercial society ; and in this frame of reference the role of the "natural history" is especially conspicuous. For it is through a generalised comparison of such a society with earlier forms that he seeks to provide a basis for appraisal. Here the "causes of labour" are now treated as ends or as norms for judgment, and the growth of economic activity itself is now related to other important areas of social experience. When viewed as a whole it may indeed be said that Hume's economic essays display a procedure which parallels that found within the *Treatise* itself. For even in its more technical parts, for example Book I, his method is historical in that he seeks the simplest components and relationships underlying the human understanding through an analysis of what he believes to be a life-history of individual experience ; while various portions of Book III, which deal with the development of justice, provide one of the more striking examples of the method of natural social history.[2]

Because of its general significance for an understanding

---

[1] This also explains Hume's attempt to reconcile divergent views. See, e.g., below, pp. lxiii–lxvii, lxx–lxxii, lxxvii–lxxviii, lxxxiii ; and cf. Johnson, *op. cit.*, for some different and in part dubious constructions of the "synthetic" elements in Hume.

[2] This was first pointed out to me by Professor R. S. Crane.

Introduction

of Hume's economic thought—as well as for general
taxonomic purposes—this threefold classification of the
material of his essays will be used as the scaffolding for
the remaining discussion. Before turning to this, one
further general question remains to be considered. It
has been said that in his treatment of "politics" as one
of the "moral sciences" Hume sought systematically to
develop laws of behaviour based on his "science of man".
To what extent did he believe that generalisations so
arrived at in this field would serve as a truly reliable basis
for prediction? It is not surprising to find that Hume
had a good deal to say on this issue. The relevant statements appear in a variety of contexts and are not wholly
organised. But on the whole it would seem appropriate
to say that his position in this regard was one of guarded
optimism.

Considering the most general principles underlying his
methodology, as is well known, in his *Treatise* (specifically
Book I) Hume had argued that the notion of causality was
not self-evident but was derived wholly from experience.
As he had pointed out, the ideas of cause and effect, as
"distinct ideas", were separable from one another, or we
can "conceive any object to be non-existent this moment,
and existent the next, without conjoining to it the distinct
idea of a cause or productive principle". What is conceivable, however, is possible ; and any principle is
"demonstrable" only if its opposite is shown to be impossible. Hence, the necessity of a cause cannot be
demonstrated as can an idea whose verification depends
solely upon its logical relations to other ideas.[1] Belief in
casual relations he therefore regarded as essentially a
"habit" based upon a psychological process. All that he
could find, more particularly, was that from the repeated
observation of recurring and spatially contiguous events
("constant conjunctions") the mind, simply through a
non-rational associative mechanism, so firmly linked the

[1] *Treatise*, pp. 79-80.

xxvi

impression of an object with the idea of its usual attendant, that the appearance of the former induced a belief in the necessary coexistence of the latter.[1] However, if we have no *a priori* justification for our "beliefs" (if our convictions concerning the uniformity of nature rest in fact on nothing but faith), none the less, he pointed out, as active minds continually facing the necessity of adjusting to experience we have no alternative to their acceptance.[2] As a means of enlarging our understanding of the existential relations between things, we can therefore do nothing but continue to investigate experience with a view to ascertaining further "constant conjunctions".

This, in brief, was the methodological basis of Hume's "philosophical scepticism". And it was this primarily which led him to a study of history. As he recognised, experimentation in the laboratory sense in the "moral sciences" is impracticable. "When I am at a loss to know the effects of one body upon another in any situation, I need only put them in that situation, and observe what results from it. But should I endeavour to clear up after the same manner any doubt in moral philosophy, by placing myself in the same case with that which I consider, 'tis evident this reflection and premeditation would so disturb the operation of my natural principles, as must render it impossible to form any just conclusion from the phaenomenon". Our "experiments" concerning human behaviour must therefore be derived "from a cautious observation of human life and [we must take] them as they appear in the course of the world, by men's behaviour in company, in affairs, and in their pleasures".[3]

---

[1] More particularly, Hume held that one believed in the necessary coexistence of the usual attendant because, through association, the idea of this latter acquired some of the "force" or "vivacity" of the present impression. Cf. *op. cit.*, p. 96.

[2] A good statement of this dilemma appears in his *An Enquiry concerning Human Understanding*, p. 38.

[3] *Treatise*, p. xxiii. And as he says in his essay "Of the Study of History": "I must add, that history is not only a valuable part of knowledge, but opens the door to many other parts, and affords materials to most of the

It would seem clear, however, that with regard to the principles of human nature Hume believed that history had already provided sufficient "experiments" for the formation of at least reasonably reliable propositions. Indeed, from various of his remarks, it would appear that he thought the uniformity in man's basic structural characteristics to be so marked that "history informs us of nothing new or strange in this particular",[1] which in his terms would mean that propositions concerning them would be "proofs" or "entirely free from doubt and uncertainty".[2]   Also this would apply not only to all the elements in human nature but to important relations between them that were operative in the process of human development itself, such as the "great force of custom and education, which mould the human mind from its infancy and form it into a fixed and established character".[3]

The laws of behaviour obviously represent a different class of propositions, since they require not merely an understanding of the principles of human nature but also, if we are to be able to predict how man will behave, a high "constant conjunction" between certain of these principles and a discrete set of conditions.   And in this regard Hume displays considerably more caution.   Recognising the complex interrelationship between man's passions and the manifold forces of his environment, he frequently stresses the wide variability of human behaviour. "Those who consider the periods and revolutions of human

---

[1] Cf. *Enquiry concerning Human Understanding*, p. 83.
[2] *Treatise*, p. 124.
[3] *Enquiry concerning Human Understanding*, pp. 84-5.

---

sciences. And indeed, if we consider the shortness of human life, and our limited knowledge, even of what passes in our own time, we must be sensible that we should be for ever children in understanding, were it not for this invention, which extends our experience to all past ages, and to the most distant nations ; making them contribute as much to our improvement in wisdom, as if they had actually lain under our observation. A man acquainted with history may, in some respect, be said to have lived from the beginning of the world, and to have been making continual additions to his stock of knowledge in every century". *Phil. Wks.*, VOL. IV, p. 390.

kind, as represented in history, are entertained with a spectacle full of pleasure and variety, and see, with surprize, the manners, customs, and opinions of the same species susceptible of such prodigious changes in different periods of time".[1] And here he emphasises that historical evidence will frequently reveal little more than what appears as wholly "chance" occurrence, and that at best it will often afford a basis only for "probabilities"—or propositions which are not free of "contrariety in our experience and observation".[2]

To turn to his observations specifically on the field of "politics", here one likewise finds an emphasis on the difficulty of establishing reliable generalisations. He thus warns that in this area "all general maxims . . . ought to be established with the greatest caution" ; and in another place, again pointedly stressing the wide historical variation in man's behaviour, he states :

I am apt . . . to entertain a suspicion that the world is still too young to fix many general truths in politics which will remain true to the latest posterity. We have not as yet

[1] *Phil. Wks.*, VOL. III, p. 163. Cf. also below, p. 5, and the essay "A Dialogue" in *Hume's Enquiries*, pp. 324 ff., where the variability of moral behaviour is the major theme. The important question of the relation between Hume's emphasis on *changing* behaviour patterns and the *uniformities* of human nature cannot be fully considered here. But it may be noted that it has received inadequate treatment in the literature. For example, it has been argued that Hume's belief in these uniformities necessarily led him to treat human *behaviour* as *fully* uniform over time, [Cf. J. B. Black, *The Art of History* (London 1926), pp. 97–8] and, less sweepingly, that his insights into genuine cultural change were arrived at "in spite of his psychology". Cf. Bryson, *op. cit.*, pp. 107–8. While there are several and not unimportant instances of actual contradiction between the two (his treatment of avarice as universal in one context and as largely a historical product in another, cf. below, pp. ciii, 21), one, however, cannot properly ignore the many instances where, *in conformity with his own methodology*, Hume sought to reveal cultural change as a product of changing conditions impinging on human nature. Though a modern cultural anthropologist would be reluctant to accept Hume's detailed blueprint of man's nature, even the extent to which the behaviour-variations now emphasised are fully incompatible with his "psychology" is a difficult question which requires careful discrimination among its various elements.

[2] *Treatise*, p. 131.

had experience of three thousand years ; so that not only the art of reasoning is still imperfect in this science, as in all others, but we even want sufficient materials upon which we can reason. It is not fully known, what degree of refinement, either in virtue or vice, human nature is susceptible of ; nor what may be expected of mankind from any great revolution in their education, customs or principles. . . . Trade was never esteemed an affair of state till the last century ; and there scarcely is any ancient writer on politics, who has made mention of it.[1]

It would seem evident, none the less, that of all areas of human behaviour Hume believed the field of "politics" to be the most fruitful for scientific analysis. As he asserts in one place : "So great is the force of laws, and of particular forms of government, and so little dependence have they on the humours and tempers of men, that consequences almost as general and certain may sometimes be deduced from them, as any which the mathematical sciences will afford us".[2] Elsewhere he attributes this determinacy to the dependence of much "political" behaviour upon mass passions. Passions of this character, as he states, are usually so "gross" or "stubborn" that they are not affected, or not affected as much, by the more subtle and imperceptible influences that frequently govern behaviour-patterns applicable to small numbers of individuals. Likening this to the varying reliability of the results obtained when a die is thrown a few and then a large number of times, he thus points out that "what depends upon a few persons is, in great measure, to be ascribed to chance, or secret and unknown causes : What arises from a great number, may often be accounted for by determinate and known causes". On this basis he contrasts the "rise and progress of commerce" with the development of intellectual activity :

> . . . it is more easy to account for the rise and progress of commerce in any kingdom, than for that of learning ; and a

---

[1] *Phil. Wks.*, VOL. III, pp. 156–7.   [2] *Op. cit.*, p. 99.

state, which should apply itself to the encouragement of the one, would be more assured of success, than one which should cultivate the other. Avarice, or the desire of gain, is an universal passion, which operates at all times, in all places, and upon all persons. But curiosity, or the love of knowledge, has a very limited influence, and requires youth, leisure, education, genius and example, to make it govern any person. You will never want booksellers, while there are buyers of books : But there may frequently be readers where there are no authors.[1]

From the confidence with which they are presented, there is every indication, too, that Hume believed that the generalisations of his own economic analysis were at the very least respectable approximations to accurate descriptions of experience. In this connexion it should be noted that it is with a justification of the use of generalisations in domestic "politics", which he here contrasts with the chance-ridden field of foreign diplomacy, that Hume introduces the economic essays.[2]

[1] *Op. cit.*, p. 176.　　　　　[2] Cf. below, pp. 3–4.

Chapter II

THE OUTLINES OF THE NATURAL HISTORY:
HUME'S ECONOMIC PSYCHOLOGY

WE have said that the most basic level of Hume's economic thought takes the form of a natural history of the "rise and progress of commerce" in which he seeks to explain the development of economic activity through the impact of changing environmental forces on certain human passions. This is properly to be regarded as the most basic level because, as noted, it is here that his economic thought is most fundamentally joined to his general treatment of the passions in his "science of man" as this is presented in the *Treatise*. Though viewed in all its aspects this history is not presented in a simple form, actually its major outlines and most general psychological foundations appear in the first essay "Of Commerce", where he considers the proposition that commerce, in promoting human happiness, likewise promotes the power of the state. This, as he observes, was already a familiar proposition, and part of his analysis finds a general parallel in portions of the earlier literature which dealt with the relation between the growth of economic incentives and the growth of industry.[1] What Hume seeks, however, is to re-evaluate this general proposition in a broad psychological and historical context ; and, as his treatment as a whole forms an important basis for so much that follows, it is well that it should be given attention at the outset.

[1] Though Hume does not make this explicit, his position departs from the common view that indulgence in luxury weakens the power of the state by breeding idleness and contributing to an unfavourable balance of trade. On this view only "properly" directed commerce would enhance both the wealth and power of the state. There were others, however, who did not see any opposition between indulgence in luxury and the power of the state.

The general historical setting for his treatment of the issue is fixed in a brief opening statement on the nature of the different general levels of economic evolution in which he refers to the stages of hunting and fishing, agriculture and commerce and industry, and notes that the latter presupposes an advance of agricultural technology sufficient to provide surpluses for an urban population. Here he questions whether, in absorbing these surpluses in the satisfaction of individual wants, it may not in fact be said that commerce undermines the power of the state. Pointedly emphasising the wide variability of behaviour-patterns, he refuses to dismiss this view entirely. Specifically, as he points out, it finds substantial support in the record of the ancient Greek and Roman republics, whose relatively prodigious capacity to raise and support armies he attributes directly to a strict husbanding of surpluses for state use. None the less, he contends, this must be regarded as a special case, and as such scarcely a reliable basis for policy formation. For since this policy necessarily depended on the force of public spirit it was entirely contrary to man's "natural bent". It is properly to be treated as the product of an "extraordinary concurrence of circumstances" (i.e. the freedom and confined areas of these countries and the martial spirit of the age, all of which combined to engender an *amor patriae* of singularly high order). As he points out more fully in the *Treatise*, while man is not wholly selfish (and in fact is very largely concerned with the interests of his family and friends), it is only the "weakest" part of his attention that "reaches to strangers". For their interest, in a word, he is "not easily induc'd to perform any action . . . except with a view to some reciprocal advantage, which [he] had not hope of obtaining but by such a performance".[1]

Short of turning society into a perpetual armed camp, it is then upon commerce that, in the "more natural and

[1] Cf. *Treatise*, pp. 488, 519.

usual course of things", the state must in fact rely for the source of its own power. For, wanting the appeal to the stronger private passions, not only would economic activity shrink and agricultural surpluses disappear, but ultimately a "habit of indolence" would ensue. On the other hand, as commerce evoked ever-increasing effort it would inevitably lead to a "habit of industry". During a time of emergency, instead of having to face the task of coaxing an increase in effort from a sluggish people, the state thus has the much easier task of persuading the labourer to devote part of an already habitual measure of effort to its use. Trade and industry, in short, are "really nothing but a stock of labour, which, in times of peace and tranquility, is employed for the ease and satisfaction of individuals ; but, in the exigencies of state, may, in part, be turned to public advantage". It should be noted that in his concluding comments Hume draws special attention to the stimulating influence of foreign commerce which, as he points out, usually precedes the expansion of domestic trade.[1] This strategic role of foreign trade in a nation's economic development he attributes to several factors : the impact on human wants of novel items of luxury,[2] the effect on both the activity and size of the merchant class of the high profits derived from exploiting the new import demand as well as the new foreign markets for domestic output, and the encouragement to home economic growth resulting from the imitation of both foreign products and techniques of production.

In the essay "Of Commerce", Hume's discussion, as indicated, is of a highly general order. His context here leads him primarily to consider the broad character of the motives underlying economic activity and to emphasise

---

[1] Cf. below, pp. 13–14.

[2] In the *Treatise* (pp. 422–3) Hume emphasises the general enlivening effect of "novelty". This he attributes to the "agitation of the spirits" caused by the difficulty in directing attention to something new. As noted below, in a more general sense "liveliness" is of considerable importance in Hume's economic psychology as a whole.

the importance of habit and custom in its development. Consequently, particular "causes of labour" are mentioned only in a somewhat passing fashion. However, if one considers the second essay—"Of Refinement in the Arts" —where Hume gives more pointed attention to the relation between the development of commerce and human happiness, a much more thorough statement of these "causes of labour" (here considered specifically as ends) is found. Because of its general significance for his economic psychology (and consequently for much of the remainder of his analysis) it is perhaps well to quote this statement at length :

Human happiness, according to the most received notions, seems to consist in three ingredients ; action, pleasure, and indolence : And though these ingredients ought to be mixed in different proportions, according to the particular disposition of the person ; yet no one ingredient can be entirely wanting, without destroying, in some measure, the relish of the whole composition. Indolence, or repose, indeed, seems not of itself to contribute much to our enjoyment ; but, like sleep, is requisite as an indulgence to the weakness of human nature, which cannot support an uninterrupted course of business or pleasure. That quick march of the spirits, which takes a man from himself, and chiefly gives satisfaction, does in the end exhaust the mind, and requires some intervals of repose, which, though agreeable for a moment, yet, if prolonged, beget a languor and lethargy that destroys all enjoyment. Education, custom, and example, have a mighty influence in turning the mind to any of these pursuits ; and it must be owned, that, where they promote a relish for action and pleasure, they are so far favourable to human happiness. In times when industry and the arts flourish, men are kept in perpetual occupation, and enjoy, as their reward, the occupation itself, as well as those pleasures which are the fruit of their labour. The mind acquires new vigour ; enlarges its powers and faculties ; and by an assiduity in honest industry, both satisfies its natural appetites, and prevents the growth of unnatural ones, which commonly spring up, when nourished by ease and idleness. Banish those arts from society, you deprive men both of action and of pleasure ; and leaving nothing but

xxxv

indolence in their place, you even destroy the relish of indolence which never is agreeable, but when it succeeds to labour, and recruits the spirits, exhausted by too much application and fatigue.[1]

From this passage three "causes of labour" emerge : the desire for "pleasure", the desire for "action", and the desire for the "quick march of the spirits", which is expressed through both action and pleasure and which may be termed, more simply, the desire for "liveliness". To these is to be added "avarice" or the "desire for gain" which Hume earlier mentions in his treatment of the "natural history" in "Of Commerce".

No further comment is required on the desire for "pleasure", which is employed throughout the essays only in a most general sense to denote the entire complex of passions gratified by the consumption of wealth, although it may be noted that in the *Treatise* Hume stresses the importance of pride in this regard.[2] With respect to the remaining passions, each of which has a more distinctive counterpart in his science of man, the relations between the treatment in the essays and the *Treatise* warrant more detailed consideration. For, apart from revealing the extent to which Hume's economic psychology represented a systematic application of his principles of human nature to the "moral science" of economics, this will be seen to add important new dimensions to that part of the analysis which appears in the essays, thus serving to clarify the significance of each of the passions involved as well as the interrelations among them all.

The desire for action. The general model for Hume's treatment of economic activity as a satisfying form of "action" appears in a section of Book II of the *Treatise* entitled "Of curiosity or the love of truth", a passion which Hume tells us he deems worthy of separate and detailed analysis because "'tis an affection of so peculiar

---

[1] Cf. below, pp. 21-2.   [2] Cf. *Treatise*, pp. 309 ff.

a kind, that 'twou'd have been impossible to have treated of it under any of those heads, which we have examin'd, without danger of obscurity and confusion".[1]

At the outset he emphasises that the pleasure derived from scholarly pursuits consists basically not in the attainment of valid knowledge as such, but rather "in the action of the mind, and the exercise of the genius and understanding in the discovery or comprehension of any truth". For the pursuit of truth to prove gratifying, however, two conditions are required. The undertaking, first, must offer a genuine challenge to our capacities :

What is easy and obvious is never valu'd . . . We love to trace the demonstrations of mathematicians ; but shou'd receive small entertainment from a person, who shou'd barely inform us of the proportions of lines and angles, tho' we repos'd the utmost confidence both in his judgment and veracity. In this case 'tis sufficient to have ears to learn the truth. We are never oblig'd to fix our attention or exert our genius.[2]

It is essential, secondly, that the truth should possess some measure of utility :

'Tis easy to multiply algebraical problems to infinity, nor is there any end in the discovery of the proportions of conic sections ; tho' few mathematicians take any pleasure in these researches, but turn their thoughts to what is more useful and important.[3]

However, to assert that the truth must be useful, he continues, would appear to lead us into paradox. For, while it is clear that the enjoyment of the activity requires that it be directed toward a worthy objective, it has been seen that it is not this objective, but simply the activity itself, which serves as the true end of this passion :

The difficulty on this head arises from hence, that many philosophers have consum'd their time, have destroy'd their

[1] *Op. cit.*, p. 448.   [2] *Ibid.*   [3] *Op. cit.*, pp. 449-50.

health, and neglected their fortune, in the search of such truths, as they esteem'd important and useful to the world, tho' it appear'd from their whole conduct and behaviour, that they were not endow'd with any share of public spirit, nor had any concern for the interests of mankind. Were they convinc'd, that their discoveries were of no consequence, they wou'd entirely lose all relish for their studies, and that tho' the consequences be entirely indifferent to them ; which seems to be a contradiction.[1]

This difficulty may be resolved if it be borne in mind that "when we are careless and inattentive, the same action of the understanding has no effect upon us, nor is able to convey any of that satisfaction, which arises from it, when we are in another disposition". Consequently, "if the importance of the truth be requisite to complete the pleasure, 'tis not on account of any considerable addition, which of itself it brings to our enjoyment". Rather, belonging in that class of "desires and inclinations, which go no farther than . . . images of passions",[2] and which may arise even from the faintest association of an object with its utility, the sole function of this concern with the importance of the truth is to provide that small but crucial margin of interest necessary to "fix the attention" on some objective, and so evoke organised and integrated effort. Philosophers, in a word, may find the quest for

---

[1] *Op. cit.*, p. 450.

[2] For a passion of this order to emerge even the most "remote" associative process, through which the mind links the object to its utility, will suffice. In an illustration Hume here invokes the process of "sympathy". As he points out, even the enemy of a particular fortified community may, through a "sympathy" with its inhabitants, experience some pleasure in perceiving the way in which the fortifications are "fitted to attain their end". (*Treatise*, p. 450 : see also Hume's references to sympathy in his treatment of the basis for our esteem of the wealthy. *Op. cit.*, pp. 258, 361, 616.) Adam Smith pointedly extended Hume's doctrine, using it to argue that the "love of contrivance" induces us to "value the means more than the end" for which it is contrived ; thus, he contended, the value attached to articles of luxury is generally far out of proportion to their true worth. Cf. his *Theory of Moral Sentiments* (London 1792), PART IV, chap. I. For a fuller discussion of Hume's doctrine of sympathy and its relation to Smith's, cf. below, pp. xcix–ci, ci *n*.

worthless truth insipid and yet be entirely non-humanitarian, since the value of the truth here takes on significance only as an instrument or, to use a well-recognised term, as an "instrumental end", in effectuating the desire to give expression to intelligence in a meaningful fashion.

In a generalisation of his analysis Hume then shows that in every major particular the pursuit of knowledge is akin to hunting and gaming :

'Tis evident, that the pleasure of hunting consists in the action of the mind and body ; the motion, the attention, the difficulty, and the uncertainty. 'Tis evident likewise, that these actions must be attended with an idea of utility, in order to their having any effect upon us. A man of the greatest fortune, and the farthest remov'd from avarice, tho' he takes pleasure in hunting after partridges and pheasants, feels no satisfaction in shooting crows and magpies ; and that because he considers the first as fit for the table, and the other as entirely useless. Here 'tis certain, that the utility or importance of itself causes no real passion, but is only requisite to support the imagination ; and the same person, who overlooks a ten times greater profit in any other subject, is pleas'd to bring home half a dozen woodcocks or plovers, after having employ'd several hours in hunting after them.[1]

It has been remark'd, that the pleasure of gaming arises not from interest alone ; since many leave a sure gain for this entertainment : Neither is it deriv'd from the game alone ; since the same persons have no satisfaction, when they play for nothing : But proceeds from both these causes united, tho' separately they have no effect. 'Tis here, as in certain chymical preparations, where the mixture of two clear and transparent liquids produces a third, which is opaque and colour'd.[2]

To return to the economic essays, the parallel between Hume's treatment of the desire for action within the

---

[1] *Treatise*, pp. 451–2.

[2] Ibid. As is evident, Hume does not recognise what may be called the "pure game", or one in which the "end" has no independent value, but is conceived wholly for the purpose of making the activity interesting.

context of his "natural history" and his analysis of the love of truth is seen to be completed in an important passage in the essay "Of Interest". For here Hume makes clear that in its relation to economic activity as a form of interesting pursuit, the desire for wealth is in the nature of a desire for "profit" or "gain", and in the context this is explicitly opposed to the "real" passion for the "pleasures" derived from the consumption of wealth. Viewed in the light of his more general analysis, wealth is thus implicitly treated as the full equivalent of the "woodcocks and plover" of the *Treatise*.

There is no craving or demand of the human mind more constant and insatiable than that for exercise and employment ; and this desire seems the foundation of most of our passions and pursuits. Deprive a man of all business and serious occupation, he runs restless from one amusement to another ; and the weight and oppression, which he feels from idleness, is so great, that he forgets the ruin which must follow him from his immoderate expenses. Give him a more harmless way of employing his mind or body [specifically "lucrative employment" or the pursuit of "gain"], he is satisfied, and feels no longer that insatiable thirst after pleasure.[1]

Although in the context in which this appears Hume is speaking more particularly of the activity of the merchant, it would seem evident from several of his comments that he likewise meant this to apply to labour in general.[2] The question arises concerning the extent to which the analysis is applicable to various types of labour. There is nothing in Hume's treatment, however, which touches on this question. On the basis of the character of his discussion as a whole, it would seem clear that although he refers to particular types of activity, the gratification that he had in mind was not conceived to flow primarily from the physical or mental operations involved in

[1] Cf. below p. 53.
[2] This is apparent, for example, in the passage cited above, p. xxxv, from "Of Refinement in the Arts". Cf. also below, p. lxxxii.

specific economic tasks but rather from the broader activity designated as the "pursuit of gain", or the more inclusive process of advancing one's economic standing. In one place, in a context related to the above, he emphasises the importance of a close connexion between "every particular exertion of industry" and the "gain"—as in the case of the merchant [1]—but, more generally, it would seem that he assumed that in the society of his time economic advancement was an effective possibility for the majority of men and supposed that this would suffice to create a broad interest in economic activity.

A recognition of the relationship between Hume's treatment of economic activity as intrinsically gratifying and his *Treatise* model also throws light on his treatment in the essays of "difficulty", "obstacles", and "necessity". For here, in considering the influence of the latter on the development of industry, he argues that additional obstacles to want-satisfaction frequently generate an expansion of effort so great as to produce an increase in scales of living far exceeding pre-existing levels. Since what is referred to is the evocation of a positive desire to overcome hardship, the analysis finds its obvious analogue in the relationship more explicitly drawn between "difficulty" and interesting action in the *Treatise*.

What is the reason, why no people, living between the tropics, could ever yet attain to any art or civility, or reach even any police in their government, and any military discipline ; while few nations in the temperate climates have been altogether deprived of these advantages ? It is probable that one cause of this phenomenon is the warmth and equality of weather in the torrid zone, which render clothes and houses less requisite for the inhabitants, and thereby remove, in part, that necessity, which is the great spur to industry and invention.[2]

---

[1] Cf. below, p. 53. Among contemporary economists the "game" aspect of economic activity has been most emphasised by Frank H. Knight. Cf., for example, his *Ethics of Competition* (London 1935), pp. 60 ff.

[2] Cf. below, pp. 17-18.

Perhaps the best statement of the position that economic activity reflects a conscious seeking out of difficulties is to be found in another essay, where he likens labour to hunting :

They [the hunters] leave behind, in their own houses, and in the neighbouring plains, animals of every kind, whose flesh furnishes the most delicious fare, and which offer themselves to the fatal stroke. Laborious men disdains so easy a purchase. He seeks for a prey, which hides itself from his search, or flies from his pursuit, or defends itself from his violence.[1]

In the economic literature of the period the view that difficulty stimulated industry was very widely held, empirical evidence in this regard often being drawn from the achievements of the Dutch. Though apparently only in more general form, some earlier economic writers also suggested that economic activity was essentially congenial to man.[2] For the most part, however, the prevailing view was different. More generally it was argued that man (or at least the mass of labour) was natively indisposed toward economic activity and a sharp contrast was often drawn between the latter and the indulgences that leisure would make possible. In considering the relation-

[1] Cf. his essay "The Stoic" (subtitled "The Man of Action and Virtue") in *Phil. Wks.*, VOL. III, p. 206, and also below, p. xcvii. It may be noted that in taking this view as well as his more general position concerning the importance of "action", Hume was well aware of various parallels in the writings of Virgil. For example, the statement quoted before the above is followed by the quotation "*curis acuens mortalia corda*" which is taken from the *Aeneid*, IV.158–9. Again, in a passage in the *Treatise*, where he speaks of the "invigorating" effects of "opposition", he introduces a quotation from the *Georgics*, I.123. Cf. *Treatise*, p. 433. The opening passages of "The Stoic", moreover, bear a striking resemblance, even in the wording, to the *Aeneid*, IV.108–09. (Cf. *Phil. Wks.*, VOL. III, p. 203). A further general parallel, of which Hume may have been aware, appears in Joseph Addison, *The Sir Roger de Coverley Papers* (London 1896), esp. p. 74. Though not presenting as detailed a psychological analysis as Hume, Adam Ferguson, in his later work on civil society, likewise argued that man needs action, and, to fulfil this desire, deliberately seeks difficulties. Cf. his *Essay on the History of Civil Society* (London 1768), pp. 63–4.

[2] Cf., for example, Defoe, *A Plan of the English Commerce*, p. 35.

ship between difficulty and work attitudes, these writers seem to have supposed consequently that the repetition of labour (compelled by difficulty) could, alone, through its effect on habit, create a disposition toward industry.[1] In this, moreover, their position also conflicted with Hume's view of habit itself. For, as he argues in the *Treatise*, while mere repetition may render a painful act tolerable owing to the increased "facility" of performing it ("passive habit"), it can never produce "an inclination and tendency towards it" ("active habit"), if to human nature the act is "entirely disagreeable". Indeed, if the habit is founded on nothing but repetition, an increased facility beyond a point actually diminishes its force "by rendering the motion of the spirits faint and languid".[2] To assert therefore that through its influence on habit difficulty engenders a continuous and enduring expansion of industry is, in his view, to imply a fundamental propensity toward the type of action involved.

It may be noted that Hume's view also differed from the main stream of classical doctrine as subsequently developed by Smith and Ricardo. They too argued that, in terms of man's basic predispositions, economic activity was disagreeable and irksome. In a sense they carried the principle further, since in their view, the "pain cost" of labour—construed to apply to all units of effort —was one of the principal foundations of exchange

---

[1] Statements of this character are to be found in the many arguments in support of "schools of industry" and an early disciplining of children for the tasks of gainful employment. See Furniss, *The Position of the Laborer in a System of Nationalism*, pp. 109 ff. Perhaps one of the clearest general statements is that of Sir William Temple. "Men naturally prefer ease before labour, and will not take pains if they can live idle ; though when, by necessity, they have been inured to it, they cannot leave it, being grown a custom necessary to their health, and to their very entertainment". Cf. *The Works of Sir William Temple* (London 1814), p. 165. In one place Hume quotes this statement in support of his own view on the relation between difficulty and economic activity. Cf. below, p. 83. However, he does not explain the more basic differences between his position and Temple's.

[2] *Treatise*, pp. 423-4.

xliii

value.[1] Indeed, although at least as early as Marshall's time distinctions between the attitudes toward different units of effort begin to appear in the literature [2] (and now, on several grounds, it is generally recognised that economic activity may prove intrinsically rewarding), yet as late as 1915 Taussig could still write that "the economist commonly tells us that [work] is an effort undergone because compensated by wages and profits, a 'disutility', a sacrifice. Underlying almost all economic theory is the assumption that work is an irksome thing, done for pay and in proportion to pay".[3]

Avarice or the desire for gain. If one considers Hume's writings as a whole, two different interpretations of avarice are found. One construction appears in his more general treatment in the *Treatise*, where reference to this passion is made in passing and primarily for purposes of illustrating a more general principle. Here the motive to acquire hoards is traced to the association or the identification of money with the pleasure it will purchase [4]:

[1] "The real price of every thing, what every thing really costs to the man who wants to acquire it, is the toil and trouble of acquiring it". "If among a nation of hunters, for example, it usually costs twice the labour to kill a beaver which it does to kill a deer, one beaver should naturally exchange for or be worth two deer. It is natural that what is usually the produce of two days' or two hours' labour, should be worth double of what is usually the produce of one day's or one hour's labour [of equal "hardship"]". Adam Smith, *The Wealth of Nations*, ed. E. Cannan (New York 1937), pp. 30 and 47 respectively. See also D. Ricardo, *The Principles of Political Economy and Taxation* (Everyman Series, London 1937), pp. 5 ff.

[2] Cf. Alfred Marshall, *Principles of Economics* (London 1936), pp. 140-1, 830.

[3] F. W. Taussig, *Inventors and Money Makers* (New York 1915), pp. 55-6. Taussig himself, however, argues that this view is wanting in so far as it ignores the role of the "instinct of contrivance" and the "instinct of devotion" or public spirit, both of which he believes to have been dominant motives in the case of the major inventors of the past, e.g. Cartwright, Ericcson, Edison. *Op. cit.*, pp. 21-2, 102-3. The "instinct of play" and the "instinct of the chase", construed in a narrow and rather literal sense, however, are not deemed significant as economic incentives. *Op. cit.*, pp. 9-10.

[4] One of the clearest statements of this view in Hume's time is to be found in a work by John Gay, the early expounder of the principle of association. See his "Dissertation Concerning the Fundamental Principle of Virtue or Morality", in *The English Philosophers from Bacon to Mill*, ed. E. A. Burtt (New York), p. 783.

A miser receives delight from his money ; that is, from the *power* it affords him of procuring all the pleasures and conveniences of life, tho' he knows he has enjoy'd his riches for forty years without ever employing them ; and consequently cannot conclude by any species of reasoning, that the real existence of these pleasures is nearer, than if he were entirely depriv'd of all his possessions. But tho' he cannot form any such conclusion in a way of reasoning concerning the nearer approach of the pleasure, 'tis certain he imagines it to approach nearer, whenever all external obstacles are re-remov'd . . .[1]

The second interpretation is presented in his more pointed discussion of avarice as a "cause of labour", where it assumes an essentially different form. For here it is linked not to the desire for pleasure but rather to the pursuit of "lucrative employment" *qua* action. Since in its latter relation wealth serves as "instrumental end", or as the goal of the action, the implication is, clearly, that the passion for gain involved is essentially in the nature of a desire to accumulate symbols of successful endeavour. This may be seen in an extension of the passage, previously quoted from the essay "Of Interest", where Hume refers to man's "craving for exercise and employment".

Give him a more harmless way of employing his mind or body, he is satisfied, and feels no longer that insatiable thirst after pleasure. But if the employment you give him be lucrative, especially if the profit be attached to every particular exertion of industry, he has gain so often in his eye, that he acquires, by degrees, a passion for it, and knows no such pleasure as that of seeing the daily increase of his fortune.[2]

A more general treatment of this phenomenon likewise appears in his further elaboration of the *Treatise* analysis of the love of truth. Thus after pointing out that the fundamental motive here at work is the desire for action, while the desire for the apparent "end" is but an "image" of a passion, he adds that in the course of the pursuit and

[1] *Treatise*, p. 314. Italics in text.   [2] Cf. below, p. 53.

through the "natural course of the affections", however, we develop an interest in the end itself as a token of the action successfully consummated :

Upon this head [the desire for success] I shall make a general remark, which may be useful on many occasions, *viz.* that where the mind pursues any end with passion ; tho' that passion be not deriv'd originally from the end, but merely from the action and pursuit ; yet by the natural course of the affections, we acquire a concern for the end itself, and are uneasy under any disappointment we meet with in the pursuit of it.[1]

And subsequently he adds :

To make the parallel betwixt hunting and philosophy more compleat, we may observe, that tho' in both cases the end of our action may in itself be despis'd, yet in the heat of the action we acquire such an attention to this end, that we are very uneasy under any disappointments, and are sorry when we either miss our game, or fall into any error in our reasoning.[2]

In a word, had Hume gone on to point out that as a consequence of having "plover and woodcock" so often in his eye, the hunter acquires a passion to preserve and mount his day's bag, his *Treatise* discussion would have provided a fully analogous and general model for this aspect of his treatment of the "passion for gain" in his economic psychology. It may be noted, however, that had he done so, he might have broken away from the classification of the desire for gain as a separate passion, which was common to his own period, and treated it as

[1] *Treatise*, p. 451. This phenomenon Hume reduces to the operation of the principle of "parallel direction", one of the two laws of association shown to underlie relations between passions. The essence of this doctrine is that passions are joined by a similarity in their "general bent or tendency" such that when one increases in intensity it tends to evoke all others of a related nature. Cf. *Treatise*, pp. 384-5.

[2] *Op. cit.*, p. 452. Hume seems to imply here that the heat of the pursuit not only intensifies our interest in attaining the end, but is the source of our interest in success itself. This is difficult to understand, since it would seem clear that an interest in the attainment of the end is intrinsic to its status as "instrumental end" and would emerge as soon as an appropriate end entered consciousness.

an instance of a more inclusive passion akin to what is now termed the "acquisitive instinct".

The desire for liveliness. As seen in the passage from the essay "Of Refinement in the Arts" Hume observes that both "action and pleasure" are further gratifying in that they provide "that quick march of the spirits, which takes a man from himself". What is most interesting to observe here is that in speaking of the quick march of the spirits, Hume is referring not merely to the sense of "liveliness" which comes from gratifying one's wants (either through action or pleasure). Rather, contrasted with "indolence", which is likened to "sleep"[1] or "no passion", this experience likewise embraces the sense of emotional excitement intrinsic to a state of active passion as such. In distilling the quality "liveliness" from both action and pleasure Hume, in a word, is recognising that passions are themselves objects of a passion, or that economic behaviour involves not merely a desire for want-gratification but further reflects a desire to *have* and *pursue* wants.[2]

In more general form this is brought out with perhaps even more clarity in the *Treatise*.

Those, who take a pleasure in declaiming against human nature, have observ'd, that man is altogether insufficient to support himself; and that when you loosen all the holds, which he has of external objects, he immediately drops down into the deepest melancholy and despair. From this, say they, proceeds that continual search after amusement in gaming, in hunting, in business; by which we endeavour to forget ourselves, and excite our spirits from the languid state, into

[1] Cf. above, p. xxxv.

[2] Thomas Hobbes likewise had earlier observed that desire itself is essential to human well-being. "Nor can a man any more live, whose desires are at an end, than he whose senses and imagination are at a stand. Felicity is a continual progress of the desire, from one object to another; the attaining of the former, being still but the way to the latter". See his *Leviathan* in *The English Works of Thomas Hobbes*, ed. Sir William Molesworth (London 1839), VOL. III, p. 85. A similar view is likewise found later during the period in Adam Ferguson, *Civil Society*, pp. 61, 64, 67–88.

which they fall, when not sustain'd by some brisk and lively emotion. To this method of thinking I so far agree, that I own the mind to be insufficient, of itself, to its own entertainment, and that it naturally seeks after foreign objects, which may produce a lively sensation, and agitate the spirits. On the appearance of such an object it awakes, as it were, from a dream : The blood flows with a new tide : The heart is elevated : And the whole man acquires a vigour, which he cannot command in his solitary and calm moments.[1]

It is interesting to note, moreover, that in further comments on the nature of the desire for liveliness he takes the view that so distressing is a passionless state that, as a refuge from its abysmal vacuity, man finds welcome relief in the excitement provided even by painful emotions. "No matter what the passion is : Let it be disagreeeable, afflicting, melancholy, disordered ; it is still better than that insipid languor, which arises from perfect tranquility and repose".[2] And similarly in the *Treatise* analysis of the love of truth, after pointing out that the "difficulty, variety, and sudden reverses of fortune" of the game are sources of satisfaction, he adds "Human life is so tiresome a scene, and men generally are of such indolent dispositions, that whatever amuses them, tho' by a passion mixt with pain, does in the main give them a sensible pleasure".[3]

It may be observed, finally, that Hume's treatment of action and pleasure as substitutable media for the expression of a desire for liveliness provides the basis for an interpretation of the relations between idleness and an excessive indulgence in pleasure more adequate than that commonly entertained in the economic literature of his own time. As seen, this question figured prominently in the mercantilist discussion of the alleged prevalence of idleness among the poor ; this and their "tippling and

---

[1] *Treatise*, pp. 352–3. It will be recalled that in his statement in "Of Refinement in the Arts" the general invigorating effect of lively sensations is likewise treated as a causal factor in the development of economic activity. See above, p. xxxv.
[2] *Phil. Wks.*, VOL. III, p. 259.　　　　[3] *Treatise*, p. 452.

carousing" being generally regarded by the mercantilist writers as the principal socio-economic evil of the period. However, whereas they commonly viewed indulgence in "the pleasures of idleness" as the fulfilment of a natural craving,[1] Hume recognises it as symptomatic of frustration —that is as an attempt to compensate through pleasure for the want of liveliness resulting from a thwarting of the desire for interesting action. To recall his statement in the passage previously quoted from the essay "Of Interest":

> Deprive a man of all business and serious occupation, he runs restless from one amusement to another ; and the weight and oppression, which he feels from idleness, is so great, that he forgets the ruin which must follow him from his immoderate expenses. Give him a more harmless way of employing his mind or body, he is satisfied, and feels no longer that insatiable thirst after pleasure.[2]

The primacy of "instinct". In the course of the discussion it has been observed that Hume makes frequent reference to the "pleasures" associated with the various "causes of labour" and that he uniformly employs the term "pleasures" when referring to the gratifications derived from the consumption of wealth. The question therefore arises whether, in the later tradition of Bentham and Mill and the main stream of nineteenth-century psychological hedonism, Hume regarded these "causes of labour" as but instances of an all-inclusive Desire for Pleasure, or whether he meant them to be construed as essentially distinct and independent motives.

On this issue Hume's analysis leaves no room for doubt that his intention was the latter. Thus in his general treatment of the "direct" passions in the *Treatise*, after considering those whose object is pleasure or the avoidance of pain (desire, aversion, hope, grief, sorrow), he observes that "beside good and evil, or in other words,

---

[1] Cf. Furniss, *op. cit.*, chap. 6.

[2] The most explicit treatment of dissipation among labourers is found in his essay "Of Taxes". Cf. below, p. 85*n*.

pain and pleasure, the direct passions frequently arise from a natural impulse or instinct, which is perfectly unaccountable".[1] As they cannot be reduced to other elements, these affections are thus in the nature of direct attractions to objects. As such, they "produce good and evil, and proceed not from them, like the other affections".

A later and fuller analysis which appears in his defence of the reality of a native benevolence, and where he emphasises the extensive influence of these "instincts" as sources of the "pleasures" we pursue, provides perhaps the best single statement of his position :

There are bodily wants or appetites acknowledged by every one, which necessarily precede all sensual enjoyment, and carry us directly to seek possession of the object. Thus, hunger and thirst have eating and drinking for their end ; and from the gratification of these primary appetites arises a pleasure, which may become the object of another species of desire or inclination that is secondary and interested. In the same manner there are mental passions by which we are impelled to seek particular objects, such as fame or power, or vengeance without any regard to interest ; and when these objects are attained a pleasing enjoyment ensues, as the consequence of our indulged affections. Nature must, by the internal frame and constitution of the mind, give an original propensity to fame, ere we can reap any pleasure from that acquisition, or pursue it from motives of self-love, and desire of happiness. If I have no vanity, I take no delight in praise : if I be void of ambition, power gives me no enjoyment : if I be not angry, the punishment of an adversary is totally indifferent to me . . . Were there no appetite of any kind antecedent to self-love, that propensity could scarcely ever exert itself ; because we should, in that case, have felt few and slender pains or pleasures, and have little misery or happiness to avoid or to pursue.[2]

---

[1] *Treatise*, p. 439. All passions other than the "direct" are classified as "indirect". Most generally the latter differ from the former in that their evocation involves an associative process—specifically the process which Hume terms the "double relation of ideas and impressions". Cf., for example, his treatment of pride and humility. *Treatise*, pp. 277 ff.

[2] *An Enquiry concerning the Principles of Morals*, pp. 301-2.

In recognition of the full implications of this doctrine, Hume argues elsewhere that, impelled by instinct, man may repeatedly, and with a complete foreknowledge of the consequences, adopt a course of action detrimental to himself. "Men often act knowingly against their interest : For which reason the view of the greatest possible good does not always influence them".[1]

Although "instinct" psychology has given way to a greater stress on the conditioning influence of social forces, it need scarcely be said, in the light of the continuing emphasis on "irrational" (i.e. not pleasure-orientated) elements in human behaviour, that Hume's analysis is more "modern" than the school of psychology which dominated much subsequent British thought. Within the field of economics, as is well known, the growing awareness of the questions raised in part by Hume's type of approach long ago led to a general abandonment of the nineteenth-century liaison with psychological hedonism.[2] "Utility" is no longer equated with "pleasure", or is explicitly construed in a most general sense, that is, simply as want-fulfilment.[3]

The preceding discussion has been primarily concerned with specific aspects of Hume's economic psychology. In concluding, however, it is well to call attention

---

[1] *Treatise*, p. 418.

[2] As illustrative of this liaison the position of Stanley Jevons is as explicit as any of the period. "Pleasure and pain are undoubtedly the ultimate objects of the calculus of economics. To satisfy our wants to the utmost with the least effort, to procure the greatest amount of what is desirable at the expense of the least that is undesirable, in other words, to maximise pleasure, is the problem of economics". See his *Theory of Political Economy* (London 1911), p. 40.

[3] Perhaps the best of the early statements of this is to be found in H. J. Davenport, *The Economics of Enterprise* (New York 1913), pp. 99–100. It is sometimes supposed, as J. R. Hicks explicitly asserts, that indifference-analysis is indispensable to "an economics free of utilitarian assumptions". See his *Value and Capital* (Oxford 1939), p. 18. Obviously whether one uses "preference" or the more conventional "utility" analysis has no bearing on this issue. The concept "preference" is equally open to a hedonic construction, if one chooses to invoke it.

to certain of its more general aspects which are properties of its notably multi-dimensional character. Of obvious significance in this connexion is the manner in which his analysis, even within its rather brief compass, displays an awareness of the complex interrelations between passions, or of the essentially organic character of human experience. Thus, beyond their direct influence, the pleasures of consumption operate indirectly as the instrumental end which renders economic activity a suitable vehicle for the desire for action ; in both capacities the desire for wealth is treated as the basis for the development of avarice ; action and pleasure are seen as avenues for the expression of a desire for liveliness ; and this relation of substitutability is employed to explain the phenomenon of dissipation. Moreover, as this process is considered in a historical framework, his treatment further serves to draw attention to the relation between particular "causes of labour" and changing circumstance in the formation of a general pattern of "habit and custom".

Equally noteworthy is the way in which his analysis conveys an appreciation of the ineffable density of human behaviour and an understanding of the opposing forces on which it rests. Thus—to gather various parts of his treatment together—man produces in order to attain "pleasures" ; enjoying the difficulties encountered in the activity itself, however, he not only delights in those pursuits which show genuine promise of thwarting his desire to consume but, in the course of the "game", conceives a passion to withhold and preserve his acquisitions from use. He wishes his wants gratified, but, likewise enjoying the emotional excitement of having wants, he desires his wants unsatisfied, and finding himself too heavily taxed with "tranquility" will seek refuge if necessary even in the bitter-sweet pleasure of pain. He desires Pleasure (and one might add, priding himself on his "reason", he deceives himself into believing this is all he desires), but, drawn toward objects for no "reason" other than that he wants them, he is likewise a creature of "instincts" who for the sake of their fulfilment may "knowingly neglect every consideration of ease, interest, or safety".[1] Perhaps the whole is best summarised by Hume himself when, in the course of discussing the conflicting emotions evoked by love and marriage, he is prompted to exclaim : "These principles of human nature, you'll say, are contradictory : But what is man but a heap of contradictions !"[2] Hume was primarily of a "scientific" turn of mind ; but it is notable that in an analysis devoted to scientific generalisation he should preserve so acute an awareness of the pluralism and variety of human experience, or, contrariwise, that insights more commonly encountered in the literary arts should find their expression within the framework of his uniformities.

[1] *An Enquiry concerning the Principles of Morals*, p. 302.
[2] *Phil. Wks.*, VOL. III, p. 238.

Chapter III

THOUGH relatively brief by present standards, Hume's political economy treats five of the major questions of his period : monetary theory, interest theory, the problem of free versus controlled markets, the shifting and incidence of taxes and fiscal policy. Presented as a collection of essays on different subjects, the analysis does not appear in anything like the form of a treatise. Rather does it take the form of a running critical commentary on the economic thought of the period. It is this highly self-conscious critical purpose, among other things, that makes Hume especially interesting reading. Indeed there is relatively little in his political economy that is not discussed within a controversial frame of reference, so that almost every essay reads as a kind of debate in which Hume pointedly seeks to expose and rectify what he regards as the main economic errors of his day.

Though the subject matter is variegated, the major part of his political economy finds its unity in the vantage point from which the different aspects of prevailing doctrine are examined. As has been said, what Hume here repeatedly seeks to emphasise are the economic implications of evolutionary sequence and in particular the evolutionary sequence of the "natural history". In a word, the bulk of his treatment springs from a consideration of one central question : Do various commonly received beliefs concerning market relations prove valid when analysed in the light of economic development and the factors—psychological and otherwise—with which it is associated ?

Monetary theory. One may consider first Hume's monetary theory, which, reflecting the emphasis of his own

liv

period, is the most extensive and detailed part of his political economy. It has been noted that the monetary literature of the time contained both mercantilist and classical elements—a marked emphasis on money either because of its intrinsic desirability or because it stimulated trade, and the view that a greater quantity of money produced nothing beyond a proportionate increase in the price-level. As will become apparent, the position which Hume adopts in this regard does not lend itself to unambiguous statement. It is clear, however, that one of the dominant features of his analysis is his emphasis on the classical view. At the opening of the essay "Of Money" he thus draws the distinction between money and wealth. While acknowledging that specie is of use in foreign transactions, he then argues that from the internal point of view "the greater or less plenty of money is of no consequence ; since the prices of commodities are always proportioned to the plenty of money".[1] If the use which Hume makes of the quantity theory is examined, the pervasiveness of his historical emphasis becomes clear. For in virtually every instance in which he employs this doctrine it is found that in thus belittling the "greater or less plenty of money" as such, he is in one way or another seeking primarily to redirect attention to the monetary significance of "the greater number of people and their greater industry", or, as he says in another place, to the "change in the manners and customs" to which this is related.

This may be seen in what is generally regarded as one of the most important parts of his monetary analysis—his formulation of the quantity-theory specie-flow doctrine which is contained in his essay "Of the Balance of

---

[1] Cf. below, p. 33. In a letter to the Abbé Morellet, in which he criticises the latter's commodity theory of the value of money, Hume pointedly emphasises that the choice of a medium of exchange is a matter of convention and that the use of a scarce commodity is essential only as a means of checking promiscuous increases in supply. Cf. below, pp. 214-16.

Trade". [1] The substance of his argument, as is well known, is that through its effects on the price-levels of different trading nations, the amount of specie in each automatically tends toward an equilibrium at which a nation's exports equal its imports. More particularly, as Hume points out, should the quantity of specie depart from this equilibrium in an upward (downward) direction, its price-level relative to others would rise (fall), it would develop an excess of imports (exports), and a return outflow (inflow) of specie would ensue, until the resulting adjustment of price-levels had corrected the inequality of the trade balance. [2] In the literature this doctrine has received greatest attention as perhaps the most cogent of the early statements demonstrating the self-defeating character of the mercantilist

[1] Hume's first statement of this doctrine appears in a letter to Montesquieu (cf. below, p. 188). Commenting more generally on the relation between Hume and Montesquieu, Feilbogen points out that the titles of Hume's economic essays find their counterpart in various book and chapter headings of Montesquieu's *Spirit of the Laws*. Sigmund Feilbogen, "Smith und Hume", in *Zeitschrift für die gesamte Staatswissenschaft*, XLVI (1890), 707 and *n*. Although there is evidence to suggest that Montesquieu was perhaps especially stimulating to Hume, it is obviously difficult to evaluate this since the questions they consider in common were likewise general issues of the day. Apart from serving as the most immediate occasion for Hume's statement of the quantity-theory specie-flow doctrine, Montesquieu's *Spirit of the Laws* seems most important in connexion with Hume's essay on population (cf. below, p. lxxix), and parts of his essay on public credit (cf. below, p. lxxxiv *n*, and p. lxxxv *n*). Part of his essay on taxes may also have been addressed to a portion of Montesquieu's BK. XXII. With regard to the remainder of Hume's analysis, if there is any relation between the two works it would appear to be mainly of a formal character.

[2] Hume recognises the importance of the velocity of circulation, noting that the law would not hold in the event that the new specie was hoarded. Cf. below, p. 75. He also recognises the role played by exchange rates in the adjustment process. Cf. below, p. 64*n*. It is interesting to note that, as part of a more general criticism of Hume's quantity-theory specie-flow doctrine James Oswald argued that the price-effects postulated by Hume were not inevitable, and in this connexion he calls attention, in the manner of Ohlin, to the income-effects of the specie-flows. "The increased quantity of money would not necessarily increase the price of all labour and commoditys ; because the increased quantity, not being confined to the home labour and commoditys, might, and certainly would, be sent to purchase both from foreign countreys ; which importation, unless obstructed by arbitrary and absurd laws, would keep down the prices of commoditys to the level of foreign countreys". Cf. below, p. 191. Moreover, Hume

attempts to increase the domestic specie-supply through restrictions on international trade. However, while Hume gives considerable attention to this more mechanical part of the doctrine, one finds that at the very opening of the essay he pointedly links the argument as a whole to the question of economic growth. Thus in the early passages, after commenting on the general fear among nations "that all their gold and silver may be leaving them", he asserts that the object of his analysis is "to form a general argument, that may prove the impossibility of this event as long as we preserve our people and industry".[1] It may be observed that throughout the analysis he makes it more pointedly clear that by "industry" he means fundamentally the level of industrial development. Thus, in employing the quantity theory in the body of his argument, it is to price-levels as determined by the proportion which specie bears to "art and industry", "skill and ingenuity", and the like, that he repeatedly directs attention ; and the argument is further illustrated by cases involving nations and regions of different productive capacities. Two may be cited :

Men naturally flock to capital cities, sea ports, and navigable rivers. There we find more men, more industry, more commodities, and consequently more money . . . [2]

What immense treasures have been spent, by so many nations, in Flanders, since the revolution, in the course of three long years! . . . But what has become of it ? Is it in the narrow compass of the Austrian provinces ? No surely : It has most of it returned to the several countries whence it came, and has followed that art and industry, by which at first it was acquired.[3]

[1] Cf. below, p. 62.   [2] Cf. below, p. 66.
[3] Cf. below, p. 77. Also pp. 64–5.

---

himself recognises the validity of this point and assimilates it to his own analysis of the mechanism of adjustment. Thus, in commenting on this in his reply to Oswald, he states : "Here, then, is the flowing out of the money already begun". Cf. below, p. 197. An earlier writer who stressed the role of income changes in the adjustment process was Isaac Gervaise. Cf. Viner, *Studies in the Theory of International Trade*, pp. 79–83.

In brief, what Hume is seeking to show is that with regard to one of the most widespread objects of concern to the mercantilists, the quantity of money itself, it is to historical conditions exclusively that we must look for the ultimate determining factors.[1]

Again we may consider a doctrine which appears near the opening of the essay "Of Money" on the heels of his first statement of the quantity theory.[2] Here, in seeking further to expose the errors of the mercantilist position, Hume is led to argue that a greater quantity of money may not merely be a matter of indifference to a country but "may even sometimes be a loss to a nation in its commerce with foreigners". The point which he has in mind at this juncture is simply the adverse effect on a nation's trade balance and output of the higher relative prices resulting from an influx of specie. However, developing the argument within a broader frame of reference, he then goes on to link this to the question of economic development, here specifically to the relative rates of economic growth of nations at different levels of development. As he points out, it might be supposed that owing to the various advantages it enjoys—its "superior industry and skill . . . and the greater stocks, of which its merchants are possessed"—a wealthy nation would be in a position to expand its trade and industry indefinitely at the expense of its more backward neighbours. However, this tendency, he argues, is not only checked but ultimately reversed by the two-sided price-effect of the specie-flow from the poor to the wealthy nation. The rich country with rising prices ultimately loses its leadership to the poor country with

---

[1] It is to be noted that North too had argued that the quantity of money was positively correlated with the state of trade and the level of economic activity. In North, however, the process of adjustment remains somewhat obscure. It does not appear that he relates the question to price movements or the balance of trade at all or that he is speaking of an equilibrium in the international supply of specie. Rather does his explanation seem to refer to some type of process that takes place wholly within a nation. Cf. R. North, *Discourses upon Trade* (Baltimore 1907), pp. 33, 35, 36.

[2] Cf. below, pp. 34–5.

falling prices. This is presented in the form of a generalised law of growth and decay which governs the relations between all trading nations; and, in so far as it ensures that opportunities for expansion will pass from one nation to another, Hume regards the forces involved as a "happy concurrence of causes".[1]

Though this doctrine further illustrates Hume's emphasis on the relation between money and the international aspects of economic development, it should be recognised as one of the decidedly weaker parts of his treatment of this question. Perhaps out of too zealous a desire to discredit the mercantilist position, he overstrains his case and fails to give adequate attention to the "real" factors which he usually stresses in this connexion. More particularly, in supposing that prices generally would necessarily rise in the advanced country (relative to those in the poor country) he inappropriately treats its acquisition of specie as a windfall (or, as in "Of the Balance of Trade", as due to import restrictions). As Josiah Tucker was to note, he overlooks that, under the stated conditions, "every Augmentation of such Money [would be] a Proof of a preceding Increase of Industry".[2] Also, assuming that prices would change in the manner supposed, the argument rests on a crude and essentially conflicting

[1] Later, however, adopting a less cosmopolitan perspective, he points out that, as a means of halting the loss of its industry to others, a sterilisation of specie flowing into the country would be in order. It may be noted that, as stated in the text above, there is a rather marked resemblance between Hume's analysis and Cantillon's. Cantillon, however, does not treat the acquisition of specie as a product of a nation's more rapid economic development, but as the result of the opening of new mines. Also, apparently assuming an indefinite continuation of the output from the mines, Cantillon does not carry his analysis beyond the point where the ensuing rise in prices has increased imports and caused a decline in the nation's industry. In a word, no oscillations in the location of industry are posited. Cf. R. Cantillon, *Essai sur la nature du commerce en general*, trans. Henry Higgs (London 1931), pp. 161 ff.

[2] Josiah Tucker, *Four Tracts on political and commercial Subjects* (Gloucester 1774), p. 44. Tucker's criticism extended far beyond this point, however, and was more fundamentally concerned with the implications of Hume's argument for the free-trade position. Cf. below, pp. 199–205.

version of the quantity-theory specie-flow doctrine. For
Hume fails to observe that, as soon as any price effects
of the specie flows from the poor to the advanced country
might have caused a reversal of their respective trade-
balance positions, the direction of the specie flow would
likewise have been reversed. The short-run price effects
of this (as is implicitly recognised in "Of the Balance of
Trade") would alone preclude the long-run oscillations
in the location of industry which he posits.

As illustrative of Hume's stress on economic growth,
more important than the two arguments considered are
the two "observations" which make up the larger part
of the essay "Of Money". The former two are essentially
of a negative character in that they presuppose that from
the domestic point of view a larger quantity of money is
useless or seek to show that it is positively pernicious.
The two "observations" are of a more constructive nature,
for, while still joined to an attempted refutation of the
mercantilist position, they are principally designed to
show the manner in which money or monetary process
may make an important contribution to a nation's welfare.
We may consider the second of these observations first.[1]

Here Hume is concerned with the issue of the relationship between money and the wealth (and power) of the
state ; and in order to highlight the novelty of his view,
he poses the problem in the form of a paradox. In many
areas of Europe, he points out, "money is so scarce" that
taxes must be paid in kind ; and, as the sovereign receives
"small benefits from impositions so paid, it is evident
that such a kingdom has little force even at home : and
cannot maintain fleets and armies to the same extent,
as if every part of it abounded in gold and silver". As is
commonly supposed to be the case, this would seem to
indicate that the difficulty is caused by the scarcity of
money. But such a view obviously conflicts with "that
principle of reason that the quantity of gold and silver

[1] Cf. below, pp. 40–6.

lx

is in itself altogether indifferent". In resolving the paradox, Hume again turns to a discussion of economic development which, spanning the period from the "first and more uncultivated ages of any state" to a substantially developed commercial economy, parallels his opening analysis in the essay "Of Commerce". In a lengthy passage, what he here seeks to emphasise is the transformation from a barter to a money economy brought about by the growth of specialisation and exchange. And in so far as money enhances the wealth and power of the state, it is its *more general use*, as against its quantity, that he finds to be of significance. This view he bases on a twofold argument. First, the more widespread the distribution of money holdings, the greater the proportion of total revenue that can be raised in the more useful form of general purchasing power ; for, as he observes more pointedly elsewhere, the ability to raise taxes tends to vary inversely with the burden of the tax liability.[1] Secondly, the replacement of a barter by a money economy increases the quantity of goods "which comes to market", or the commodity-demand for money, and, if the quantity of money remains unchanged, this will produce a decrease in the general price-level. In the more advanced economics, therefore, the sovereign is better off not only because he "may draw money by his taxes from every part of the state ; [but] what he receives, goes farther in every purchase and payment".[2]

Though not entirely without parallel, it would appear on the basis of available studies that Hume's pointed emphasis on the economic implications of the growth of a money economy was unusual for his time.[3] It is to be

---

[1] Cf. below, p. 15. [2] Cf. below, p. 45.

[3] It is sometimes claimed that the effects of the transformation from a barter to a money economy played an important role in mercantilist monetary theory. Their emphasis on an increased quantity of money, it is said, was largely based on a desire to check the evils of falling prices which they feared would result from the greater commodity demand for money. Recent authorities have questioned this. Viner can find no evidence of this view in the English mercantilist writings and he argues that this inter-

observed, however, that since it assumes that the quantity of money remains unchanged, Hume's analysis (in particular his second point pertaining to the decrease in price-levels) does not explain the actual historical phenomenon under consideration and is essentially of a hypothetical or analytical character. For during the period involved the more advanced countries were acquiring substantial quantities of specie. Hume subsequently recognises this, but, changing the grounds of his argument, he points out that in these countries the increased commodity-demand for money (together with the expanded output resulting from their rapid economic development) had kept prices from rising as much as might otherwise have been expected. In contrast to the analysis in the essay "Of the Balance of Trade", as well as in his treatment of the relations between poor and rich countries, he does not note, however, that the acquisition of specie was itself a function of their economic development (having been acquired from poorer countries, most specifically Spain), and that a price-raising, equally with a price-lowering, tendency was a result of this same historical process. Two further shortcomings of the argument may be noted. There is no qualification for whatever increase in the money-demand for commodities might have occurred in the transition from a barter to a money economy ; and Hume does not note that the use of money as a medium of exchange is not entirely independent

---

pretation is also dubious on more general grounds. During the period in which the English mercantilists were most active, he points out, England had already developed a full money economy, and he also questions whether the mercantilists generally regarded falling prices as an evil. Cf. Viner, *op cit.*, pp. 33–6. Hecksher finds that two writers (Becher and Petty) showed concern over the difficulties which barter caused, specifically with regard to the payment of taxes. More broadly speaking, he does not entirely discount the possibility that a link between "mercantilism as a monetary system and the difficulties of the transition to a money economy" may have been implicit in some mercantilist thinking, but he states that this was "apparently only very slender". Cf. Hecksher, *Mercantilism*, VOL. II, pp. 219–21.

of, but, up to some point at least, depends on the quantity available.

Of the two "observations" the first [1] is of greater significance. For here Hume further considers the relation between money and the wealth of the community as a whole. This is likewise introduced in the form of a paradox arising out of a particular historical phenomenon. In this case it involves the reconciliation of the quantity theory with the fact, which he accepts as evidence of true causal relation, that the influx of specie into western European countries since the discovery of the American mines was followed by a general expansion of industry.

Here he distinguishes between the ultimate effect of a higher absolute quantity of money as such and the effect of the process of change to a larger quantity of money. It is to the former alone that the quantity theory applies. In the interim period and "before the money circulates through the whole state and makes its effect be felt on all ranks of the people" the monetary expansion in fact has two beneficial influences. The first is a pure employment effect. In this regard Hume makes explicit his initial assumption of less than full employment and it also should be noted that his analysis contains a relatively detailed and highly lucid account of the multiplier process. In a step by step fashion he traces the manner in which the increase in the quantity of money (supposed hypothetically to fall initially into the hands of the employer) increases the demand for labour, consumer income, and thus generates an expansion of employment and output throughout the economy as a whole.[2]

Though in itself not regarded as unimportant, this effect is not the one to which Hume gives primary em-

[1] Cf. below, pp. 36–40.
[2] An even more detailed treatment of the multiplier process is to be found in Cantillon. However, unlike Hume, Cantillon treats the effects of an increase in the quantity of money as largely inflationary from the outset and gives primary emphasis to its influence on the distribution of income. Cf. Cantillon, *op. cit.*, pp. 163–7.

phasis. Rather is he concerned to stress the essentially historical influence of the increase in the money supply, that is its impact on the "spirit of industry" itself. As he sums up the effects of the entire multiplier process, in response to the increased market demand the effort forthcoming from all classes of the population will eventually expand. ". . . we shall find that [the money] must first quicken the diligence of every individual, before it encreases the price of labour". In his final comment he then argues :

> From the whole of this reasoning we may conclude, that it is no manner of consequence, with regard to the domestic happiness of a state, whether money be in a greater or less quantity. The good policy of the magistrate consists only in keeping it, if possible, still encreasing ; because, by that means, he keeps alive a spirit of industry in the nation and encreases the stock of labour, in which consists all real power and riches.[1]

Viewed in the light of the historical phenomenon which Hume is attempting to explain, it is apparent that the protracted increase in the gold supply of the European nations takes its place as one factor responsible for the change in behaviour patterns underlying the growth of their economic activity. Though its emphasis is somewhat different, his analysis may be said to resemble the stress, in the literature of a later period, on the causal relation between the growth of pecuniary incentives and the development of a money economy as such.

It is clear, however, that in this "observation" Hume has become entangled in serious difficulties. Seeking to preserve the quantity theory, he has supposed that the beneficial effects of any monetary expansion would ultimately be transitory, or that the net effect of the process would be a pure price increase. He apparently assumes that this would be caused by an eventual increase in wage costs. Even his treatment of the first impact of

[1] Cf. below, pp. 39-40.

the expansion of the money supply conflicts with this supposition. For, as he here assumes a condition of less than full employment, there is no obvious reason why the resulting increase in output should be wholly ephemeral.[1] Needless to say, his adherence to the quantity theory is especially incompatible with the second part of his analysis, since here he has been concerned to emphasise that a basic change of habits of industry is involved. Hume has directed attention away from the "plenty of money" as such to the dynamics of monetary change, but in the process he has seriously undermined the basis of his attack on the mercantilist position.[2]

It may be noted that this unresolved ambiguity of his analysis appears in an especially conspicuous form in his summary of the quantity-theory specie-flow doctrine at the conclusion of the essay "Of the Balance of Trade".

[1] In the literature Hume's doctrine has been widely misinterpreted and possibly because of this the above-noted deficiency has been overlooked. Virtually all observers see it as an analysis of the benefits of inflation, the latter being construed either in a general sense or as differential price increases with emphasis on the inflation of unit profit margins. To mention but a few, cf. E. A. J. Johnson, *Predecessors of Adam Smith*, pp. 166–7, and J. Viner, *Studies in the Theory of International Trade*, p. 44. Careful examination will show that, far from holding that the rising prices were in any sense beneficial, Hume seemed to assume that—caused by belated wage increases—they produced or were symptomatic of a *decline* in employment. The output expansion is ascribed directly to the increase in purchasing power. It develops before any "alteration [of prices] is perceived" (p. 38), with receivers of increased incomes finding "every thing at the same price as formerly" (ibid.), and with the price rise occurring after a long delay during which, as appears clear, wages have first begun to rise (ibid.). Roll further compounds the usual error by gratuitously reading a class bias into the analysis. Hume was "quite happy" that the price rise was "at the expense of labour". Cf. his *History of Economic Thought* (New York 1939), p. 121.

[2] It is difficult to gauge the extent to which the historical effect of an increased money supply may have played a role in mercantilist thought, since their references to the relation between money and trade and industry are usually of a highly general nature. This effect does not explicitly appear in the most thorough of the treatments of the relation between money and trade (i.e., those of Potter and Law) where apparently it is the pure employment influence which is stressed. Though relatively vague and fragmentary, some of Petty's remarks—when brought together—seem to suggest a view similar to Hume's. Cf. *The Economic Writings of Sir William Petty*, ed. C. H. Hull (Cambridge 1899), VOL. I, pp. 36 and 60.

Here he first states : "In short, a government has great reason to preserve with care its people and its manufactures. Its money, it may safely trust to the course of human affairs, without fear or jealousy". But then he adds : "Or if it ever give attention to this latter circumstance [money] it ought only be so far as it affects the former".[1] This should be read specifically in connection with a portion of a letter of Hume to James Oswald which, written in response to Oswald's criticism of the manuscript of the essay, explicitly qualifies the quantity-theory specie-flow doctrine in conformity with his treatment of a protracted or gradual increase in the money supply.[2]

In view of these considerations, it is evident that Hume's emphasis on historical process is not only the most general element in his monetary theory, but also that it comprises its only consistent feature. As it was the purpose of underscoring the significance of this process that led him to belittle the domestic benefits of the "plenty of money", so was the objective of stressing the importance of this process his major guiding principle in his treatment of the positive influences of money on the economy. While he largely wrote as though he had successfully reconciled these two different phases of his analysis, his argument suggests that he was not unaware of the difficulties which they had created.[3] It is the historical perspective alone which is common to both the negative

---

[1] Cf. below, p. 77.

[2] Oswald had objected to Hume's position for its failure to recognise that, owing to its stimulating effects, a new acquisition of specie might remain within a country. Conceding Oswald's point qualifiedly, Hume writes : "I agree with you, that the increase of money, if not too sudden, naturally increases people and industry, and by that means may retain itself : but if it do not produce such an increase, nothing will retain it except hoarding". Cf. below, pp. 198–9.

[3] Indeed in one place Hume finds himself acknowledging—with evident embarrassment—that even the absolute quantity of money (here specifically credit) might prove stimulating. In this regard as well it is a historical influence which he stresses. Speaking of the development of the practice of note issue by banks, he asserts that by this means "a stock of five thousand pounds was able to perform the same operations as if it were six or seven ; and merchants were thereby enabled to trade to a greater extent, and to

and positive aspects of his treatment and primarily in this that one finds the logic of his contradictions.

Interest theory. Interest theory, in Hume's time, was in much the same state as monetary theory. The majority of the writers—representing the mercantilist position—had argued that interest was wholly a monetary phenomenon and, as a means of lowering the cost of borrowing, had repeatedly emphasised the desirability of an increased quantity of money.[1] There were, however, a few dissenting voices—in this case, it would appear, fewer than in the field of monetary theory proper—who, anticipating the later classical view, had contended that interest-rates were determined exclusively by the supply and demand for real capital.[2] Hume's position on this issue parallels his monetary theory in virtually every major respect. As there, he opens with an attack on the mercantilist position. Money, he repeats, is sought by borrowers only to acquire goods and services. A larger quantity of money will, however, not affect the wealth available for loan but will only raise prices.[3] If the supply of loanable funds is increased, the result therefore will simply be a proportionate increase in the demand, leaving the interest-rate unaffected.[4] Again, however, for Hume this is but the point of departure. He wishes to show that ultimately it is only through changes in the demand and supply of real savings that the rate of interest may be affected ; but he is more fundamentally concerned to show that the supply and demand are themselves conditioned by the

[1] The major supporters of the doctrine were Malynes, Misselden, Petty, Davenant and, considering one part of his position, Locke. Cf. Hecksher, *Mercantilism*, VOL. II, pp. 199 ff.

[2] Among those who took this position were Massie, Barbon, and North.

[3] As in his monetary theory, Hume makes clear that he is abstracting from the presumed interim effects of an increase in the money supply. Cf. below, p. 48.   [4] Cf. below, pp. 48–9.

---

require less profit in all their transactions". Cf. below, p. 71. As he adds later : "This renders the commodity cheaper, causes a greater consumption, quickens the labour of the common people, and helps to spread art and industry throughout the whole society". Cf. below, pp. 93–4.

effect of the development of trade upon economic motivation. His interest theory is, in fact, introduced as another "observation", in which, as against the quantity of money, he will prove that the phenomenon in question is reducible to "changes in manners and customs".[1] Indeed, it may be said that his analysis here represents the most complete embodiment of the "natural history" to be found in his political economy ; for in this case all the major laws of behaviour of this history are directly invoked in the formulation of his own doctrine.

To summarise his position,[2] Hume opens by considering an agrarian economy, where, as he points out, capital is likely to be scarce and the interest-rate high. This he traces to the nature of the class structure of the society—the division of the population into the landed aristocracy on the one hand and the peasantry on the other. The peasantry, it is clear, are not a source of capital since they "have no means, nor view, nor ambition of obtaining above a bare livelihood". As to the landowner, typically he makes heavy demands on available savings. The view that the idle landowner was characteristically given to extravagant consumption-expenditure was not new to the literature. Hume, however, seeks to explain this behaviour-pattern, and here the relation of his analysis to his treatment of economic motivation is clearly apparent ; for it represents a pointed application of his previously considered view concerning the causes of dissipation in general. As he points out, since the landowner is an idle rentier, he cannot gratify his natural desire for liveliness through economic pursuits. Overindulgence in pleasure, therefore, is his principal means of escape from an otherwise empty and tedious existence.

. . . as the spending of a settled revenue is a way of life entirely without occupation, men have so much need of somewhat to fix and engage them, that pleasures, such as they

---

[1] Cf. below, p. 46.   [2] Cf. below, pp. 49–56.

are, will be the pursuit of the greater part of the landholders, and the prodigals among them will always be more numerous than the misers. In a state, therefore, where there is nothing but a landed interest, as there is little frugality, the borrowers must be very numerous. : . . .

Continuing with his psychological analysis, he then seeks to show that as commerce develops the rate of interest necessarily tends to fall. First, owing to the influence of "lucrative employment" on the spending habits of the new merchant class, the development of trade promotes frugality. Here he invokes the twofold effect of "action".[1] By providing a more satisfactory avenue for the fulfilment of the desire for liveliness, lucrative employment not only diminishes the desire for pleasure, but, as it whets the desire for the objective symbolising success in the pursuit, it induces a love of gain. It is thus "an infallible consequence of all industrious professions to beget frugality, and make the love of gain prevail over the love of pleasure". Introducing what was to become the familiar distinction between "productive" and "unproductive" labour, he argues that the income received by the merchant (unlike that of the "lawyer" and "physician") is not compensated by reductions elsewhere. As the increase in output which he promotes and his share are both considerable, his savings thus represent large net additions to the supply. "By a necessary consequence", therefore, an expansion of commerce "produces lowness of interest".

Hume calls attention to a third, and ancillary, factor affecting the rate of interest—the rate of profit. The returns on both the latter, he points out, are in the nature of alternative costs. "No man will accept of low profits, where he can have high interest : and no man will accept of low interest, where he can have high profit". The growth of commerce, however, not only lowers

[1] It is at this juncture that Hume introduces the important passage on the "craving for exercise and employment" considered above, pp. xl, xlv.

interest-rates but has the independent effect of lowering the rate of profit too ; for "when commerce has become extensive and employs large stocks, there must arise a rivalship among the merchants, which diminish the profits of trade . . ." As debt and equities are substitutable forms of investment, in thus lowering the returns on both "an extensive commerce . . . is always assisted in its diminution of the one, by the proportional sinking of the other".[1] Hume argues that the reduction in the rate of profit itself promotes economic growth because, by lowering prices, it encourages consumption and thus stimulates the spirit of industry generally. As it is instrumental in encouraging investment and further reducing the rate of profit, a lower rate of interest would obviously be beneficial as well. Hume, however, does not single out the rate of interest for any emphasis in this connexion, since here it is in no sense a strategic factor subject to direct manipulation. Rather, like the rate of profit, it exerts its influence only as a product of economic development itself.[2]

This covers the dominant portion of Hume's interest analysis. Needless to say, since Hume's doctrine rests on the quantity theory, much the same questions concerning the role of money arise here as in his monetary analysis. And here too, where he again attempts to treat qualifying elements in terms of his historical perspective, it is not surprising to find the same unresolved ambiguity. Thus

---

[1] As an exception to the general rule, Hume notes that the rate of interest might also fall owing to a "sudden and great check to commerce". He observes, however, that since the decline here is accompanied by unemployment, this type of case is easily distinguishable from the secular decline. Cf. below, pp. 55–6.

[2] In so far as it views interest rates as a product of economic growth Hume's interest theory shares an emphasis found in Dudley North's treatment. Cf. North, *op. cit.*, p. 18. In other ways there is a similarity. Though he does not present a psychological or historical analysis comparable to Hume's, North stresses the influence on interest rates of the concentration of capital in the hands of the wealthy as commerce and industry develop. Cf. *op. cit.*, p. 17.

in the concluding portion of the essay, where he seeks to explain the reasons for the mercantilist error on the interest question, he cites the tendency of interest rates to fall in various European countries which had been acquiring specie. On quantity-theory specie-flow grounds he at first contends that the acquisition of the specie was wholly a product of their economic development and thus was only a joint consequence of the same factor responsible for the fall in interest rates.[1] But later, though he remains consistent in his error that its net ultimate effect would be a pure price increase, he acknowledges that in the course of its influx the increased specie was indirectly a true causal factor. By promoting the economic growth it helped to produce the change in spending and saving patterns which caused the fall in interest rates.[2]

A further qualification likewise arises from his attempt to explain the reasons for the mercantilist treatment of interest in monetary terms. Here he alludes to the cases of Spain and ancient Rome which, as he points out, experienced a fall in interest rates after they had acquired specie by conquest. This he grants was due directly to the increased money supply. But, contrasting it with the enduring influence of economic growth, he notes that this effect was temporary and argues that under the circumstances it could not be otherwise.[3] As he contends, in these instances the interest rate declined because the specie (since acquired by conquest) originally fell into few hands and for a time thus produced both the same concentration of money holdings and the same increased supply of loanable funds that would normally result from the growth of economic activity. However, since such growth did not occur (presumably because of an unfavourable social environment), the later rise in interest rates was inevitable. Habits had remained unchanged,

[1] ". . . the same industry, which sinks the interest, commonly acquires great abundance of the precious metals". Cf. below, p. 56.
[2] Cf. below, p. 59.   [3] Cf. below, pp. 57–8.

the specie (spent with the usual extravagance) proliferated throughout the economy in accordance with the old pattern, and the net effect necessarily was a pure price increase and the restoration of the initial supply and demand relations on loans.

Abstracting from its particular psychological interpretation, it is noteworthy that the relation of this part of Hume's interest theory to the central portion conforms to the distinction, commonly drawn in the literature of a later period, between ephemeral monetary influences on interest rates and those that reflect the state of economic development and the long run return on real capital. Though only by implication, here too however Hume concedes more to the mercantilists than he recognises. More particularly, he would have to acknowledge that directly through monetary means (or credit control) the rate of interest could be deliberately manipulated and, in view of his recognition of the relationship between the returns on debt and equities, that control of the former under favourable social conditions could be employed to stimulate investment and economic growth. The real capital basis of the long-term rate is preserved. But his (qualified) position implies that, causally speaking, the latter cannot always be sharply separated from the short-term rate. As in his monetary theory, it is clear that Hume's treatment of historical process explains the manner in which his analysis, both explicitly and inadvertently by implication, cuts across any single doctrinal classification applicable to the period.

The free-trade issue. When considered in the light of the broad policy questions of his period, perhaps the most important part of Hume's political economy is his treatment of the free-trade issue. It is obvious that this was a matter of great concern to Hume, and while much of his analysis appears in concentrated form, statements germane to the question are to be found in various parts of his writings. In the critical literature considerable attention

has been given to the free-trade elements in Hume's
doctrine. None the less the impression generally given by
the literature is misleading. Either by the nature of the
context in which it is considered or more explicitly, what is
often emphasised is the purely static aspect of Hume's
treatment, i.e., his recognition that trade involves the
exchange of goods for goods and his opposition to tariffs
on the ground that they prevent nations from enjoying
the products of their different human and material endow-
ments.[1] From the standpoint of doctrinal history this is
of course significant, and, as will be noted subsequently,
all that Hume had to say on this aspect of the issue has not
been recognised. But in his treatment in the essays this
is but a part, and a relatively minor part, of his analysis.
For here what concerns Hume most is the mercantilist
view that protection is needed if foreign expansion is not
to undermine home employment and the development
of home industry. As has been seen, this view was associated
with the belief that the economic opportunities of the
world were rigidly limited.

In the light of the dominant focus of Hume's economic
thought, this provides him with an unusually pertinent
issue. His response is fully characteristic. It is thus
economic development which is singled out as the
principal basis for the analysis of the question. This
applies in two senses. It is regarded as a major independent standard for judgment on the effects of foreign
trade and it is virtually entirely within the context of
historical considerations that the employment issue is
discussed. By placing economic growth at the centre
of the analysis Hume seeks to give it the more thorough
consideration that he thinks it merits and at the same
time he also seeks to meet the mercantilist argument on
its own grounds. This may be seen in a brief summary
of his argument in the essay "Of the Jealousy of Trade",
where the issue is considered in greatest detail.[2]

[1] Cf. below, pp. 67, 75, 79.   [2] Cf. below, pp. 78–82.

The historical framework of his treatment is made clear in the opening passages of the essay. Here, "In opposition to [the] narrow and malignant opinion" that all trading nations are rivals and cannot flourish except at one another's expense, he asserts that the "encrease of riches and commerce in any one nation, instead of hurting, commonly promotes the riches and commerce of all its neighbours ; and that a state can scarcely carry its trade and industry very far, where all the surrounding states are buried in ignorance, sloth and barbarism". This thesis he bases on two general grounds. The first is essentially a repetition of an argument previously considered in connexion with his more general treatment of the "natural history". We have seen that, owing to the peculiar force of its varied stimuli, Hume ascribes a strategic place to the role played by foreign trade in the development of the "spirit of industry".[1] Here he singles out for special emphasis the relationship between the foreign and domestic rate of technological development, arguing that it is commonly forgotten that such development in England was originally based on an "imitation of foreigners" and that were it not for their "continued instructions" and the constant stimulation provided by "emulation and novelty", her industrial arts would "fall into a state of languor". He then calls attention to the relation between the growth of foreign income and the demand for home exports : ". . . if our neighbours have no art or cultivation, they cannot take [our exports] ; because they will have nothing to give in exchange". This, he emphasises, parallels the case of trade between individuals, where "The riches of the several members of a community contribute to encrease my riches whatever profession I may follow".

What then of the case of an expansion abroad which competes directly with home industry ? Considering first the question of maintaining employment in the face of

[1] Cf. above, p. xxxiv.

competition resulting from a *general* growth of industry abroad, he argues that owing to the heterogeneity of factor-endowments among nations, no country need fear that a development of this nature will rob it of all its markets as long as it remains sufficiently "industrious and civilised" to exploit its own resources effectively—especially as he adds, when it is considered that foreign demand grows concomitantly with foreign income. Similarly, a nation has little cause to fear that foreigners can seriously encroach upon the market for its staple—which is after all the commodity in which it enjoys a special advantage—unless, through "idleness" or "bad government", it permits its leadership in the field to go by default. It would appear that Hume supposes that resource-endowment is so highly specialised, or that an early start in production is so important, that a single commodity cannot become the staple of two or more countries. Implicitly assuming that the foreign country's production of the staple is but part of a more general industrial expansion, he likewise argues here that, since this will be associated with a growth of foreign income, the resulting increase in demand might extend to the domestic staple as well and so might prevent a decline or even generate an increase in its domestic output. But even if the demand for the staple should fall, he continues, it need not be feared that the nation will suffer sustained unemployment as long as it preserves its "spirit of industry", for, granting the latter, resources may "easily be diverted" to a wide variety of other products "for which there appears to be a demand". In fact, since the emulation among nations "serves . . . to keep industry alive", the exposure to foreign competition will itself condition a nation for a rapid diversion of resources. It may be noted that on similar grounds Hume elsewhere supposes that effective resource diversion would be possible even if foreign markets substantially disappeared,[1] while here the re-allocation envisaged seems in some

[1] Cf. below, pp. 14-15.

part to contemplate new export demand. Finally, he points out that, in virtue of its influence on the spirit of enterprise, foreign competition will likewise minimise those market impacts which create a need for large scale resource diversion. As he emphasises, economic development itself promotes a wider diversification of resource-use. Consequently it provides insulation against "those revolutions and uncertainties, to which every particular branch of commerce will always be exposed".

In view of the more current revival of interest in under-developed nations and their international relationships all this has an obvious modern flavour. In its general outline, if not in its awareness of the more technical aspects of the problem, Hume's analysis foreshadows fundamental aspects of the contemporary liberal's answer to renewed proposals for protection as a means of alleviating the difficulties associated with disparate rates of national economic development.

In considering Hume's analysis as a whole, however, it is to be noted that on the basis of historical and other considerations he too displayed some protectionist thinking. It is clear, in fact, that his final position as formulated in the essay "Of the Jealousy of Trade" represented the culmination of much groping on the issue. (It will be recalled that this essay appeared six years after the other economic essays.) In earlier essays such as "Of Commerce" and "Of the Balance of Trade" there is indeed much that anticipates his final view. But on the other hand there is his treatment of the poor-country/rich-country question in the essay "Of Money". There he sees the long run interest of nations as unalterably opposed and can find comfort only in the supposition that, owing to the presumed effects of specie-flows, each country would have its exclusive opportunity to enjoy the advantages of economic development. As this type of perspective logically opens the way for the protectionist argument, it largely explains his well-known concession to the case for tariffs in the essay "Of the Balance of Trade", a concession which has generally appeared to be wholly *ad hoc* in character.[1] Though it would seem that Hume had long contemplated publishing a defence of free trade along the lines taken in the essay "Of the Jealousy of Trade",[2] there is evidence that his full renunciation of protectionism owed not a little to a discussion of his original poor-country/rich-country argument with Josiah Tucker.[3]

In appraising Hume's final position itself it should be observed that even here there is some evidence of the old doubts which, in view of the nature of the problem, is readily understandable. To some extent this is reflected in a tendency to overargue his case, which suggests that he was striving to convince himself virtually as much as the reader : e.g. his concern to show that a country preserving its spirit of industry could not lose the market for its staple and his equally deep concern to make clear that its readjustment to this eventuality would be "easy". There is also some more direct indication that Hume was not entirely certain that industriousness alone would render resource diversion simple. Thus near the conclusion of the essay he recognises the exception of the limiting case where such diversion is impossible. This is illustrated by the position of the Dutch who, presumably because of a highly specialised factor endowment, he supposes incapable of developing substitutes for their middleman and carrier function in international trade.[4]

In view of all these considerations it would appear that, with respect both to particular cases and for com-

---

[1] It appears especially *ad hoc* because it follows his pronouncement that tariffs are useless on quantity-theory specie-flow grounds and pernicious on grounds of interference with desirable exchange. As he states : "All taxes, however, upon foreign commodities, are not to be regarded as prejudicial or useless, but those only which are founded on the jealousy above-mentioned. A tax on German linen encourages home manufactures, and thereby multiplies our people and industry. A tax on brandy encreases the sale of rum and supports our southern colonies". Cf. below, p. 76.

[2] Cf. below, pp. 201-2.   [3] Cf. below, pp. 199-205 and 205n.

[4] Cf. below, p. 81.

paratively short or intermediate periods, Hume remained more fully aware of the possible costs of free trade than is readily apparent in his argument. Despite his well-pointed emphasis on the pertinence of historical factors to the different aspects of the issue, it would seem that his final repudiation of protectionism was based rather more largely on a further consideration of the general pre-quisites and longer run implications of international economic development itself. Perhaps the essence of his position is best reflected in a plea for liberalism at the conclusion of the essay, a statement which has frequently been noted for its cosmopolitan spirit.

Were our narrow and malignant politics to meet with success, we should reduce all our neighbouring nations to the same state of sloth and ignorance that prevails in Morocco and the coast of Barbary. But what would be the conse-quence? They could send us no commodities: They could take none from us: Our domestic commerce itself would languish for want of emulation, example and instruction: And we ourselves should soon fall into the same abject con-dition to which we had reduced them. I shall therefore venture to acknowledge, that, not only as a man, but as a British subject, I pray for the flourishing commerce of Germany, Spain, Italy, and even France itself. I am at least certain that Great Britain, and all those nations, would flourish more, did their sovereigns and their ministers adopt such enlarged and benevolent sentiments towards each other.[1]

Though it is to digress from the main theme of this study, before leaving Hume's treatment of the free-trade issue some further attention should be given the static aspect of his argument. In the economic essays, whenever he deals with the increase of real income that free trade would bring about at any given level of resource-use, Hume uniformly couches his treatment in terms of inter-national trade. As indicated, he emphasises the gains that would accrue to nations from the exchange of the products of their different factor-endowments. Since

---

[1] Cf. below, pp. 81–2.

attention has been confined to the essays, it has thus appeared that, whatever else its merits, Hume's statement of the liberal position overlooked the important welfare-implications of free domestic markets to which Adam Smith gave such pointed attention in dealing with the problem of internal resource-allocation. As an addendum, it may be noted therefore that in numerous references to the domestic market-regulations of the guild and mercantilist period which appear in his later *History of England* Hume addresses himself directly to this issue ; and, although introduced *ad hoc* and comparatively fragmentary, his commentaries here, moreover, leave little doubt that he had essentially grasped this aspect of classical doctrine as well. For, taken collectively, not only do they contain a condemnation of domestic market-restrictions as un-equivocal as any found in the *Wealth of Nations*,[1] but several further reveal a clear insight into the major functions of a free price-mechanism. To illustrate, when speaking of price-regulation during the reign of Henry VII, he says :

> In order to promote archery, no bows were to be sold at a higher price than six shillings and fourpence . . . The only effect of this regulation must be, either that the people would be supplied with bad bows, or none at all. Prices were also affixed to woollen cloth, to caps and hats : and the wages of labourers were regulated by law. It is evident, that these matters ought always to be left free, and be entrusted to the common course of business and commerce.[2]

In another passage where he attacks the imposition of price-ceilings on farm commodities during a period of short crops, he asserts :

---

[1] Statements of this character are innumerable and appear in several of the volumes. Among the practices attacked are the chartering of royal monopolies, wage and interest regulation as well as general price control, restrictions regarding apprenticeship and control of the movement of labour. See his *History of England* (Boston 1852), VOL. I, p. 275 ; VOL. II, pp. 74, 316–18, 447 ; VOL. IV, pp. 140, 335–6, 338, 366 ; VOL. V, pp. 195, 328.   [2] *Op. cit.*, VOL. III, p. 73.

Introduction

Parliament [was] not sensible that such an attempt was impracticable and that [even] were it possible to reduce the price of provisions by any other expedient than by introducing plenty, nothing could be more pernicious and destructive to the public. Where the produce of a year, for instance, falls so far short as to afford a full subsistence only for nine months, the only expedient for making it last all the twelve, is to raise the prices ; to put the people by that means on short allowance, and oblige them to save their food till a more plentiful season . . . In reality the increase of prices is a necessary consequence of scarcity ; and laws, instead of preventing it, only aggravate the evil by cramping and restraining commerce.[1]

Taken in conjunction with these statements, the following, however, is especially significant. For it not only treats the allocation question in a context which more directly involves the problem of alternative resource use but further posits, although in somewhat different and again partially historical terms, the harmony of private and public interest of Smith's celebrated "invisible hand" statement.

Most of the arts and professions in a state are of such a nature, that, while they promote the interests of the society, they are also useful or agreeable to some individuals ; and, in that case, the constant rule of the magistrate, except, perhaps in the first introduction of any art, is to leave the profession to itself, and trust its encouragement to those who reap the benefits of it. The artisans, finding their profits to rise by the favour of their customers, increase as much as possible their skill and industry ; and as matters are not disturbed by any injudicious tampering the commodity is always sure to be at all times nearly proportioned to the demand.[2]

Among the pre-Smithian writers there were of course others who, with varying insight into its implications, had

[1] *Op. cit.*, VOL. II, p. 172.
[2] *Op. cit.*, VOL. III, p. 128. This *laissez-faire* policy is contrasted with the need for special inducements to attract labour to occupations which give "no particular advantage or pleasure", e.g. ecclesiastical and military pursuits and the magistracy.

recognised this relationship between the economic interest of the individual and society, and in his *Lectures on Justice, Police, Revenue and Arms* (which preceded Hume's *History of England*), it would seem clear that Smith himself had already perceived the essentials of this doctrine.[1] In its relatively detailed treatment of the price-mechanism Hume's analysis, however, deserves recognition as one of the best of the early statements, and it is possible too that, in addition to the influence of his essays, the statements in his *History of England* may likewise have contributed to the further development of Smith's doctrine.[2] As is apparent from various references in the *Wealth of Nations*, Smith was very well acquainted with Hume's *History*.[3]

The shifting and incidence of taxes. In his analysis of the shifting and incidence of taxes—in particular as presented in the first part of his essay "Of Taxes"[4]—Hume considers

[1] In addition to containing relevant quotations from the *Lectures*, Cannan's introduction to the *Wealth of Nations* refers to some pertinent observations by Dugald Stewart. Cf. pp. xxx, xxxi, xliii.

[2] It has sometimes been argued that in his various references to "natural liberty", which appear in contexts in which he is discussing the wisdom of limiting government action, Smith was implying that state intervention was to be avoided because, as in the language of Locke, it violated man's "natural rights". His concessions to the necessity for state intervention would thus be regarded as particular and special qualifications of a more general and rationalistic philosophical principle. This view cannot be evaluated here. But it may be noted that Hume's position does not at all allow for such an interpretation. His treatment of the principles of human nature permits no place for anything comparable to "natural rights" and he never accepts anything but "utility" as the criterion for evaluating social policy. (Cf. below, pp. xci–xcii.) Also in one place, where he treats the issue in a general fashion, he takes a most favourable view of the role of government in society—treating it as the main vehicle for accomplishing social objectives which, owing to the shortsighted self-interest of individuals, would otherwise not be realised. Cf. *Treatise*, p. 539.

[3] It is of interest to note, in fact, that although he introduces it in a different context, Smith quotes directly from the last quoted passage cited from Hume's *History of England*. Cf. *The Wealth of Nations*, pp. 742–3.

[4] Though the second part of the essay is not directly relevant here, it is of considerable importance from the viewpoint of doctrinal history, since here Hume criticises the physiocratic view that all taxes are ultimately shifted to land. While his own position is not entirely consistent, his argument is especially interesting because it effectively calls into question the physiocratic acceptance of the subsistence theory of wages and its supposition that entrepreneurial activity in trade and industry does not

a psychological issue involved in a view commonly taken by the mercantilist writer$. This is the argument that excises affecting labour would be fully absorbed because "each encrease of public burdens encreases proportionably the industry of the people". Hume's position on this is twofold, and in its dual aspect its relation to his treatment of the growth of economic activity is fully apparent.

On the one hand, alluding to the generally stressed effect of "difficulty" on the spirit of industry, he in part supports this argument. We have seen that this aspect of his analysis is related to his emphasis on the desire for action, and hence indirectly for difficulty itself, as a basic economic incentive. As he points out, since "some natural necessities or disadvantages", such as relatively infertile land "render [a people] more opulent and laborious, than others, who enjoy the greatest advantages", "why may not artificial burdens have the same effect"? [1]

On the other hand, he argues that the stimulating effect of difficulty operates only within certain limits. Here—warning that continually increasing taxes eventually undermine the spirit of industry—he emphasises the importance of the opposite desire for the rewards of economic activity. As he states, it is essential that taxes "be laid on gradually, and affect not the necessaries of life", since "exorbitant taxes, like extreme necessity, destroy industry by producing despair; and even before they reach this pitch, they raise the wages of the labourer and manufacturer, and heighten the price of all commodities". Needless to say, the resulting despair would also reflect a loss of interest in the activity as such. It is apparent that

---

[1] Cf. below, p. 84.

yield a surplus. This part of the essay, moreover, formed the basis of a direct exchange with Turgot who, on the tax issue, was one of the outstanding exponents of the physiocratic position. In view of the fundamental differences in perspective between Hume and the physiocrats, it is not surprising to find that the exchange scarcely provided a basis for a clear joining, much less a resolution, of the issue. Cf. below, pp. 206–13.

on these grounds Hume thought that prevailing taxes were already too high, for he adds that "'tis to be feared that taxes all over Europe, are multiplying to such a degree, as will entirely crush all art and industry ; tho', perhaps, their first increase, together with other circumstances, might have contributed to the growth of these advantages".[1]

It would appear that in taking this combined view Hume reconciled two positions on the incidence question which usually had not been joined in this way or which even more commonly represented antithetical views found in isolation from each other. If the mercantilist "utility of poverty" school generally de-emphasised or overlooked the oppressive effects of high levies, those who drew attention to the shiftability of excises typically ignored (except for the short run) [2] the possible stimulating effects of moderate levies. Foremost among these latter were writers like Mun and the physiocrats and later both Smith and Ricardo who, on a subsistence or an accustomed standard of living theory of wages, argued that any tax affecting labour would necessarily lead to an eventual reduction in its supply.'[3]

Fiscal policy. While in part devoted to a general analysis of deficit finance, Hume's treatment of fiscal policy (in the essay "Of Public Credit") is more largely concerned with the specific question of large debt. Of all aspects of his political economy this bears the least direct relationship to the "natural history". None the less, it deserves atten-

---

[1] Cf. below, p. 85n.

[2] For example, Sir Walter Harris accepted the view that a reduction in real wages might prove stimulating in so far as it induced an attempt to preserve pre-existing living scales ; but on subsistence grounds he argued that this could only be temporary. Cf. his *Remarks on the affairs and trade of England and Ireland* (London 1691), pp. 53-4. It is reasonable to suppose that this was generally implicit in those views which emphasised the shiftability of excises.

[3] Though he generally accepts the subsistence doctrine (cf. *The Wealth of Nations*, pp. 815-16), it may be noted that in one place Smith distinguishes between excises affecting the luxuries and the necessities consumed by the poor and argues that the former would be absorbed through retrenchment. *Op. cit.*, pp. 822-3.

tion here because in every sense it displays the same characteristics as the rest of his political economy. Throughout, one finds that a historical perspective predominates. Moreover, of all parts of his political economy this affords the most striking illustration of Hume's awareness, as a "moral" scientist, of the relations between developments in different areas of social experience. Indeed, so marked is the stress on these relations that it may be said that his analysis is virtually as much a sociological and political tract as a study in fiscal policy.

Viewed most broadly the essay falls into two parts. The first takes the form of a summary treatment of the advantages and disadvantages of public credit. In the former the historical emphasis is apparent in his major argument. Here he observes that by providing a profitable and highly liquid investment-outlet (a new "kind of money") for the merchants' idle funds and for those whose investment preferences would otherwise lead them to divert all their mercantile funds to land, the development of the new security-market lowers the rate of profit. By lowering commodity prices, this induces an expansion of consumption, promotes increased labour-effort and encourages general technological innovation.[1] This emphasis is also apparent in his treatment of the disadvantages, where he relates the growth of the debt to

---

[1] Cf. below, p. 93. In a letter to Montesquieu, who had stated that he knew of "no advantages" to be gained from public debt, Hume makes the same point. Cf. below, p. 189. Blackstone had similarly pointed out that a government security could be "employed in any beneficial undertaking, by means of this its transferable quality ; and yet producing some profit when it lies idle and unemployed". Blackstone, *Commentaries on the Laws of England* (London 1855), BK. I, chap. 8. It should be noted, however, that Hume's point here conflicts with the position taken in his interest theory, for there he treats debts and equities as substitutes. This latter view had been specifically applied to public debt by Drake, who argued that, owing to the attraction of the high interest on the securities, such debt causes commercial stagnation. Cited in S. Matsushita, *The Economic Effects of Public Debts* (New York 1929), p. 15. For a somewhat similar view cf. Charles Davenant, *An Essay upon Ways and Means of supplying the War* (2nd edn., London 1695), pp. 43–4. In his above-cited letter to Montesquieu, Hume also refers to the position of Milford Lonsdale, who had argued

such matters as population movements from the provinces to the capital (and hence to the difficulty of preserving political stability), to the growth of a class of idle rentiers and to the opportunities for foreign control of domestic assets.[1]

In the second and larger part of the essay the similarity between this analysis and his political economy as a whole is even more fully apparent. As is indicated at the opening of the essay, Hume was persuaded that Britain's rising national debt—which, owing to her wars and poor debt-management, had been rapidly increasing for some time—was but a prelude to a further and indefinite increase.[2] This he bases on the view that to expect a public minister to exercise judicious restraint in the use of his borrowing powers is to expect the politically impossible. A minister will inevitably seek "to make a great figure during his administration without exciting any public clamour against himself. . . . It would scarcely be more imprudent to give a prodigal son a credit in every banker's shop in London, than to empower a statesman to draw bills, in this manner, upon posterity". As it is interesting to note, the view had already been expressed that "the public is no weaker upon account of its debts, since they are mostly due among ourselves; and bring as much property to one as they take from another".[3] Though his

---

[1] The last two points, and especially the former, were more common causes for concern. See Blackstone, *op. cit.*, pp. 297-8 ; Montesquieu, *Spirit of the Laws*, BK. XXII, chap. 17 ; C. Davenant, *op. cit.*, p. 111.

[2] During the preceding half-century the various wars in which England had been engaged had approximately quadrupled her total internal obligations. As would appear from all accounts, moreover, virtually no progress had been made toward retirement, the various sinking-funds established for this purpose being employed instead—apparently in a routine fashion—to defray current operating expenses. Cf. W. Cunningham, *The Growth of English Industry and Commerce in modern Times* (Cambridge 1925), VOL. II, pp. 423-4.   [3] This position had been taken by Melon.

---

along more modern lines that through its expansionary effects on the money supply the issuance of government securities stimulates industry by lowering the interest rate. He regards the validity of this view as "very doubtful".

earlier references to the disadvantages of public debt bear on this position, it is in this latter part of the essay that Hume undertakes in a pointed fashion to refute this doctrine. Thus what he seeks to show is that the inevitable continued rise in debt will not only have the gravest consequences for society but will ultimately terminate in total bankruptcy—a forecast which clearly had considerable basis in the many European debt repudiations (both of the open variety and through the route of currency-debasement and inflation) and which found echo in the expression of a general concern by others.[1] While Hume's prediction concerning the course of Britain's debt was not mistaken (it continued to rise fairly uniformly and quite rapidly),[2] it is apparent that in forecasting bankruptcy he underestimated Britain's correlative—if not permissive —capacity to bear debt ; though it is interesting to note that in a humorously worded escape-clause he makes allowance for this possibility.[3]

But, what is most interesting, it is apparent that this prediction itself is in all essential respects a "natural history of the rise and fall of public credit". In his maxim concerning the nature of ministers Hume has provided the "natural" basis for the rise of the debt. After tracing the constantly increasing tax-burdens required to service the mounting debt, the eventual cause of the collapse is seen in a rapid and large expansion of revenue-needs occasioned

---

[1] Cf., for example, *The Wealth of Nations*, p. 863.

[2] For a detailed discussion of the course of England's debt during this and subsequent periods, see E. Hamilton, "Origin and Growth of the National Debt in Western Europe", *American Economic Review, Proceedings*, vol. xxxvii, No. 2 (May 1947), pp. 118–30.

[3] As he states in speaking of the predicted bankruptcy, "One would incline to assign to this event a very near period, such as half a century, had not our fathers' prophecies of this kind been already found fallacious, by the duration of our public credit, so much beyond all reasonable expectation. When the astrologers in France were every year foretelling the death of Henry IV. *These fellows*, says he, *must be right at last*. We shall, therefore, be more cautious than to assign any precise date ; and shall content ourselves with pointing out the event in general". Cf. below, p. 105*n*. A similar word of caution appears in Smith's *Wealth of Nations*, p. 882.

by a war emergency. Three variants of the demise are noted : the "natural [most usual] death" itself, in which, having exhausted all sources of revenue in servicing the debt, the state repudiates its obligations by seizing the funds set aside for retirement[1]; a "violent death", in which the state, out of a misguided devotion to public faith, persists in using its retirement-funds to repay the debt and so falls prey to the invader[2]; and death at the hands "of the doctor", where, seeking the required funds by an emergency capital levy, the state further taxes the already overburdened property holders themselves and, thus "tampering" with the credit structure, precipitates the collapse.[3]

Here, where he traces the collateral effects of the continually increasing debt, the sweep of Hume's perspective is especially conspicuous. Some of the influences noted represent further extensions of points made in his opening treatment of the disadvantages of public debts. For example, he argues that, as the securities are highly liquid, the extravagance which will accompany the idleness fostered among their wealthy owners will mean a disruption of the continuity of possessions and with it a disruption in the continuity of cultural refinement, or whatever is left of it among this group.[4] In this context special emphasis is given to various political influences. Thus, having argued that the increased tax-burdens would ruin the landowner (and would eventually lead to a full socialisation of land), he points out that this would destroy the "independent magistracy" or "middle power" between the monarch and the people.[5] The resulting tendency toward political absolutism would be further strengthened, he argues, by the necessity of giving government the requisite power to extract additional revenue from an increasingly recalcitrant people, in particular the wealthier security-holder himself who now realises that his

[1] Cf. below, p. 104.   [2] Cf. below, p. 106.   [3] Cf. below, p. 102.
[4] Cf. below, p. 98.   [5] Cf. below, p. 99.

"earnings" from the securities are simply becoming payments from himself.[1] Interestingly enough in tracing the political effects of the rising debt, Hume is led to argue that the heavy debt-service requirements might conflict with the demands of an appropriate employment policy.

> Though a resolution should be formed by the legislature never to impose any tax which hurts commerce and discourages industry, it will be impossible for men, in subjects of such extreme delicacy, to reason so justly as never to be mistaken, or amidst difficulties so urgent, never to be seduced from their resolution. The continual fluctuations in commerce require continual alterations in the nature of the taxes ; which exposes the legislature every moment to the danger both of wilful and involuntary error. And any great blow given to trade, whether by injudicious taxes or by other accidents, throws the whole system of government into confusion.[2]

Hume also offers a prognostication for the period following the collapse. If couched in highly cynical terms, this obviously reflects an accurate reading of the relevant history. He thus insists that, despite the clear teachings of the debt experience, the public's incurable gullibility should make it a simple matter for the government to re-establish a system of public credit as flourishing as its predecessor. "Mankind are, in all ages, caught by the same baits : The same tricks played over and over again, still trepan them. The heights of popularity and patriotism are still the beaten road to power and tyranny ; flattery to treachery ; standing armies to arbitrary governments ; and the glory of God to the temporal interest of the clergy".[3]

Population. Though it has obvious economic relevance, as it is presented Hume's population theory is only partially related to his own treatment of the various issues of political economy. His analysis appears in the essay "Of the Populousness of Ancient Nations", which in its own right

[1] Cf. below, p. 100.   [2] Cf. below, p. 99.   [3] Cf. below, p. 104.

ranks as one of the major eighteenth-century historical studies of the population issue. Here Hume critically appraises (and is led to dispute) the thesis—popularised by Montesquieu—that the world population had fallen since antiquity.[1]

Hume introduces a wide variety of considerations both empirical and theoretical. With regard to the latter he excludes all argument based on "general physical causes" on grounds of insufficiency of reliable evidence.[2] Among the non physical factors considered are several of a major order. Perhaps the most general is the view that "it seems natural to expect that wherever there are most happiness and virtue, and the wisest institutions, there will also be the most people".[3] •Principally with this in view he then relates population growth to the distribution of income, the extent to which political power is decentralised, the size of the political unit, the conditions and extent of domestic and international peace, the institution of slavery,[4] and—alluding to the welfare implications of the growth of economic activity—he calls attention to the relation often referred to in his political economy, i.e. between "people" and "industry".

All our later improvements and refinements, have they done nothing towards the easy subsistence of men, and consequently toward their propagation and increase? Our superior skill in mechanics; the discovery of new worlds, by which commerce has been so much enlarged; the establishment of posts, and the use of bills of exchange: these seem all extremely useful to the encouragement of art, industry, and

---

[1] The main arguments of Montesquieu with which Hume takes issue in this essay are to found in BK. XXIII of his *Spirit of the Laws*. A discussion of the relationship between Hume's and Montesquieu's treatment which runs largely in terms of a comparison of the similarities in both texts is to be found in Roger Oake, "Montesquieu and Hume", in *Modern Language Quarterly*, II (March, 1948), pp. 25–41. In a treatment of the same issue which dealt largely in terms of the same influences, Robert Wallace in turn dissented from Hume's position. Cf. his *Dissertation on the Numbers of Mankind in Ancient and Modern Times* (Edinburgh 1753). And cf. below, p. 184n.

[2] Cf. below, pp. 108–9.

[3] Cf. below, p. 112.

[4] Cf. below, pp. 112–43.

populousness. Were we to strike off these, what a check should we give to every kind of business and labour, and what multitudes of families would immediately perish from want and hunger? And it seems not probable, that we could supply the place of these new inventions by any other regulation or institution.[1]

Some scattered comments in this essay have a decidedly Malthusian flavour—for example : "The prolific virtue of men, were it to act in' its full extent, without that restraint which poverty and necessity impose on it, would double the number every generation".[2] It is to be presumed that it was these that Malthus had in mind when he mentioned Hume as one among several (Wallace, Price, ·Smith) whose work contributed to the development of his own doctrine.[3] It would seem clear, however, that —appearing in *ad hoc* form—these comments do not accurately represent Hume's general position. His recognition of the importance of other conditions affecting population growth implies a more pluralistic view than the stress on "poverty and necessity" would suggest. Also in his essay "Of Taxes", and especially in its latter portion where he criticises the physiocratic position on incidence, he pointedly rejects the subsistence theory of wages. This moreover is more fully consistent with his general emphasis, in his treatment of economic development, on the rise in scales of living. Various of his comments would in fact seem to suggest the belief that with the growth of capital and the advance of technology an expanding population would itself contribute to the rise of *per capita* income.[4]

[1] Cf. below, p. 146. A similar view is found elsewhere in the literature. Cf., for example, Nicholas Barbon, *A Discourse of Trade*, p. 25.

[2] Cf. below, pp. 128–9 ; also pp. 111–12.

[3] T. R. Malthus, *An Essay on the Principle of Population* (London 1890), p. xxxv.

[4] See, for example, his various comments pertaining to this in the essay "Of the Balance of Trade".

Chapter IV

HUME'S ECONOMIC PHILOSOPHY

THERE remains to be considered the normative level of Hume's economic thought where, discussing the controversial issue of luxury, he seeks to frame a comprehensive appraisal of a commercial society. Owing to the compartmentalisation of social disciplines, this aspect of his analysis (as in the case of his economic psychology) has generally received little attention in the histories of economic doctrine. In view of his background and his general concern with both moral theory and practical moral issues (at least one writer has held that from the outset this was his fundamental concern),[1] it would have been surprising, however, had Hume failed to give full attention to so important an ethical issue of his time.[2] Considered in one of the opening essays—"Of Refinement in the Arts"— where he elaborates and further adds to the points made in the more special context of the essay "Of Commerce", it occupies in fact a key position in his economic thought ; and, though this question is separated from the more positive issues of his analysis, it is clear that he regarded its treatment as a *sine qua non* in the study of economic activity.

Viewed in its setting, Hume's analysis is addressed to the extreme prevailing positions on luxury, and it takes the form of an attempt to mediate between them. As he makes clear at the outset—and in conformity with his own moral theory—it is ultimately in terms of its implications for human welfare, or of its utility, that luxury must be

[1] Norman Kemp Smith, *The Philosophy of David Hume* (London 1941).
[2] It is interesting to note that Hume, in fact, presents an abridged summary statement of his position on the luxury issue in his *Enquiry concerning the Principles of Morals*. Cf. p. 181.

judged.[1] The "monkish" view which regarded luxury, *qua* sense indulgence, as sinful *in se*, he thus immediately dismisses as a type of perversion. What does concern him are two other of the contemporary extremes : on the one hand, the position of the "men of severe morals" who regarded even "innocent" or the most moderate luxury as the root of evil, and on the other the opposite "libertine" view, which saw even the most excessive forms of luxury as a social blessing. With regard to these he takes a threefold position : (1) far from being reprehensible, the ages of "refinement", i.e. "innocent" luxury, are in fact the "happiest and most virtuous", (2) where luxury is excessive, it must be recognised as "the source of many ills", but (3) even vicious luxury is preferable to a society entirely without luxury. It is to be noted that in his general criticism of the unqualified views on the luxury question Hume takes the position of the historical relativist on matters of moral judgment, pointing out that "any degree of [luxury] may be innocent or blameable, according to the age, or country, or condition of the person. The bounds between the virtue and the vice cannot here be exactly fixed, more than in other moral subjects".[2]

[1] Presented initially in Book III of the *Treatise*, the moral theory was recast in simplified form in the *Enquiry* on morals. As he argues, most of the "private virtues"—prudence, patience, etc.—are regarded as morally estimable because they are "useful to the person himself", while benevolence and justice command approval as "social virtues" because they are "useful to others". In the resolution of all issues affecting society, moreover, it is "this circumstance of public utility which is ever principally in view ; and whenever disputes arise, either in philosophy or common life, concerning the bounds of duty, the question cannot, by any means, be decided with greater certainty, than by ascertaining, on any side, the true interests of mankind. If any false opinion, embraced from appearances, has been found to prevail ; as soon as farther experience and sounder reasoning have given us juster notions of human affairs, we retract our first sentiments, and adjust anew the boundaries of moral good and evil". *Enquiry concerning the Principles of Morals*, p. 180. It is to be noted, however, that certain qualities are regarded as virtues because of their "immediate agreeability" either to the possessor or to others and without any regard to their "utility or any tendency to further good". *Op. cit.*, sects. 7, 8.

[2] As he states in "A Dialogue", where the historical variability of customs and moral sentiments is the major theme of his analysis, "A degree

It is also noteworthy that in speaking of the "libertine" view he had most specifically in mind Mandeville's paradox of the *Fable of the Bees*, where, in his deliberately outraging attack on the traditional rationalist morality, Mandeville had argued that as it stimulated employment, even the most extravagant self-indulgence was socially praiseworthy. Here, where Hume seeks to restore the legitimacy of discriminative moral judgment within the framework of utilitarian ethics, it is to be observed that he bases his position ultimately on principles which had earlier been stated in his *Treatise*.[1]

We have said that what is most generally significant here is the important role which the "natural history" plays in his analysis. For, now extended to embrace major non-economic areas of human experience, it forms the basis of the whole of his treatment of "refinement" and, making up the largest part of the essay, it forms the most important basis for his more general judgment of luxury as well. In this case the analysis is so highly organised that, once the outlines of this history are recognised, the relevant relationships become immediately apparent. To summarise this portion of his argument, Hume opens by seeking to show that "refinement" is conducive to individual happiness. It is at this juncture,

---

[1] This principle is that our standard for moral judgment always depends upon the usual behaviour of people or on "the common and natural course of the affections". Cf. *Treatise*, pp. 483–4. Mandeville's position is thus rejected because in arguing that vicious or self-indulgent expenditure is necessary to stimulate employment, he does not recognise that conformity with the usual, i.e. "virtuous", behaviour does not involve a sharp reduction in expenditure, but the *same* expenditure more fully directed toward furthering the interests of family, friends and the poor. So conceived then, to designate selfish expenditure as vicious does not entail any inconsistency between the demands of the private and social interest. Cf. below, pp. 30–1.

---

of luxury may be ruinous and pernicious in a native of Switzerland, which only fosters the arts, and encourages industry in a Frenchman or Englishman. We are not, therefore, to expect, either the same sentiments, or the same laws in Berne, which prevail in London or Paris". Cf. *Hume's Enquiries*, p. 337.

where he gives detailed attention to the appropriate standards for evaluation, that he refers to the four "ingredients of human happiness" (pleasure, action, liveliness and indolence)—the desires for the first three of which are, in other contexts, treated as the principal "causes of labour" which are both more fully activated and rewarded by the expansion of trade and industry.[1] As in these other contexts, in more pointedly considering these passions as ends he again stresses their organic relations : ". . . though these ingredients ought to be mixed in different proportions, according to the particular disposition of the person ; yet no one ingredient can be entirely wanting, without destroying, in some measure, the relish of the whole composition". In a second major argument he then joins the growth of economic activity to the growth of intellectual and general cultural refinement, contending that "industry, knowledge [in the field of the liberal as well as the mechanical arts] and humanity, are linked together by an indissoluble chain, and are found, from experience as well as reason, to be peculiar to the more polished, and, what are commonly denominated, the more luxurious ages". Lastly, he argues that commerce is likewise beneficial from the political point of view. Here, going well beyond his argument in the essay "Of Commerce", he adduces a wide range of important considerations, including the effect of the growth of commerce on a nation's spiritual as well as its economic capacity for defence, the relation between the general growth of knowledge and an understanding of the more mechanical techniques of political administration, and the impact of the growth of both knowledge and humanity on the prevalence of faction and hence on internal political harmony itself. What absorbs him most, however, is the common argument (drawn from the experience of Rome) that by encouraging venality and corruption in government, luxury destroys political liberty ; and here, in a

[1] Cf. above, pp. xxxv–xxxvi.

detailed analysis, he attempts to show that the truth lies with the very reverse of this thesis.

Some aspects of his argument concerning the effects of "refinement" are deserving of special attention. With regard to his treatment of individual happiness, it is interesting to note that the pluralistic prescription here presented is deliberately designed to accommodate the principal philosophies of "The Good Life" as Hume interprets them in an earlier series of essays. These are entitled respectively "The Epicurean", "The Stoic", "The Platonist", and "The Sceptic".[1] More particularly, in light of our earlier analysis of Hume's economic psychology, it should be apparent that in its most basic terms this prescription (action and pleasure, indolence and liveliness) represents a composite of broad categories of opposites— striving versus realisation, and states of no passion versus states of emotional excitement. The former dichotomy will be recognised in the opposition which Hume draws between the view of the Stoic [2] and that of the Epicurean, while the latter represents the contrast between the ultimate desideratum of the Platonist (i.e. "contemplation", or, more generally, "perfect tranquility and repose") and the major element common to the position of both the Stoic and the Epicurean. Moreover this pluralism itself represents a direct application of the position which is outlined in the opening passage of the essay "The Sceptic". Because it so aptly expresses the spirit under-

[1] The subtitles of the first three are respectively "the man of elegance and pleasure", "the man of action and virtue", and "the man of contemplation and philosophical devotion". Cf. *Phil. Wks.*, vol. iii, pp. 197–231. Of this series of essays Hume says that his "intention . . . is not so much to explain accurately the sentiments of the ancient sects of philosophy as to deliver the sentiments of sects that naturally form themselves in the world, and entertain different ideas of human life and happiness. I have given each of them the name of the philosophical sect, to which it bears the greatest affinity". *Op. cit.*, p. 197n.

[2] As indicated by its subtitle, throughout his treatment of the position which he characterises as that of the Stoic, Hume accords a central place to the value of positive striving to overcome difficulty and does not refer to the more usually emphasised passive endurance of adversity.

lying this part of his economic philosophy, this may well be quoted at some length.

I have long entertained a suspicion, with regard to the decisions of philosophers upon all subjects, and found in myself a greater inclination to dispute, than assent to their conclusions. There is one mistake, to which they seem liable, almost without exception ; they confine too much their principles, and make no account of that vast variety, which nature has so much affected in all her operations . . .

But if ever this infirmity of philosophers is to be suspected on any occasion, it is in their reasonings concerning human life, and the methods of attaining happiness. In that case, they are led astray, not only by the narrowness of their understandings, but by that also of their passions. Almost every one has a predominant inclination, to which his other desires and affections submit, and which governs him, though, perhaps, with some intervals, throughout the whole course of his life. It is difficult for him to apprehend that any thing, which appears totally indifferent to him, can ever give enjoyment to any person, or can possess charms, which altogether escape his observation. His own pursuits are always, in his account, the most engaging : The objects of his passion, the most valuable : And the road, which he pursues, the only one that leads to happiness.

But would these prejudiced reasoners reflect a moment, there are many obvious instances and arguments, sufficient to undeceive them, and make them enlarge their maxims and principles. Do they not see the vast variety of inclinations and pursuits among our species ; where each man seems fully satisfied with his own course of life, and would esteem it the greatest unhappiness to be confined to that of his neighbour ? Do they not feel in themselves, that what pleases at one time, displeases at another, by the change of inclination ; and that it is not in their power, by their utmost efforts, to recall that taste or appetite, which formerly bestowed charms on what now appears indifferent or disagreeable ? [1]

When viewed in terms of the dichotomy represented by the position of the Platonist on the one hand and the Epicurean and Stoic on the other, it is apparent that

[1] *Op. cit.*, pp. 213-14.

Hume's position is far less sympathetic to the former than to the latter. For, as one might expect from his general emphasis on "liveliness"—and as he makes explicit in his treatment of the four ingredients—it is only as a respite from the "quick march of the spirits" that he regards complete repose as at all gratifying. As the Epicurean says to the man of contemplation :

Miserable, but vain mortal ! Thy mind be happy within itself ! With what resources is it endowed to fill so immense a void, and supply the place of all thy bodily senses and faculties ? Can thy head subsist without thy other members ? In such a situation,

> *What foolish figure must it make ?*
> *Do nothing else but sleep and ake.*[1]

Although the question is not considered in the essay "Of Refinement in the Arts", there would likewise seem to be no doubt that as between the positions of the Stoic and the Epicurean it was the former's emphasis on meaningful striving that Hume regarded as more ultimately significant for human well-being. His position on the central importance of action, both intrinsically and as a complement to the enjoyment of "pleasure", is brought out clearly in the following :

Though the tempers of men be very different, yet we may safely pronounce in general, that a life of pleasure cannot support itself so long as one of business, but is much more subject to satiety and disgust. The amusements, which are the most durable, have all a mixture of application and attention in them ; such as gaming and hunting. And in general, business and action fill up all the great vacancies in human life.[2]

And, says the Stoic in addressing himself to the enlightenment of the Epicurean :

In vain do you seek repose from beds of roses : In vain do you hope for enjoyment from the most delicious wines and

[1] *Op. cit.*, p. 199.   [2] *Op. cit.*, p. 220.

fruits . . . Your pleasure itself creates disgust. The mind, unexercised, finds every delight insipid and loathsome ; and ere yet the body, full of noxious humours, feels the torment of its multiplied diseases, your nobler part is sensible of the invading poison, and seeks in vain to relieve its anxiety by new pleasures, which still augment the fatal malady.[1]

In the light of this it is not improbable then that Hume is voicing his own view when, in a general paraphrase of the Stoic's position, he treats all forms of disciplined action as facets of the *summum bonum* represented by a more inclusive striving for a greater harmony between human desires themselves. It is clear that what Hume here has in mind is essentially the view, now commonly emphasised in justifying a free society, that it is the striving for self-fulfilment that is ultimately the most important single human value.

Can no particular pleasure be attained without skill ; and can the whole be regulated without reflection or intelligence, by the blind guidance of appetite and instinct ? Surely then no mistakes are ever committed in this affair ; but every man, however dissolute and negligent, proceeds in the pursuit of happiness, with as unerring a motion, as that which the celestial bodies observe, when, conducted by the hand of the Almighty, they roll along the ethereal plains. But if mistakes be often, be inevitably committed, let us consider their causes ; let us weigh their importance ; let us inquire for their remedies. When from this we have fixed all the rules of conduct, we are *philosophers :* When we have reduced these rules to practice, we are *sages.*

Like many subordinate artists, employed to form the several wheels and springs of a machine : Such are those who excel in all the particular arts of life. *He* is the master workman who puts those several parts together ; moves them according to a just harmony and proportion : and produces true felicity as the result of their conspiring order.

While thou hast such an alluring object in view, shall that labour and attention, requisite to the attainment of thy end, ever seem burdensome and intolerable ? Know, that this

[1] *Op. cit.,* p. 206.

labour is the chief ingredient of the felicity to which thou aspirest . . .[1]

It has been noted that, as part of his second major argument, Hume links the growth of a spirit of industry to the growth of "humanity". In view of the attention given to Adam Smith's recognition of the social origins of a sense of morality (in his *Theory of Moral Sentiments*),[2] it is of some importance to observe that here, although technically on somewhat different grounds, Hume likewise perceives that the cohesive moral forces which preserve mutually satisfactory relationships in society are themselves largely a product of society's influence. As he points out, owing to the improvement of tastes and the growth of knowledge which accompany economic development, individuals increasingly seek each other out to enjoy the give-and-take that springs from the sharing of a common fund of experience and from the growing sense of belonging to a common social tradition. "They flock into cities ; love to receive and communicate knowledge ; to show their wit or their breeding ; their taste in conversation or living, in clothes or furniture. . . . Both sexes meet in an easy and sociable manner : and the tempers of men, as well as their behaviour, refine apace". Consequently, "beside the improvements which they receive from knowledge and the liberal arts, it is impossible but they must feel an encrease of humanity, from the very habit of conversing together, and contribute to each other's pleasure and entertainment".

The more technical foundations of this position are to be found in Hume's philosophy, in particular in his treatment of "sympathy". Hume defines "sympathy" as an

[1] *Op. cit.*, pp. 205–6.

[2] See, for example, J. H. Tufts, "The Individual and his Relation to Society as reflected in the British Ethics of the 18th Century", in *Psychological Review*, VI (May 1904), esp. pp. 49–50, and Glenn R. Morrow, "Adam Smith : Moralist and Philosopher", in *Adam Smith, 1776–1926*, ed. J. Hollander (Chicago 1928), pp. 175 ff.

associative mechanism through which the mind, primarily on the basis of resemblance, infuses the "idea" of the emotions of others with the "liveliness" intrinsic to the impression of "self".[1] As the vehicle for the growth of a sense of morality it would appear to be operative in a twofold fashion. Most generally, as he argues in the *Treatise*, the evocation of a benevolent response to others depends in large measure on the vivacity of our perception of their emotions. Thus pain, but weakly sympathised with, is likely to produce aversion, since the reaction in this case is conditioned wholly by the disagreeable nature of the passion sympathised with. When sympathy is intense, however, "the conception is not confin'd merely to its immediate object, but diffuses its influence over all the related ideas, and gives [one] a lively notion of all the circumstances of that passion, whether past, present or future, possible, probable, or certain".[2] By entering into another's emotions fully, in a word, we cannot avoid becoming interested in his total welfare. Most fundamentally then, the encouragement given to "humanity" by the development of a more closely knit society may be traced to its influence in widening the basis for the association of "self" with others, or in deepening the sympathetic process through which we participate in the immediacy of their experience.[3] Also, as Hume recognises, we

[1] *Treatise*, pp. 317–20. The role of "liveliness" in this context bears a direct relationship to all its other roles in Hume's treatment of human nature. As noted above (p. xlvii) "action" itself is regarded as desirable not merely for its intrinsic liveliness, but because this in turn enlivens all related experiences (cf. *op. cit.*, pp. 353, 433–4) ; the effect of "novelty" (cf. above p. xxxiv *n*) is also reduced to liveliness ; while this is also central to Hume's doctrine of "belief", which is defined as "a lively idea related to a present impression". *Op. cit.*, pp. 93, 98, 209.

[2] *Op. cit.*, p. 386. It is here that Hume first introduces the process of "parallel direction" (cf. above, p. xlvi *n*) as a means of showing how "strong pity", through a "similarity in general bent and tendency" necessarily leads to love.

[3] As he adds elsewhere, "as the benevolent concern for others is diffused, in a greater or less degree over all men, and is the same in all, it occurs more frequently in discourse, and the blame and approbation, consequent

"sympathise with others in the sentiments they entertain of us".[1] Thus, nourished by a growing concern over our reputation in society, "this constant habit of surveying ourselves, as it were, in reflection, keeps alive all the sentiments of right and wrong, and begets, in noble natures, a certain reverence for themselves as well as others, which is the surest guardian of every virtue".[2]

Among the last group of arguments (which concerns the development of the state) the most noteworthy is that portion dealing with the relation between the economic revolution of his general period and political liberty—which is presented as part of his refutation of the argument that the latter is undermined by a materialistic society. For here in a remarkably lucid statement he emphasises the point (which Adam Smith drew upon later) [3] that it

---

[1] *Treatise*, p. 499.

[2] *Enquiry concerning the Principles of Morals*, p. 276. In so far as it calls attention to the moralising effects of public opinion, Hume's treatment is similar to Adam Smith's. Cf. his *Theory of Moral Sentiments* (London 1792), pp. 160 ff. But Smith's doctrine of sympathy differs from Hume's in that it would appear to be more largely of an egoistic character. For him it would seem that our reaction to an emotion sympathised with is, at least to an appreciable degree, conditioned by an induced experience of the same emotion. Cf. *op. cit.*, p. 6. Though Hume's doctrine (specifically in the *Treatise*) has also often been held to be egoistic in origin, as he treats it, "sympathy" does not make *another's* experience *my* experience, but simply renders *my* idea of another's experience more vivid. It thus presupposes the evocation of a native benevolence. Cf. E. B. McGilvary, "Altruism in Hume's *Treatise*", in *Philosophical Review*, XII (May 1903), p. 272. Hume's position should also not be identified with Smith's related doctrine of the "impartial spectator" which involves a sympathy with what we imagine *ought* to be the judgment of others and rests on a natural "love of virtue" or "conscience". Cf. Smith, *op. cit.*, p. 162. Hume denies that the "love of virtue" is irreducible and argues that all moral judgment ultimately rests on utility considerations. Cf. *Treatise*, pp. 478–80.

[3] Cf. *The Wealth of Nations*, p. 385. Smith here refers not only to this point but to other of the beneficial political changes that Hume had traced to the growth of commerce. Smith regards these as "by far the most important of all" the effects of commerce. "Mr. Hume is the only writer who, so far as I know, has hitherto taken notice of [them]".

---

on it, are thereby roused from that lethargy into which they are probably lulled, in solitary and uncultivated nature". *Enquiry concerning the Principles of Morals*, p. 275.

was the growth of economic decentralisation and individualism associated with this revolution that was primarily responsible for the growth of political liberty and parliamentary government. Thus, after directing attention to the manner in which the feudal hierarchy inevitably bred general subservience, he stresses the political effect of the emancipation of the peasant and, in particular, the influence on the authority of the Commons of the new merchant class, "the middling rank of men". As he states in explaining the liberating implications of the latter's class interest and ideology, these are "the firmest basis of public liberty", for they "submit not to slavery, like the peasants, from poverty and meanness of spirit ; and having no hopes of tyrannising over others, like the barons, they are not tempted, for the sake of that gratification, to submit to the tyranny of their sovereign. They covet equal laws, which may secure their property, and preserve them from monarchical, as well as aristocratical tyranny".[1]

The discussion has stressed those aspects of Hume's economic philosophy which exhibit its continuity with his own psychology and general historical perspective. In viewing it more generally, it is well to note, however,

---

[1] It may be noted that in other writings of his Hume emphasises the necessity of preserving "authority", and this has led to considerable discussion of whether he was more inclined to the Whig or Tory point of view, with evidence being adduced from both the essays and his *History of England* to support one emphasis or the other. A reading of both, however, clearly seems to indicate that, although perhaps especially in the *History* his Tory side may have predominated, on the whole Hume was primarily concerned with a *proper balance* between "liberty and authority". See in particular, "Of the Liberty of the Press", in *Phil. Wks.*, VOL. III, p. 11 ; "Whether the British Government Inclines More to Absolute Monarchy, or to a Republic", *op. cit.*, p. 122 ; and "Of the Parties of Great Britain", *op. cit.*, p. 133, where, as one writer has pointed out, Hume sees both the Whig and Tory as recognising the desirability of liberty and authority, though with a little different stress on each. For a further discussion of this see Ernest C. Mossner, "Was Hume a Tory Historian ?" in *Journal of the History of Ideas*, II (April 1941), pp. 225–36 ; and Marjorie Grene, "Hume : Sceptic and Tory ?" in *Journal of the History of Ideas*, IV (June 1943), pp. 333–48.

that it also contains some serious lacunae and contradictions. For example, though he has emphasised that
luxury whets the appetite for both "pleasure" and "gain",
in answering the charge that it undermines political liberty
by promoting venality and immorality in government he
denies that there is any functional relation between luxury
and greed. Falling back on a universalistic position, he
contends that avarice is equally intense at all times ;
and here, incongruously gauging the relative intensity of
the general desire for wealth in different time periods by
the desire for "particular" pleasures in any given time
period, he invokes the principle of the relativity of all
-value. "The value which all men put upon any particular
pleasure, depends on comparison and experience ; nor is
a porter less greedy of money, which he spends on bacon
and brandy, than a courtier, who purchases champagne
and ortolans".[1] It is apparent that in taking this view
he exposes his position to the argument—earlier stressed
by Hutcheson and Shaftesbury—that there is no net gain
to be derived from the pursuit of the "pleasures" of luxury.

Again, at one critical juncture, where he argues that
the evils of refinement are likely to be far outweighed by
its benefits, he bases his position chiefly on the general
proposition that "The more men refine upon pleasure, the
less they indulge in excess of any kind ; because nothing
is more destructive to true pleasure than such excesses".[2]
This would seem to presuppose that there is some highly
rational element in human nature which once exposed
to "refinement" inevitably leads one to the continued
pursuit of "true" pleasure—a view which is not readily
reconcilable with his own and the Stoic's emphasis on the
difficulty of controlling the instinctive and irrational
elements in human behaviour. But more important, in
treating "refinement" as a kind of self-perpetuating state
conducive to nothing but further "virtue and happiness",
it leaves one at a loss to explain the origin not only of the

[1] Cf. below, p. 27.   [2] Cf. below, p. 23.

"evils" here mentioned but of all those serious "excesses" which he wishes to recognise in correcting the position of the "libertine".[1] In the light of these considerations, one is inclined to suspect that, although his defence of luxury was philosophically more discriminating than Mandeville's, in part Hume was here over-indulging his own patent and often expressed distaste for the excesses of religious "enthusiasm".[2]

None the less it may perhaps be said that Hume's analysis displays his capacities as a moral scientist and historian more fully than any other portion of his writings of comparable size. In common with others of his own period, Hume possessed relatively little knowledge of the culture of the middle ages. Though he was more generally aware of the historical variability of "customs and manners" and the necessity of appraising them in the light of relevant conditions, he too apparently regarded this period as largely or wholly "barbarous". His portrayal of the progress represented by "refinement", especially in such respects as the growth of social relations, thus appears exaggerated in view of what is now known. But it is probably no over-statement to say that in its grasp of various of the distinctive contributions of his own age and their ideological founda-tions and as a statement of the liberal social philosophy his treatment deserves recognition as an early classic.

[1] Though emphasised in a general fashion, it may be noted that these "excesses" themselves are given much less detailed attention than the advantages of luxury. As the manner in which these excesses develop and their relation to previous advantages are treated only in a summary fashion, this further enhances the sense of discontinuity between a con-dition of "refinement" and "vicious" luxury. However, this largely appears to be a by-product of a belief that, beyond a demonstration that the evils could consistently be regarded as such (in refutation of Mandeville), they were of such common knowledge as to require little comment. While his broadest purpose was to correct both extreme positions on luxury, it would seem clear that Hume felt that, in restoring a more balanced view on the issue, the more pressing need lay in a correction of the oversights of the traditional morality.

[2] On this cf., for example, *Enquiry concerning the Principles of Morals*, p. 270.

Chapter V

CONCLUDING COMMENTS

THROUGHOUT this study major emphasis has been given to the psychological and historical aspects of Hume's economic thought because this provides the most meaningful basis for interpreting what he was generally seeking to accomplish as an economist. As we have seen, there is virtually no major portion of his treatment which can be considered apart from either or both of these aspects of his analysis ; and, so conceived, it is apparent that his economic essays reflect a very significant measure of unity in both purpose and method. Indeed, if one may say, with Teggart, that the natural history of the eighteenth century was "not some curious aberration of thought but a most serious effort to lay the foundations for a strictly scientific approach to man", it is clear that a very substantial part of Hume's economic thought (along with other phases of his general inquiry) represents an unusually striking exemplification of this approach.

We have seen that an interest in the psychological and historical aspects of economic activity is likewise to be found among the earlier writings. Taken collectively, the evidences of this are by no means unimportant, and there is every reason to suppose that Hume drew upon this portion of the literature—as he doubtless drew upon the more general and largely philosophical writings of the period—in elaborating his own position. This study has not attempted an exhaustive analysis of all the particular relations between Hume and his predecessors on this score. However, in evaluating a work as a whole, it is ultimately not particular doctrines, but the general quality and breadth of analysis which are of primary importance ; and on these grounds Hume clearly appears to be deserving of special distinction.

Owing to his philosophical perspective—together with his insight as an economist—Hume was able to see the relevant relations more clearly and fully and (if not always with full internal consistency) to develop their implications with unusual cogency. This is evident in several ways : in the scope and penetration of his economic psychology ; in his skill in relating to each other the various general aspects of economic development ; and, perhaps most importantly, in the use which he makes of these elements and their relationships. In systematically treating psychology and history as the joint centres of his analysis of a wide range of major issues of theory and policy, he contributed much to an understanding of their significance for the study of economic activity as a whole.

If one considers the period immediately following Hume, it is particularly interesting to compare his economic analysis with Adam Smith's in this general regard. Like Hume, Smith—who was his close friend—came to economics from philosophy. Like Hume's essays, the *Wealth of Nations* contains numerous psychological allusions and much historical material. Owing to its larger scope, its historical material is, in fact, far more voluminous than that contained in Hume's essays. While much of this is of a detailed and illustrative character, much of it likewise deals pointedly with general and theoretical aspects of economic development (the first three Books are, in their major outline, concerned with this question), and it is evident that in many places Smith's and Hume's treatments in this respect overlap. Yet on these scores there are important differences between the two. As in the case of his historical material, a good deal of Smith's treatment of psychology is relatively particularistic and, reflecting its comparatively subsidiary place in his analysis, is notably less systematic than Hume's. But, most importantly, Smith, generally speaking, does not consider the subjective aspects of behaviour patterns as historical variables. He is prone to regard them as universals.

In view of the hazards of characterising so complex and kaleidescopic a work as the *Wealth of Nations* in any simple form, one may have some special reservations apropos Bagehot's comment that Smith always assumed that there was a Scotsman in every man. Accepting the fable of the Scotsman, there is ample indication, however, that Bagehot's interpretation is substantially applicable even to those portions of Smith's analysis which are specifically concerned with historical sequence. Smith's well-known ascription of the development of commerce and the division of labour to an innate disposition to "truck and barter" is reflected in other historical contexts as well, including Book III, where, in a general parallel of Hume's treatment, he deals with the "progress of opulence". Thus, owing to its effect on the spirit of industry, Hume regards the relatively early growth of both foreign and domestic commerce as essential to the general growth of both agriculture and industry. Smith, on the other hand, treats the early development of commerce as an institutional dislocation which slows down the rate of economic growth [1]; and, here tacitly assuming an underlying persistence of a highly developed spirit of industry, he is led to argue on other grounds that such growth is best furthered when the greater part of society's capital is first devoted to an extensive exploitation of agriculture.[2]

[1] *The Wealth of Nations*, p. 392. Whatever the validity of his view concerning the desirability of what took place, it should be noted that Smith here presents a very thorough discussion of the various forces associated with the growth of commerce and industry. A careful examination of his analysis will show several affinities to Hume's briefer treatment. *Op. cit.*, pp. 361–96.

[2] *Op. cit.*, pp. 356–60. The chapter title here is "Of the Natural Progress of Opulence". In this context "natural" does not mean the "usual", as in Hume's case, but the "best", or what would ensue under optimal conditions.

The same or related differences are likewise to be found in those portions of Smith's analysis which most closely approximate to the main classifications of Hume's political economy, particularly so since here Smith's generalised treatments of history (which largely appear in separate sections) play a notably less significant role than in Hume's case. There are several such contexts in Smith where generalised history is important—for example his treatment of the public-debt issue, where he traces the origin and development of public borrowing and its implications for the growth of agriculture and industry,[1] and, more notably, part of the central portion of his analysis of the free-trade issue where he emphasises the effect of the opening of foreign markets on the profitability of introducing further refinements in the division of labour.[2] This latter consideration, however, substantially exhausts the developmental content of his analysis of the free-trade issue. In his theoretical treatment Smith gives at least equal emphasis to the purely static aspect of the gains in real income resulting from international specialisation and exchange[3]; and, though he too considers the effect of foreign competition on home employment (and also in terms of the feasibility of factor reallocation), this question is treated largely without reference to historical conditioning influences.[4] Similarly, though it contains valuable descriptive material on the money-supply, the development of banking facilities, and the like, his monetary theory proper is largely of an

---

[1] *Op. cit.*, pp. 859 ff.

[2] *Op. cit.*, p. 416. This is an application of the well-known principle elaborated earlier in his chapter "That the Division of Labour is Limited by the Extent of the Market" (pp. 17 ff).

[3] *Op. cit.*, p. 415 and pp. 420 ff.

[4] *Op. cit.*, esp. pp. 436–7. Smith too emphasises the ease of resource diversion, though in the preceding pages he shows that he is not unaware of the difficulties which this would involve. It may be noted, however, that his emphasis here is sharply in conflict with an early statement in which, neglecting the possibility of factor re-allocation entirely, he seems to imply that employment would fall by the full extent of the shrinkage in foreign markets. Cf. *op. cit.*, p. 353.

analytical nature and displays no fundamental theoretical relation to his earlier discussion of the development of a money economy.[1]

Perhaps the sharpest contrast between Hume and Smith in this regard, however, is to be found in their respective treatments of the accumulation of capital. As we have seen, Hume argues that the effective desire to save is a function of both the opportunity to improve one's economic position and the means by which income is earned, and through these considerations he traces the growth in the intensity of this desire from the oppressed peasant-idle landowner feudal stage to the largely mercantile economy of his own time. In what appears to be a pointed rejection of Hume's position on avowedly universalistic grounds, Smith argues that there is no reason why, generally speaking, all groups at all times should not be equally frugal. No-one, he maintains, is given to prodigality except sporadically, for there is in all of us the more basic and stronger "desire of bettering our condition, a desire which, though generally calm and dispassionate, comes with us from the womb, and never leaves us until we go into the grave".[2] Though in his interest theory Smith acknowledges a debt to Hume, what he assimilates is thus little more than the purely mechanical aspects of Hume's doctrine, that is the view that interest-rates are determined by the supply and demand for real capital.

In the light of these considerations, one may say that, despite its pronounced emphasis on economic development, Smith's approach to its more general aspects is less basically genetic or evolutionary than Hume's, or, stated

---

[1] *Op. cit.*, pp. 27 ff. and 270 ff.

[2] *Op. cit.*, pp. 324-5. At the opening of his interest theory (p. 333), Smith modifies this doctrine ; for here he allows—as in fact he elsewhere insists (pp. 390-1)—that the landowner is a spendthrift. It may also be noted that Smith's view as to the universality of an intense desire to improve one's lot conflicts with his earlier recognition (p. 81) that the diligence of the labourer is a function of his opportunities for economic advancement.

differently, that it is genetic principally on a more external level. With regard particularly to his treatment of the theoretical issues of political economy, Smith clearly exhibits the tendency to abstract from historical influences which was so characteristic of Ricardo and the later classical economists.

Since the eighteenth century there have been many who have sought to give a dominant emphasis to the psychological and historical phases of economic activity. Though their theoretical framework has often been different from that common during Hume's time, and frequently their treatments have taken a wholly descriptive turn, the "historical" and "institutional" schools of the nineteenth and twentieth centuries are obvious cases in point. To stress these considerations, however, seems especially pertinent at the present time since, after long and more "orthodox" development of the special aspects of the field, economists now give every indication of a general renewal of interest in broadening the areas of their inquiry. Fed from many sources and affecting other disciplines as well, this has in part taken the form of a more acute awareness of old problems for a time regarded as subsidiary. But, as always, it most basically reflects the factual and ideological pressures of social change itself, which to a greater or lesser degree have altered the nature of the problems and their treatment.

The concern with underdeveloped areas—a product of many new forces—has inevitably led to a more detailed analysis of the factors essential to economic growth, including a wide variety of cultural conditions ordinarily regarded as "givens" in the more "orthodox" treatment ; and this has received further impetus from theoretical analyses, such as Schumpeter's, which are concerned with the more general aspects of economic growth in capitalist economies. Supported more largely by theoretical treatment (and further prompting concern with longer run issues) the revived interest in the question of full employ-

1ent has encouraged a more intensive consideration of
1e psychology underlying aggregative behaviour. In
ompelling a shift of emphasis from impersonal market
orces to the behaviour of important single units or
ollective entities, such developments as the growth of
rade-unionism, the expanding activities of the state
especially in international transactions), and the new
ght generally thrown on the area of imperfect com-
etition, have all led to the use of concepts which extend
onsiderably beyond the economic psychology traditionally
mployed in the theory of price and distribution. It is
carcely surprising, in view of the relative rapidity of
ecent institutional change, that the distinction between
1e "positive" and the "normative" aspects of economics
 in practice growing hazier ; and, as issues of economic
olicy increasingly involve questions of conflicts of values
nd the social desirability of alternative "systems",
ecessarily the supporting argument prompts more fre-
uent and explicit reference to history and its many-sided
orces.

   Although the relevant analogies can easily be over-
rawn and would lead to different constructions, few, if
1y, would deny that there are fundamental parallels
etween the present period and Hume's time ; and for this
1d other reasons more peculiar to the present scene there
 every ground to expect that the general parallels in
onomic inquiry will likewise continue to grow more
arked. If this does occur, many of the pertinent cate-
ories will doubtless be different or entirely strange to the
ghteenth-century universe of discourse ; but among the
any forerunners of broad and systematic social inquiry
ume is entitled to a rank among its most distinguished
positors. Long known for his contributions to the more
echanical aspects of the discipline, he richly deserves
 be remembered at least as much for his more funda-
ental attempt to incorporate economics into a broader
ience of human experience.

HUME'S
ESSAYS ON ECONOMICS

First published,
the essay "Of the Jealousy of Trade" in 1758,
the remainder in 1752.

LIST OF EDITIONS CITED
IN THE APPARATUS

A	*Political Discourses*, 1st edn.	1 vol.	Edinburgh 1752
B	the same, 2nd edn.	1 vol.	Edinburgh 1752
C	*Essays and Treatises on several Subjects*	4 vols.	London 1753–4
D	the same	1 vol.	London 1758
E	the same	4 vols.	London 1760
F	the same	2 vols.	London 1764
G	the same	2 vols.	London 1768
H	the same	4 vols.	London 1770
I	the same	2 vols.	London 1777

The text printed is that of the 1777 or posthumous edition, here referred to as *I*. The meaning of the symbols used in the apparatus is fully explained in the Note on the Text (below, p. 218).

2

Of Commerce

THE greater part of mankind may be divided into two classes ; that of *shallow* thinkers, who fall short of the truth, and that of *abstruse* thinkers, who go beyond it. The latter class are by far the most rare ; and I may add, by far the most useful and valuable. They suggest hints, at least, and start difficulties, which they want, perhaps, skill to pursue ; but which may produce fine discoveries, when handled by men who have a more just way of thinking. At worst, what they say is uncommon ; and if it should cost some pains to comprehend it, one has, however, the pleasure of hearing something that is new. An author is little to be valued, who tells us nothing but what we can learn from every coffee-house conversation.

All people of *shallow* thought are apt to decry even those *of solid* understanding, as *abstruse* thinkers, and metaphysicians, and refiners ; and never will allow any thing to be just which is beyond their own weak conceptions. There are some cases, I own, where an extraordinary refinement affords a strong presumption of falsehood, and where no reasoning is to be trusted but what is natural and easy. When a man deliberates concerning his conduct in any *particular* affair, and forms schemes in politics, trade, œconomy, or any business in life, he never ought to draw his arguments too fine, or connect too long a chain of consequences together. Something is sure to happen, that will disconcert his reasoning, and produce an event different from what he expected. But when we reason upon *general* subjects, one may justly affirm, that our speculations can scarcely ever be too fine, provided they be just ; and that the difference between a common man and a man of genius is chiefly seen in the shallowness or depth of the principles upon which they proceed.

3

General reasonings seem intricate, merely because they are general ; nor is it easy for the bulk of mankind to distinguish, in a great number of particulars, that common circumstance in which they all agree, or to extract it, pure and unmixed, from the other superfluous circumstances. Every judgment or conclusion, with them, is particular. They cannot enlarge their view to those universal propositions, which comprehend under them an infinite number of individuals, and include a whole science in a single theorem. Their eye is confounded with such an extensive prospect ; and the conclusions, derived from it, even though clearly expressed, seem intricate and obscure. But however intricate they may seem, it is certain, that general principles, if just and sound, must always prevail in the general course of things, though they may fail in particular cases ; and it is the chief business of philosophers to regard the general course of things. I may add, that it is also the chief business of politicians ; especially in the domestic government of the state, where the public good, which is, or ought to be their object, depends on the concurrence of a multitude of *causes ; not, as in foreign politics, on accidents and chances, and the caprices of a few persons.[1] This therefore makes the difference between *particular* deliberations and *general* reasonings, and renders subtility and refinement much more suitable to the latter than to the former.

I thought this introduction necessary before the following discourses on †*commerce, money, interest, balance of trade,*

---

[1] [Though the sets of anthitheses drawn are characteristically Humian, it is not clear whether Hume here meant "causes" or (as in earlier editions) "cases". If the former is a printer's error, it would appear that these sets of anthitheses are explicable in terms of Hume's contrast between the "grossness" of the passions governing the mass of mankind and the "delicacy" of those governing the few. Cf. above, pp. xxix–xxxi.—ED.]

* causes = cases [*A–G*].

† *commerce, money, interest, balance of trade,* &c. = *commerce, luxury, money, interest,* &c. [*A–D*].

4

&c. where, perhaps, there will occur some principles which are uncommon, and which may seem too refined and subtile for such vulgar subjects. If false, let them be rejected : But no one ought to entertain a prejudice against them, merely because they are out of the common road.

The greatness of a state, and the happiness of its subjects, how independent soever they may be supposed in some respects, are commonly allowed to be inseparable with regard to commerce ; and as private men receive greater security, in the possession of their trade and riches, from the power of the public, so the public becomes powerful in proportion to the opulence and extensive commerce of private men.[1] This maxim is true in general ; though I cannot forbear thinking, that it may possibly admit of exceptions, and that we often establish it with too little reserve and limitation. There may be some circumstances, where the commerce and riches and luxury of individuals, instead of adding strength to the public, will serve only to thin its armies, and diminish its authority among the neighbouring nations. Man is a very variable being, and susceptible of many different opinions, principles, and rules of conduct. What may be true, while he adheres to one way of thinking, will be found false, when he has embraced an opposite set of manners and opinions.[2]

The bulk of every state may be divided into *husbandmen* and *manufacturers.* The former are employed in the culture of the land ; the latter work up the materials furnished by the former, into all the commodities which are necessary or ornamental to human life. As soon as men quit their savage state, where they live chiefly by hunting and

---

[1] [Cf. above, p. xxii *n* ; and J. Viner, "Power versus Plenty as Objectives of Foreign Policy, in the Seventeenth and Eighteenth Century", in *World Politics,* 1 (Oct. 1948), 1–29.—Ed.]

[2] [For further instances of Hume's emphasis on the variability of human behaviour, cf. *Phil. Wks.,* iii, 163, and his long essay "A Dialogue" in *Enquiries,* pp. 324 ff. Also see above, pp. xxviii–xxix, xcii—Ed.]

fishing, they must fall into these two classes ; though the arts of agriculture employ *at first* the most numerous part of the society.[1] Time and experience improve so much these arts, that the land may easily maintain a much greater number of men, than those who are immediately employed in its culture, or who furnish the more necessary manufactures to such as are so employed.[2]

If these superfluous hands apply themselves to the finer arts, which are commonly denominated the arts of *luxury*, they add to the happiness of the state ; since they afford to many the opportunity of receiving enjoyments, with which they would otherwise have been unacquainted. But may not another scheme be proposed for the employment of these superfluous hands ? May not the sovereign lay claim to them, and employ them in fleets and armies, to encrease the dominions of the state abroad, and spread its fame over distant nations ? It is certain that the fewer desires and wants are found in the proprietors and labourers of land, the fewer hands do they employ ; and consequently the superfluities of the land, instead of maintaining tradesmen and manufacturers, may support fleets and armies to a much greater extent, than where a great many arts are required to minister to the luxury of particular persons. Here therefore seems to be a kind of opposition between the greatness of the state and the happiness of the subject. A state is never greater than when all its superfluous hands are employed in the service of the public. The ease and convenience of private persons require, that these hands should be employed in their

---

[1] Mons. MELON, in his political essay on commerce, asserts, that even at present, if you divide FRANCE into 20 parts, 16 are labourers or peasants ; two only artizans ; one belonging to the law, church, and miltiary ; and one merchants, financiers, and bourgeois. This calculation is certainly very erroneous. In FRANCE, ENGLAND, and indeed most parts of EUROPE, half of the inhabitants live in cities ; and even of those who live in the country, a great number are artizans, perhaps above a third.

[2] [Elsewhere Hume points out that it was in part for the purpose of gaining the advantages of the division of labour that society itself was first formed. Cf. *Treatise*, p. 485.—ED.]

6

service. The one can never be satisfied, but at the expence of the other. As the ambition of the sovereign must entrench on the luxury of individuals ; so the luxury of individuals must diminish the force, and check the ambition of the sovereign.

Nor is this reasoning merely chimerical ; but is founded on history and experience. The republic of SPARTA was certainly more powerful than any state now in the world, consisting of an equal number of people ; and this was owing entirely to the want of commerce and luxury. The HELOTES were the labourers : The SPARTANS were the soldiers or gentlemen. It is evident, that the labour of the HELOTES could not have maintained so great a number of SPARTANS, had these latter lived in ease and delicacy, and given employment to a great variety of trades and manufactures. The like policy may be remarked in ROME. And indeed, throughout all ancient history, it is observable, that the smallest republics raised and maintained greater armies, than states consisting of triple the number of inhabitants, are able to support at present. It is computed, that, in all EUROPEAN nations, the proportion between soldiers and people does not exceed one to a hundred. But we read, that the city of ROME alone, with its small territory, raised and maintained, in early times, ten legions against the LATINS. ATHENS, the whole of whose dominions was not larger than YORKSHIRE, sent to the expedition against SICILY near forty thousand men.[1] DIONYSIUS the elder, it is said, maintained a standing army of a hundred thousand foot and ten thousand horse, besides a large fleet of four hundred sail [2] ; though his territories extended no farther than the city of SYRACUSE, about a third of the island of SICILY, and some sea-port towns and garrisons on the coast of ITALY and ILLYRICUM.

---

[1] THUCYDIDES, lib. vii. 75.

[2] DIOD. SIC. lib. ii. 5. This account, I own, is somewhat suspicious, not to say worse ; chiefly because this army was not composed of citizens, but of mercenary forces.

It is true, the ancient armies, in time of war, subsisted much upon plunder : But did not the enemy plunder in their turn ? which was a more ruinous way of levying a tax, than any other that could be devised. In short, no probable reason can be assigned for the great power of the more ancient states above the modern, but their want of commerce and luxury. Few artizans were maintained by the labour of the farmers, and therefore more soldiers might live upon it. Livy says, that Rome, in his time, would find it difficult to raise. as large an army as that which, in her early days, she sent out against the Gauls and Latins.[1] Instead of those soldiers who fought for liberty and empire in Camillus's time, there were, in Augustus's days, musicians, painters, cooks, players, and tailors ; and if the land was equally cultivated at both periods, it could certainly maintain equal numbers in the one profession as in the other. They added nothing to the mere necessaries of life, in the later period more than in the former.

It is natural on this occasion to ask, whether sovereigns may not return to the maxims of ancient policy, and consult their own interest in this respect, more than the happiness of their subjects ? I answer, that it appears to me, almost impossible ; and that because ancient policy was violent, and contrary to the more natural and usual course of things. It is well known with what peculiar laws Sparta was governed, and what a prodigy that republic is justly esteemed by every one, who has considered human nature as it has displayed itself in other nations, and other ages. Were the testimony of history less positive and circumstantial, such a government would appear a mere philosophical whim or fiction, and impossible ever to be reduced to practice. And though the Roman and other ancient republics were supported on principles somewhat more natural, yet was there an

[1] Titi Livii, lib. vii. cap. 25. "Adeo in quae laboramus", says he, "sola crevimus, divitias luxuriemque".

8

extraordinary concurrence of circumstances to make them submit to such grievous burthens. They were free states ; they were small ones [1] ; and the age being martial, all their neighbours were continually in arms. Freedom naturally begets public spirit, especially in small states ; and this public spirit, this *amor patriæ*, must encrease, when the public is almost in continual alarm, and men are obliged, every moment, to expose themselves to the greatest dangers for its defence. A continual succession of wars makes every citizen a soldier : He takes the field in his turn : And during his service he is chiefly maintained by himself. This service is indeed equivalent to a heavy tax ; yet is it less felt by a people addicted to arms, who fight for honour and revenge more than pay, and are unacquainted with gain and industry as well as pleasure. [2] Not to mention the great equality of fortunes among the inhabitants of the ancient republics, where every field, belonging to a different proprietor, was able to maintain a family, and rendered the numbers of citizens very considerable, even without trade and manufactures.

But though the want of trade and manufactures, among a free and very martial people, may *sometimes* have no other effect than to render the public more powerful, it is certain, that, in the common course of human affairs,

---

[1] [For further comments on these points cf. below, pp. 128–31.—Ed.]

[2] The more antient ROMANS lived in perpetual war with all their neighbours : and in old LATIN, the term, *hostis*, expressed both a stranger and an enemy. This is remarked by CICERO ; but by him is ascribed to the humanity of his ancestors, who softened, as much as possible, the denomination of an enemy, by calling him by the same appellation which signified a stranger. *De Off.* lib. i. 12. 'Tis however much more probable, from the manners of the times, that the ferocity of those people was so great as to make them regard all strangers as enemies, and call them by the same name. It is not, besides, consistent with the most common maxims of policy or of nature, that any state should regard its public enemies with a friendly eye, or preserve any such sentiments for them as the ROMAN orator would ascribe to his ancestors. Not to mention, that the early ROMANS really exercised piracy, as we learn from their first treaties with CARTHAGE, preserved by POLYBIUS, lib. 3, and consequently like the SALLEE and ALGERINE rovers, were actually at war with most nations, and a stranger and an enemy were with them almost synonymous.

it will have a quite contrary tendency. Sovereigns must take mankind as they find them, and cannot pretend to introduce any violent change in their principles and ways of thinking. A long course of time, with a variety of accidents and circumstances, are requisite to produce those great revolutions, which so much diversify the face of human affairs. And the less natural any set of principles are, which support a particular society, the more difficulty will a legislator meet with in raising and cultivating them. It is his best policy to comply with the common bent of mankind, and give it all the improvements of which it is susceptible. Now, according to the most natural course of things, industry and arts and trade encrease the power of the sovereign as well as the happiness of the subjects ; and that policy is violent, which aggrandizes the public by the poverty of individuals.[1] This will easily appear from a few considerations, which will present to us the consequences of sloth and barbarity.

Where manufactures and mechanic arts are not cultivated, the bulk of the people must apply themselves to agriculture ; and if their skill and industry encrease, there must arise a great superfluity from their labour beyond what suffices to maintain them. They have no temptation, therefore, to encrease their skill and industry ; since they cannot exchange that superfluity for any commodities, which may serve either to their pleasure or vanity. A habit of indolence naturally prevails. The greater part of the land lies uncultivated. What is cultivated, yields not its utmost for want of skill and assiduity in the farmers. If at any time the public exigencies require, that great numbers should be employed in the public service, the labour of the people furnishes now no superfluities, by which these numbers can be maintained. The labourers cannot encrease their skill and industry on a sudden.

---

[1] [For Hume's views on the relative importance of selfishness and benevolence in human nature see *Treatise*, pp. 486-8, 491-5, 519, and above, p. xxxiii.—ED.]

Lands uncultivated cannot be brought into tillage for some years. The armies, mean while, must either make sudden and violent conquests, or disband for want of subsistence. A regular attack or defence, therefore, is not to be expected from such a people, and their soldiers must be as ignorant and unskilful as their farmers and manufacturers.

Every thing in the world is purchased by labour ; and our passions are the only causes of labour. When a nation abounds in manufactures and mechanic arts, the proprietors of land, as well as the farmers, study agriculture as a science, and redouble their industry and attention. The superfluity, which arises from their labour, is not lost ; but is exchanged with manufactures for those commodities, which men's luxury now makes them covet. By this means, land furnishes a great deal more of the necessaries of life, than what suffices for those who cultivate it. In times of peace and tranquility, this superfluity goes to the maintenance of manufacturers, and the improvers of liberal arts. But it is easy for the public to convert many of these manufacturers into soldiers, and maintain them by that superfluity, which arises from the labour of the farmers. Accordingly we find, that this is the case in all civilized governments. When the sovereign raises an army, what is the consequence ? He imposes a tax. This tax obliges all the people to retrench what is least necessary to their subsistence. Those, who labour in such commodities, must either enlist in the troops, or turn themselves to agriculture, and thereby oblige some labourers to enlist for want of business. And to consider the matter abstractedly, manufacturers encrease the power of the state only as they store up so much labour, and that of a kind to which the public may lay claim, without depriving any one of the necessaries of life. The more labour, therefore, is employed beyond mere necessaries, the more powerful is any state ; since the persons engaged in that labour may easily be converted to the public service. In a state without manufacturers, there may be the same number of hands ; but there is not the same quantity of labour, nor of the same kind. All the labour is there bestowed upon necessaries, which can admit of little or no abatement.

Thus the greatness of the sovereign and the happiness of the state are, in a great measure, united with regard to trade and manufactures. It is a violent method, and in most cases impracticable, to oblige the labourer to toil, in order to raise from the land more than what subsists himself and family. Furnish him with manufactures and commodities, and he will do it of himself. Afterwards you will find it easy to seize some part of his superfluous labour, and employ it in the public service, without giving him his wonted return. Being accustomed to industry, he will think this less grievous, than if, at once, you obliged him to an augmentation of labour without any reward. The case is the same with regard to the other members of the state. The greater is the stock of labour of all kinds, the greater quantity may be taken from the heap, without making any sensible alteration in it.

A public granary of corn, a storehouse of cloth, a magazine of arms ; all these must be allowed real riches and strength in any state. Trade and industry are really nothing but a stock of labour, which, in times of peace and tranquility, is employed for the ease and satisfaction of individuals ; but in the exigencies of state, may, in part, be turned to public advantage. Could we convert a city into a kind of fortified camp, and infuse into each breast so martial a genius, and such a passion for public good, as to make every one willing to undergo the greatest hardships for the sake of the public ; these affections might now, as in ancient times, prove alone a sufficient spur to industry, and support the community. It would then be advantageous, as in camps, to banish all arts and luxury ; and, by restrictions on equipage and tables, make the provisions and forage last longer than if the army were loaded with a number of superfluous retainers. But as these principles are too disinterested and too difficult to support, it is requisite to govern men by other passions, and animate them with a spirit of avarice and industry, art and luxury. The camp is, in this case, loaded with a superfluous retinue ; but the provisions flow in proportionably larger. The harmony of the whole is still supported ; and the natural bent of the mind being more complied with, individuals, as well as the public, find their account in the observance of those maxims.

The same method of reasoning will let us see the advantage of *foreign* commerce, in augmenting the power of the state, as well as the riches and happiness of the subject. It encreases the stock of labour in the nation ; and the sovereign may convert what share of it he finds necessary to the service of the public. Foreign trade, by its imports, furnishes materials for new manufactures ; and by its exports, it produces labour in particular commodities, which could not be consumed at home. In short, a kingdom, that has a large import and export, must abound more with industry, and that employed upon delicacies and luxuries, than a kingdom which rests contented with its native commodities. It is, therefore, more powerful, as well as richer and happier. The individuals reap the benefit of these commodities, so far as they gratify the senses and appetites. And the public is also a gainer, while a greater stock of labour is, by this means, stored up against any public exigency ; that is, a greater number of laborious men are maintained, who may be diverted to the public service, without robbing any one of the necessaries, or even the chief conveniencies of life.

If we consult history, we shall find, that, in most nations, foreign trade has preceded any refinement in home manufactures, and given birth to domestic luxury.[1]

[1] [For a comparison of Adam Smith's and Hume's views on the order of economic development see above, p. cvii.—ED.]

The temptation is stronger to make use of foreign commodities, which are ready for use, and which are entirely new to us, than to make improvements on any domestic commodity, which always advance by slow degrees, and never affect us by their novelty. The profit is also very great, in exporting what is superfluous at home, and what bears no price, to foreign nations, whose soil or climate is not favourable to that commodity. Thus men become acquainted with the *pleasures* of luxury and the *profits* of commerce ; and their *delicacy* and *industry*, being once awakened, carry them on to farther improvements, in every branch of domestic as well as foreign trade. And this perhaps is the chief advantage which arises from a commerce with strangers. It rouses men from their indolence ; and presenting the gayer and more opulent part of the nation with objects of luxury, which they never before dreamed of, raises in them a desire of a more splendid way of life than what their ancestors enjoyed.[1] And at the same time, the few merchants, who possess the secret of this importation and exportation, make great profits ; and becoming rivals in wealth to the ancient nobility, tempt other adventurers to become their rivals in commerce. Imitation soon diffuses all those arts ; while domestic manufactures emulate the foreign in their improvements, and work up every home commodity to the utmost perfection of which it is susceptible. Their own steel and iron, in such laborious hands, become equal to the gold and rubies of the INDIES.

When the affairs of the society are once brought to this situation, a nation may lose most of its foreign trade, and yet continue a great and powerful people. If strangers will not take any particular commodity of ours, we must cease to labour in it. The same hands will turn themselves towards some refinement in other commodities, which may be wanted at home. And there must always be materials

---

[1] [For Hume's interpretation of the stimulating effect of "novelty" see above, p. xxxiv *n*.—ED.]

for them to work upon ; till every person in the state, who possesses riches, enjoys as great plenty of home commodities, and those in as great perfection, as he desires ; which can never possibly happen. CHINA is represented as one of the most flourishing empires in the world ; though it has very little commerce beyond its own territories.

It will not, I hope, be considered as a superfluous digression, if I here observe, that, as the multitude of mechanical arts is advantageous, so is the great number of persons to whose share the productions of these arts fall. A too great disproportion among the citizens weakens any state. Every person, if possible, ought to enjoy the fruits of his labour, in a full possession of all the necessaries, and many of the conveniencies of life. No one can doubt, but such an equality is most suitable to human nature, and diminishes much less from the *happiness* of the rich than it adds to that of the poor. It also augments the *power of the state*, and makes any extraordinary taxes or impositions be paid with more chearfulness. Where the riches are engrossed by a few, these must contribute very largely to the supplying of the public necessities. But when the riches are dispersed among multitudes, the burthen feels light on every shoulder, and the taxes make not a very sensible difference on any one's way of living.

Add to this, that, where the riches are in few hands, these must enjoy all the power, and will readily conspire to lay the whole burthen on the poor, and oppress them still farther, to the discouragement of all industry.[1]

In this circumstance consists the great advantage of ENGLAND above any nation at present in the world, or that appears in the records of any story. It is true, the ENGLISH feel some disadvantages in foreign trade by the high price of labour, which is in part the effect of the

[1] [It is clear that Hume was of the opinion that taxes on the poor had already risen to the point where incentive was being threatened. Cf. below, p. 85*n*.—ED.]

riches of their artisans, as well as of the plenty of money : But as foreign trade is not the most material circumstance, it is not to be put in competition with the happiness of so many millions. And if there were no more to endear to them that free government under which they live, this alone were sufficient. The poverty of the common people is a natural, if not an infallible effect of absolute monarchy ; though I doubt, whether it be always true, on the other hand, that their riches are an infallible result of liberty. Liberty must be attended with particular accidents, and a certain turn of thinking, in order to produce that effect. Lord BACON, accounting for the great advantages obtained by the ENGLISH in their wars with FRANCE, ascribes them chiefly to the superior ease and plenty of the common people amongst the former ; yet the government of the two kingdoms was, at that time, pretty much alike. Where the labourers and artisans are accustomed to work for low wages, and to retain but a small part of the fruits of their labour, it is difficult for them, even in a free government, to better their condition, or conspire among themselves to heighten their wages. But even where they are accustomed to a more plentiful way of life, it is easy for the rich, in an arbitrary government, to conspire against *them*, and throw the whole burthen of the taxes on their shoulders.

It may seem an odd position, that the poverty of the common people in FRANCE, ITALY, and SPAIN, is, in some measure, owing to the superior riches of the soil and happiness of the climate ; yet there want not reasons to justify this paradox. In such a fine mould or soil as that of those more southern regions, agriculture is an easy art ; and one man, with a couple of sorry horses, will be able, in a season, to cultivate as much land as will pay a pretty considerable rent to the proprietor. All the art, which the farmer knows, is to leave his ground fallow for a year, as soon as it is exhausted ; and the warmth of the sun alone and temperature of the climate enrich it, and restore

16

its fertility. Such poor peasants, therefore, require only a simple maintenance for their labour. They have no stock or riches, which claim more ; and at the same time they are for ever dependent on their landlord, who gives no leases, nor fears that his land will be spoiled by the ill methods of cultivation. In ENGLAND, the land is rich, but coarse ; must be cultivated at a great expense ; and produces slender crops, when not carefully managed, and by a method which gives not the full profit but in a course of several years. A farmer, therefore, in ENGLAND must have a considerable stock, and a long lease ; which beget proportional profits. The fine vineyards of CHAMPAGNE and BURGUNDY, that often yield to the landlord about five pounds *per* acre, are cultivated by peasants who have scarcely bread : The reason is, that such peasants need no stock but their own limbs, with instruments of husbandry, which they can buy for twenty shillings. The farmers are commonly in some better circumstances in those countries. But the grasiers are most at their ease of all those who cultivate the land. The reason is still the same. Men must have profits proportionable to their expense and hazard. Where so considerable a number of the labouring poor as the peasants and farmers are in very low circumstances, all the rest must partake of their poverty, whether the government of that nation be monarchical or republican.

We may form a similar remark with regard to the general history of mankind. What is the reason, why no people, living between the tropics, could ever yet attain to any art or civility, or reach even any police in their government, and any military discipline ; while few nations in the temperate climates have been altogether deprived of these advantages ? It is probable that one cause of this phænomenon is the warmth and equality of weather in the torrid zone, which render clothes and houses less requisite for the inhabitants, and thereby remove, in part, that necessity, which is the great spur to

17

industry and invention. *Curis acuens mortalia corda.*[1] Not to mention, that the fewer goods or possessions of this kind any people enjoy, the fewer quarrels are likely to arise amongst them, and the less necessity will there be for a settled police or regular authority to protect and defend them from foreign enemies, or from each other.

[1] [This quotation is taken from Virg., *Aen.* See above, p. xliii *n.*—ED.]

*Of Refinement in the Arts [1]

LUXURY is a word of uncertain signification, and may be
taken in a good as well as in a bad sense. In general, it
means great refinement in the gratification of the senses ;
and any degree of it may be innocent or blameable,
according to the age, or country, or condition of the
person.[2] The bounds between the virtue and the vice
cannot here be exactly fixed, more than in other moral
subjects. To imagine, that the gratifying of any sense, or
the indulging of any delicacy in meat, drink, or apparel,
is of itself a vice, can never enter into a head, that is not
disordered by the frenzies of enthusiasm.[3] I have, indeed,
heard of a monk abroad, who, because the windows of his
cell opened upon a noble prospect, made a *covenant with
his eyes* never to turn that way, or receive so sensual a
gratification. And such is the crime of drinking CHAM-
PAGNE or BURGUNDY, preferably to small beer or porter.
These indulgences are only vices, when they are pursued
at the expense of some virtue, as liberality or charity ; in
like manner as they are follies, when for them a man

[1] [It is to be noted that, as treated by Hume, "refinement in the arts"
and "luxury" are not entirely synonymous The former is rather regarded
as a species of the latter, or, to be more specific, only as "innocent luxury".
Though in the main devoted to "innocent luxury", the essay, however, does
in fact consider "vicious" luxury as well. The various editions of the
essay show that at several points within the text Hume also substituted
the term "refinement" or its equivalent for the general term "luxury".
—ED.]

[2] [The historical variability of moral conventions is the major theme
of Hume's essay "A Dialogue". Cf. above, p. xcii n.—ED.]

[2] [For a further and especially acid comment on the excesses of religious
enthusiasm, cf. Hume's *Enquiry concerning the Principles of Morals*, in *Enquiries*,
p. 270. Though he was particularly critical of its extreme forms, on the
whole Hume was not favourably inclined to institutionalised religion in
general. Cf., for example, his comment in the essay "Of Public Credit",
below, pp. 104 ff. This is also revealed in numerous comments in his
History of England.—ED.]

* Refinement in the Arts = Luxury [A-D].

19

ruins his fortune, and reduces himself to want and beggary. Where they entrench upon no virtue, but leave ample subject whence to provide for friends, family, and every proper object of generosity or compassion, they are entirely innocent, and have in every age been acknowledged such by almost all moralists. To be entirely occupied with the luxury of the table, for instance, without any relish for the pleasures of ambition, study, or conversation, is a mark of stupidity, and is incompatible with any vigour of temper or genius. To confine one's expense entirely to such a gratification, without regard to friends or family, is an indication of a heart destitute of humanity or benevolence. But if a man reserve time sufficient for all laudable pursuits, and money sufficient for all generous purposes, he is free from every shadow of blame or reproach.[1]

Since luxury may be considered either as innocent or blameable, one may be surprized at those preposterous opinions, which have been entertained concerning it ; while men of libertine principles bestow praises even on vicious luxury, and represent it as highly advantageous to society ; and on the other hand, men of severe morals blame even the most innocent luxury, and represent it as the source of all the corruptions, disorders, and factions, incident to civil government. We shall here endeavour to correct both these extremes, by proving, *first*, that the ages of refinement are both the happiest and most virtuous : *secondly*, that wherever luxury ceases to be innocent, it also ceases to be beneficial ; and when carried a degree too far, is a quality pernicious, though perhaps not the most pernicious, to political society.

To prove the first point, we need but consider the

---

[1] [As part of his attempt to frame a wholly empirical moral theory, Hume argues elsewhere, e.g. *Treatise*, pp. 483-4, that our moral judgment of any act is based, among other things, upon a norm given by "the common and natural course of the affections". It is because of this influence that we are led to expect a man to show a certain regard for his family, his friends, and the poor.—Ed.]

effects of refinement both on *private* and on *public* life.[1]
Human happiness, according to the most received notions,
seems to consist in three ingredients ; action, pleasure,
and indolence [2] : And though these ingredients ought to
be mixed in different proportions, according to the particular disposition of the person ; yet no one ingredient
can be entirely wanting, without destroying, in some
measure, the relish of the whole composition. Indolence
or repose, indeed, seems not of itself to contribute much
to our enjoyment ; but, like sleep, is requisite as an
indulgence to the weakness of human nature, which cannot
support an uninterrupted course of business or pleasure.
That quick march of the spirits, which takes a man from
himself, and chiefly gives satisfaction, does in the end
exhaust the mind, and requires some intervals of repose,
which, though agreeable for a moment, yet, if prolonged,
beget a languor and lethargy that destroys all enjoyment.
Education, custom, and example, have a mighty influence
in turning the mind to any of these pursuits ; and it must
be owned, that, where they promote a relish for action
and pleasure, they are so far favourable to human happiness. In times when industry and the arts flourish, men
are kept in perpetual occupation, and enjoy, as their
reward, the occupation itself, as well as those pleasures
which are the fruit of their labour. The mind acquires
new vigour ; enlarges its powers and faculties ; and by
an assiduity in honest industry, both satisfies its natural
appetites, and prevents the growth of unnatural ones,
which commonly spring up, when nourished by ease and
idleness. Banish those arts from society, you deprive men
both of action and of pleasure ; and leaving nothing but
indolence in their place, you even destroy the relish of

---

[1] [The utilitarian morality which underlies this and the other normative
aspects of Hume's thought is extensively defended in *Treatise*, BK. III,
and in the *Enquiry concerning the Principles of Morals*.—ED.]

[2] [The relation of all these "ingredients" to Hume's economic psychology
as presented here and in other of his writings is considered above, pp. xxxv
and xcv–xcix.—ED.]

indolence, which never is agreeable, but when it succeeds to labour, and recruits the spirits, exhausted by too much application and fatigue.

Another advantage of industry and of refinements in the mechanical arts, is, that they commonly produce some refinements in the liberal ; nor can one be carried to perfection, without being accompanied, in some degree, with the other. The same age, which produces great philosophers and politicians, renowned generals and poets, usually abounds with skilful weavers, and ship-carpenters. We cannot reasonably expect, that a piece of woollen cloth will be brought to perfection in a nation, which is ignorant of astronomy, or where ethics are neglected. The spirit of the age affects all the arts ; and the minds of men, being once roused from their lethargy, and put into a fermentation, turn themselves on all sides, and carry improvements into every art and science. Profound ignorance is totally banished, and men enjoy the privilege of rational creatures, to think as well as to act, to cultivate the pleasures of the mind as well as those of the body.

The more these refined arts advance, the more sociable men become : nor is it possible, that, when enriched with science, and possessed of a fund of conversation, they should be contented to remain in solitude, or live with their fellow-citizens in that distant manner, which is peculiar to ignorant and barbarous nations. They flock into cities ; love to receive and communicate knowledge ; to show their wit or their breeding ; their taste in conversation or living, in clothes or furniture. Curiosity allures the wise ; vanity the foolish ; and pleasure both. Particular clubs and societies are everywhere formed : Both sexes meet in an easy and sociable manner : and the tempers of men, as well as their behaviour, refine apace. So that, beside the improvements which they receive from knowledge and the liberal arts, it is impossible but they must feel an encrease of humanity, from the very habit of conversing together, and contribute to each other's pleasure and entertainment. Thus *industry, knowledge,* and *humanity,* are linked together by an indissoluble chain, and are found, from experience as well as reason, to be peculiar to the more polished, and, what are commonly denominated, the more luxurious ages.[1]

Nor are these advantages attended with disadvantages, that bear any proportion to them. The more men refine upon pleasure, the less they indulge in excesses of any kind ; because nothing is more destructive to true pleasure than such excesses. One may safely affirm, that the TARTARS are oftener guilty of beastly gluttony, when they feast on their dead horses, than EUROPEAN courtiers with all their refinements of cookery. And if libertine love, or even infidelity to the marriage-bed, be more frequent in polite ages, when it is often regarded only as a piece of gallantry ; drunkenness, on the other hand, is much less common : A vice more odious, and more pernicious both to mind and body. And in this matter I would appeal, not only to an OVID or a PETRONIUS, but to a SENECA or a CATO. We know, that CÆSAR, during CATILINE's conspiracy, being necessitated to put into CATO's hands a *billet-doux,* which discovered an intrigue with SERVILIA, CATO's own sister, that stern philosopher threw it back to him with indignation ; and in the bitterness of his wrath, gave him the appellation of drunkard, as a term more opprobrious than that with which he could more justly have reproached him.

But industry, knowledge, and humanity, are not advantageous in private life alone : They diffuse their beneficial influence on the *public,* and render the government as great and flourishing as they make individuals happy and prosperous. The encrease and consumption of all the commodities, which serve to the ornament and pleasure of life, are advantageous to society ; because, at the same

---

[1] [For a discussion of the technical aspects of the relationship which Hume draws between the growth of society and humanity, see above, pp. xcix–ci.—ED.]

time that they multiply those innocent gratifications to individuals, they are a kind of *storehouse* of labour, which, in the exigencies of state, may be turned to public service. In a nation, where there is no demand for such superfluities, men sink into indolence, lose all enjoyment of life, and are useless to the public, which cannot maintain or support its fleets and armies, from the industry of such slothful members.

The bounds of all the EUROPEAN kingdoms are, at present, nearly the same they were two hundred years ago : But what a difference is there in the power and grandeur of those kingdoms ? Which can be ascribed to nothing but the encrease of art and industry. When CHARLES VIII. of FRANCE invaded ITALY, he carried with him about 20,000 men : Yet this armament so exhausted the nation, as we learn from GUICCIARDIN, that for some years it was not able to make so great an effort. The late king of FRANCE, in time of war, kept in pay above 400,000 men [1] ; though from MAZARINE'S death to his own, he was engaged in a course of wars that lasted near thirty years.

This industry is much promoted by the knowledge inseparable from ages of art and refinement ; as, on the other hand, this knowledge enables the public to make the best advantage of the industry of its subjects. Laws, order, police, discipline ; these can never be carried to any degree of perfection, before human reason has refined itself by exercise, and by an application to the more vulgar arts, at least, of commerce and manufacture. Can we expect, that a government will be well modelled by a people, who know not how to make a spinning-wheel, or to employ a loom to advantage ? Not to mention, that all ignorant ages are infested with superstition, which throws the government off its bias, and disturbs men in the pursuit of their interest and happiness.

Knowledge in the arts of government naturally begets

[1] The inscription on the PLACE-DE-VENDOME says 440,000.

mildness and moderation, by instructing men in the advantages of humane maxims above rigour and severity, which drive subjects into rebellion, and make the return to submission impracticable, by cutting off all hopes of pardon. When the tempers of men are softened as well as their knowledge improved, this humanity appears still more conspicuous, and is the chief characteristic which distinguishes a civilized age from times of barbarity and ignorance. Factions are then less inveterate, revolutions less tragical, authority less severe, and seditions less frequent.[1] Even foreign wars abate of their cruelty ; and after the field of battle, where honour and interest steel men against compassion as well as fear, the combatants divest themselves of the brute, and resume the man.

Nor need we fear, that men, by losing their ferocity, will lose their martial spirit, or become less undaunted and vigorous in defence of their country or their liberty. The arts have no such effect in enervating either the mind or body. On the contrary, industry, their inseparable attendant, adds new force to both. And if anger, which is said to be the whetstone of courage, loses somewhat of its asperity, by politeness and refinement ; a sense of honour, which is a stronger, more constant, and more governable principle, acquires fresh vigour by that elevation of genius which arises from knowledge and a good education. Add to this, that courage can neither have any duration, nor be of any use, when not accompanied with discipline and martial skill, which are seldom found among a barbarous people. The ancients remarked, that DATAMES was the only barbarian that ever knew the art of war. And PYRRHUS, seeing the ROMANS marshal their army with some art and skill, said with surprize, *These barbarians have nothing barbarous in their discipline !* It is observable, that, as the old ROMANS, by applying them-

[1] [Further and more extensive comments on this are to be found in the essay "Of the Populousness of Ancient Nations". Cf. below, pp. 134–43. —ED.]

selves solely to war, were almost the only uncivilized people that ever possessed military discipline ; so the modern ITALIANS are the only civilized people, among EUROPEANS, that ever wanted courage and a martial spirit. Those who would ascribe this effeminacy of the ITALIANS to their luxury, or politeness, or application to the arts, need but consider the FRENCH and ENGLISH, whose bravery is as uncontestable, as their love for the arts, and their assiduity in commerce. The ITALIAN historians give us a more satisfactory reason for this degeneracy of their countrymen. They shew us how the sword was dropped at once by all the ITALIAN sovereigns ; while the VENETIAN aristocracy was jealous of its subjects, the FLORENTINE democracy applied itself entirely to commerce ; ROME was governed by priests, and NAPLES by women. War then became the business of soldiers of fortune, who spared one another, and to the astonishment of the world, could engage a whole day in what they called a battle, and return at night to their camp, without the least bloodshed.

What has chiefly induced severe moralists to declaim against refinement in the arts, is the example of ancient ROME, which, joining, to its poverty and rusticity, virtue and public spirit, rose to such a surprising height of grandeur and liberty ; but having learned from its con-quered provinces the *ASIATIC luxury, fell into every kind of corruption ; whence arose sedition and civil wars, attended at last with the total loss of liberty. All the LATIN classics, whom we peruse in our infancy, are full of these sentiments, and universally ascribe the ruin of their state to the arts and riches imported from the East : Insomuch that SALLUST represents a taste for painting as a vice, no less than lewdness and drinking. And so popular were these sentiments, during the later ages of the republic, that this author abounds in praises of the old rigid ROMAN virtue, though himself the most egregious

* ASIATIC=*Grecian* and *Asiatic* [A–C].

instance of modern luxury and corruption ; speaks contemptuously of the GRECIAN eloquence, though the most elegant writer in the world ; nay, employs preposterous digressions and declamations to this purpose, though a model of taste and correctness.

But it would be easy to prove, that these writers mistook the cause of the disorders in the ROMAN state, and ascribed to luxury and the arts, what really proceeded from an ill modelled government, and the unlimited extent of conquests. Refinement on the pleasures and conveniences of life has no natural tendency to beget venality and corruption. The value, which all men put upon any particular pleasure, depends on comparison and experience [1] ; nor is a porter less greedy of money, which he spends on bacon and brandy, than a courtier, who purchases champagne and ortolans. Riches are valuable at all times, and to all men ; because they always purchase pleasures, such as men are accustomed to, and desire : Nor can anything restrain or regulate the love of money, but a sense of honour and virtue ; which, if it be not nearly equal at all times, will naturally abound most in ages of knowledge and refinement.

Of all EUROPEAN kingdoms, POLAND seems the most defective in the arts of war as well as peace, mechanical as well as liberal ; yet it is there that venality and corruption do most prevail. The nobles seem to have preserved their crown elective for no other purpose, than regularly to sell it to the highest bidder. This is almost the only species of commerce, with which that people are acquainted.

The liberties of ENGLAND, so far from decaying since the *improvements in the arts, have never flourished so much as during that period. And though corruption may seem to encrease of late years ; this is chiefly to be

---

[1] [For a fuller treatment of this point see *Treatise*, pp. 372-5.—ED.]

* improvements in the = origin of luxury and [*A–D*].

ascribed to our established liberty, when our princes have found the impossibility of governing without parliaments, or of terrifying parliaments by the phantom of prerogative. Not to mention, that this corruption or venality prevails much more among the electors than the elected ; and therefore cannot justly be ascribed to any refinements in luxury.

If we consider the matter in a proper light, we shall find, that a progress in the arts is rather favourable to liberty, and has a natural tendency to preserve, if not produce a free government. In rude unpolished nations, where the arts are neglected, all labour is bestowed on the cultivation of the ground ; and the whole society is divided into two classes, proprietors of land, and their vassals or tenants. The latter are necessarily dependent, and fitted for slavery and subjection ; especially where they possess no riches, and are not valued for their knowledge in agriculture ; as must always be the case where the arts are neglected. The former naturally erect themselves into petty tyrants ; and must either submit to an absolute master, for the sake of peace and order ; or if they will preserve their independency, like the *ancient barons, they must fall into feuds and contests among themselves, and throw the whole society into such confusion, as is perhaps worse than the most despotic government. But where luxury nourishes commerce and industry, the peasants, by a proper cultivation of the land, become rich and independent ; while the tradesmen and merchants acquire a share of the property, and draw authority and consideration to that middling rank of men, who are the best and firmest basis of public liberty. These submit not to slavery, like the peasants, from poverty and meanness of spirit ; and having no hopes of tyrannizing over others, like the barons, they are not tempted, for the sake of that gratification, to submit to the tyranny of their sovereign. They covet equal laws, which may

* ancient = Gothic [*A-E*].

secure their property, and preserve them from monarchical, as well as aristocratical tyranny.[1]

The lower house is the support of our popular government ; and all the world acknowledges, that it owed its chief influence and consideration to the encrease of commerce, which threw such a balance of property into the hands of the commons. How inconsistent then is it to blame so violently a refinement in the arts, and to represent it as the bane of liberty and public spirit !

To declaim against present times, and magnify the virtue of remote ancestors, is a propensity almost inherent in human nature : And as the sentiments and opinions of civilized ages alone are transmitted to posterity, hence it is that we meet with so many severe judgments pronounced against luxury, and even science ; and hence it is that at present we give so ready an assent to them. But the fallacy is easily perceived, by comparing different nations that are contemporaries ; where we both judge more impartially, and can better set in opposition those manners, with which we are sufficiently acquainted. Treachery and cruelty, the most pernicious and most odious of all vices, seem peculiar to uncivilised ages ; and by the refined Greeks and Romans were ascribed to all the barbarous nations, which surrounded them. They might justly, therefore, have presumed, that their own ancestors, so highly celebrated, possessed no greater virtue, and were as much inferior to their posterity in honour and humanity, as in taste and science. An ancient Frank or Saxon may be highly extolled : But I believe every man would think his life or fortune much less secure in the hands of a Moor or Tartar, than in those of a French or English gentleman, the rank of men the most civilized in the most civilized nations.

We come now to the *second* position which we propose

---

[1] [In the essay "Of Civil Liberty" Hume gives some attention to the effect of liberty on commerce. See *Phil. Wks.*, iii, 159–60. For a general comment on Hume's political views see above, p. cii *n.*—Ed.]

to illustrate, to wit, that, as innocent luxury, or a refinement in the arts and conveniences of life, is advantageous to the public ; so wherever luxury ceases to be innocent, it also ceases to be beneficial ; and when carried a degree farther, begins to be a quality pernicious, though, perhaps, not the most pernicious, to political society.

Let us consider what we call vicious luxury. No gratification, however sensual, can of itself be esteemed vicious. A gratification is only vicious, when it engrosses all a man's expence, and leaves no ability for such acts of duty and generosity as are required by his situation and fortune. Suppose, that he correct the vice, and employ part of his expence in the education of his children, in the support of his friends, and in relieving the poor : would any prejudice result to society ? On the contrary, the same consumption would arise ; and that labour, which, at present, is employed only in producing a slender gratification to one man, would relieve the necessitous, and bestow satisfaction on hundreds. The same care and toil that raise a dish of peas at CHRISTMAS, would give bread to a whole family during six months. To say, that, without a vicious luxury, the labour would not have been employed at all, is only to say, that there is some other defect in human nature, such as indolence, selfishness, inattention to others, for which luxury, in some measure, provides a remedy ; as one poison may be an antidote to another. But virtue, like wholesome food, is better than poisons, however corrected.

Suppose the same number of men, that are present in GREAT BRITAIN, with the same soil and climate ; I ask, is it not possible for them to be happier, by the most perfect way of life that can be imagined, and by the greatest reformation that Omnipotence itself could work in their temper and disposition ? To assert, that they cannot, appears evidently ridiculous. As the land is able to maintain more than all its present inhabitants, they could never, in such a UTOPIAN state, feel any other ills than those which arise from bodily sickness ; and these are not the half of human miseries. All other ills spring from some vice, either in ourselves or others ; and even many of our diseases proceed from the same origin. Remove the vices, and the ills follow. You must only take care to remove all the vices. If you remove part, you may render the matter worse. By banishing *vicious* luxury, without curing sloth and an indifference to others, you only diminish industry in the state, and add nothing to men's charity or their generosity. Let us, therefore, rest contented with asserting, that two opposite vices in a state may be more advantageous than either of them alone ; but let us never pronounce vice in itself advantageous. Is it not very inconsistent for an author to assert in one page that moral distinctions are inventions of politicians for public interest ; [1] and in the next page maintain, that vice is advantageous to the public? [2] And indeed it seems upon any system of morality, little less than a contradiction in terms, to talk of a vice, which is in general beneficial to society. [3]

I thought this reasoning necessary, in order to give some light to a philosophical question, which has been much disputed in ENGLAND. I call it a *philosophical* question, not a *political* one. For whatever may be the consequence of such a miraculous transformation of man-

[1] [Arguing, as he does generally, that moral distinctions are based on a native sentiment, Hume pointedly criticises this view in his *Enquiry concerning the Principles of Morals*. Cf. *Enquiries*, pp. 214-15. —Ed.]

[2] Fable of the Bees.

[3] *Prodigality is not to be confounded with a refinement in the arts. It even appears, that that vice is much less frequent in the cultivated ages. Industry and gain beget this frugality, among the lower and middle ranks of men ; and in all the busy professions. Men of high rank, indeed, it may be pretended, are more allured by the pleasures, which become more frequent. But idleness is the great source of prodigality at all times ; and there are pleasures and vanities in every age, which allure men equally when they are unacquainted with better enjoyments. Not to mention, that the high interest, payed in rude times, quickly consumes the fortunes of the landed gentry, and multiplies their necessities.

* [*This footnote not in A–F ; G in text ; H as footnote.*]

kind, as would endow them with every species of virtue, and free them from every species of vice ; this concerns not the magistrate, who aims only at possibilities. He cannot cure every vice by substituting a virtue in its place. Very often he can only cure one vice by another ; and in that case, he ought to prefer what is least pernicious to society. Luxury, when excessive, is the source of many ills ; but is in general preferable to sloth and idleness, which would commonly succeed in its place, and are more hurtful both to private persons and to the public. When sloth reigns, a mean uncultivated way of life prevails amongst individuals, without society, without enjoyment. And if the sovereign, in such a situation, demands the service of his subjects, the labour of the state suffices only to furnish the necessaries of life to the labourers, and can afford nothing to those who are employed in the public service.

Of Money [1]

MONEY is not, properly speaking, one of the subjects of commerce ; but only the instrument which men have agreed upon to facilitate the exchange of one commodity for another. It is none of the wheels of trade : It is the oil which renders the motion of the wheels more smooth and easy.[2] If we consider any one kingdom by itself, it is evident, that the greater or less plenty of money is of no consequence ; since the prices of commodities are always proportioned to the plenty of money, and a crown in HARRY VII.'s time served the same purpose as a pound does at present. It is only the *public* which draws any advantage from the greater plenty of money ; and that only in its wars and negociations with foreign states. And this is the reason, why all rich and trading countries from CARTHAGE to GREAT BRITAIN and HOLLAND, have employed mercenary troops, which they hired from their poorer neighbours. Were they to make use of their native subjects, they would find less advantage from their superior riches, and from their great plenty of gold and silver ; since the pay of all their servants must rise in proportion to the public opulence. Our small army of 20,000 men is maintained at as great expence, as a FRENCH army *twice as numerous. The ENGLISH fleet, during the late war, required as much money to support it as all the ROMAN legions, which kept the whole world in subjection, during the time of the emperors.[3]

¹ [For background material pertinent to this essay see above, pp. xiii-xv.—ED.]

² [In a letter to the Abbé Morellet (cf. below, p. 214) Hume stresses the conventional aspects of the choice of a medium of exchange.—ED.]

³ A private soldier in the ROMAN infantry had a denarius a day, somewhat less than eightpence. The ROMAN emperors had commonly 25 legions in pay, which, allowing 5,000 men to a legion, makes 125,000.

* twice = thrice [A–G].

33

The greater number of people and their greater industry are serviceable in all cases ; at home and abroad, in private and in public. But the greater plenty of money, is very limited in its use, and may even sometimes be a loss to a nation in its commerce with foreigners.

There seems to be a happy concurrence of causes in human affairs, which checks the growth of trade and riches, and hinders them from being confined entirely to one people ; as might naturally at first be dreaded from the advantages of an established commerce. Where one nation has gotten the start of another in trade, it is very difficult for the latter to regain the ground it has lost ; because of the superior industry and skill of the former, and the greater stocks, of which its merchants are possessed, and which enable them to trade on so much smaller profits. But these advantages are compensated, in some measure, by the low price of labour in every nation which has not an extensive commerce, and does not much abound in gold and silver. Manufactures, therefore gradually shift their places, leaving those countries and provinces which they have already enriched, and flying to others, whither they are allured by the cheapness

---

TACIT. *Ann.* lib. iv. 5. It is true, there were also auxiliaries to the legions ; but their numbers are uncertain, as well as their pay. To consider only the legionaries, the pay of the private men could not exceed 1,600,000 pounds. Now, the parliament in the last war commonly allowed for the fleet 2,500,000. We have therefore 900,000 over for the officers and other expences of the ROMAN legions. There seem to have been but few officers in the ROMAN armies, in comparison of what are employed in all our modern troops, except some SWISS corps. And these officers had very small pay : A centurion, for instance, only double a common soldier And as the soldiers from their pay (TACIT. *Ann.* lib. i. 17) bought their own cloaths, arms, tents, and baggage ; this must also diminish considerably the other charges of the army. So little expensive was that mighty government, and so easy was its yoke over the world. And, indeed, this is the more natural conclusion from the foregoing calculations. For money, after the conquest of ÆGYPT, seems to have been nearly in as great plenty at ROME, as it is at present in the richest of the EUROPEAN kingdoms.

of provisions and labour ; till they have enriched these also, and are again banished by the same causes.[1] And, in general, we may observe, that the dearness of every thing, from plenty of money, is a disadvantage, which attends an established commerce, and sets bounds to it in every country, by enabling the poorer states to undersel the richer in all foreign markets.

This has made me entertain a doubt concerning the benefit of *banks* and *paper-credit,* which are so generally esteemed advantageous to every nation.[2] That provisions and labour should become dear by the encrease of trade and money, is in many respects, an inconvenience ; but an inconvenience that is unavoidable, and the effect of that public wealth and prosperity which are the end of all our wishes. It is compensated by the advantages, which we reap from the possession of these precious metals, and the weight, which they give the nation in all foreign wars and negociations. But there appears no reason for encreasing that inconvenience by a counterfeit money, which foreigners will not accept of in any payment, and which any great disorder in the state will reduce to nothing. There are, it is true, many people in every rich state, who having large sums of money, would prefer paper with good security ; as being of more easy transport and more safe custody. If the public provide not a bank, private bankers will take advantage of this circumstance ; as the goldsmiths formerly did in LONDON, or as the bankers do at present in DUBLIN : And therefore it is better, it may be thought, that a public company should

[1] [This law of growth and decay conflicts with other portions of Hume's position, especially in its implication that the interests of different nations are fundamentally opposed. Cf. above, p. lxxvi ; and also the correspondence concerning this point (below, pp. 199 ff.), which indicates that in abandoning this law (as he does in fully adopting a free-trade position in the essay "Of the Jealousy of Trade") Hume was influenced by his discussion with Josiah Tucker.—ED.]

[2] [For comment on the relation of this to other of Hume's views pertaining to the desirability of a credit expansion, cf. above, pp. lxvi *n,* lxxii.—ED.]

enjoy the benefit of that paper-credit, which always will have place in every opulent kingdom. But to endeavour artificially to encrease such a credit, can never be the interest of any trading nation ; but must lay them under disadvantages, by encreasing money beyond its natural proportion to labour and commodities, and thereby heightening their price to the merchant and manufacturer. And in this view, it must be allowed, that no bank could be more advantageous, than such a one as locked up all the money it received,[1] and never augmented the circulating coin, as is usual, by returning part of its treasure into commerce. A public bank, by this expedient, might cut off much of the dealings of private bankers and money-jobbers ; and though the state bore the charge of salaries to the directors and tellers of this bank (for, according to the preceding supposition, it would have no profit from its dealings), the national advantage, resulting from the low price of labour and the destruction of paper-credit, would be a sufficient compensation. Not to mention, that so large a sum, lying ready at command, would be a convenience in times of great public danger and distress ; and what part of it was used might be replaced at leisure, when peace and tranquility was restored to the nation.

But of this subject of paper-credit we shall treat more largely hereafter. And I shall finish this essay on money, by proposing and explaining two observations, which may, perhaps, serve to employ the thoughts of our speculative politicians.*

It was a shrewd observation of ANACHARSIS [2] the SCYTHIAN, who had never seen money in his own country,

---

[1] †This is the case with the bank of AMSTERDAM.

[2] PLUT. *Quomodo quis suos profectus in virtute sentire possit.*

* +For to these only I all along address myself. 'Tis enough that I submit to the ridicule sometimes, in this age, attached to the character of a philosopher, without adding to it that which belongs to a projector. [*A–G*].   † [*This footnote not in A–B*].

that gold and silver seemed to him of no use to the GREEKS, but to assist them in numeration and arithmetic. It is indeed evident, that money is nothing but the representation of labour and commodities, and serves only as a method of rating or estimating them. Where coin is in greater plenty ; as a greater quantity of it is required to represent the same quantity of goods ; it can have no effect, either good or bad, taking a nation within itself ; any more than it would make an alteration on a merchant's books, if, instead of the ARABIAN method of notation, which requires few characters, he should make use of the ROMAN, which requires a great many. Nay, the greater quantity of money, like the ROMAN characters, is rather inconvenient, and requires greater trouble both to keep and transport it. But notwithstanding this conclusion, which must be allowed just, it is certain, that, since the discovery of the mines in AMERICA, industry has encreased in all the nations of EUROPE, except in the possessors of those mines ; and this may justly be ascribed, amongst other reasons, to the encrease of gold and silver. Accordingly we find, that, in every kingdom, into which money begins to flow in greater abundance than formerly, every thing takes a new face : labour and industry gain life ; the merchant becomes more enterprising, the manufacturer more diligent and skilful, and even the farmer follows his plough with greater alacrity and attention. This is not easily to be accounted for, if we consider only the influence which a greater abundance of coin has in the kingdom itself, by heightening the price of commodities, and obliging every one to pay a greater number of these little yellow or white pieces for every thing he purchases. And as to foreign trade, it appears, that great plenty of money is rather disadvantageous, by raising the price of every kind of labour.

To account, then, for this phenomenon, we must consider, that though the high price of commodities be a necessary consequence of the encrease of gold and silver,

37

yet it follows not immediately upon that encrease ; but some time is required before the money circulates through the whole state, and makes its effect be felt on all ranks of people. At first, no alteration is perceived ; by degrees the price rises, first of one commodity, then of another ; till the whole at last reaches a just proportion with the new quantity of specie which is in the kingdom. In my opinion, it is only in this interval or intermediate situation, between the acquisition of money and rise of prices, that the encreasing quantity of gold and silver is favourable to industry. When any quantity of money is imported into a nation, it is not at first dispersed into many hands , but is confined to the coffers of a few persons, who immediately seek to employ it *to advantage. Here are a set of manufacturers or merchants, we shall suppose, who have received returns of gold and silver for goods which they sent to CADIZ. They are thereby enabled to employ more workmen than formerly, who never dream of demanding higher wages, but are glad of employment from such good paymasters. If workmen become scarce, the manufacturer gives higher wages, but at first requires an encrease of labour ; and this is willingly submitted to by the artisan, who can now eat and drink better, to compensate his additional toil and fatigue. He carries his money to market, where he finds every thing at the same price as formerly, but returns with greater quantity and of better kinds, for the use of his family. The farmer and gardener, finding, that all their commodities are taken off, apply themselves with alacrity to the raising more ; and at the same time can afford to take better and more cloths from their tradesmen, whose price is the same as formerly, and their industry only whetted by so much new gain. It is easy to trace the money in its progress through the whole commonwealth ; where we shall find, that it must first quicken the diligence of every individual, before it encrease the price of labour.

* to advantage = to the best advantage [*A–G*].

38

And that the specie may encrease to a considerable pitch, before it have this latter effect, appears, amongst other instances, from the frequent operations of the FRENCH king on the money ; where it was always found, that the augmenting of the numerary value did not produce a proportional rise of the prices, at least for some time. In the last year of LOUIS XIV. money was raised three-sevenths, but prices augmented only one. Corn in FRANCE is now sold at the same price, or for the same number of livres, it was in 1683 ; though silver was then at 30 livres the mark, and is now at 50.[1] Not to mention the great addition of gold and silver, which may have come into that kingdom since the former period.

From the whole of this reasoning we may conclude, that it is of no manner of consequence, with regard to the domestic happiness of a state, whether money be in a greater or less quantity. The good policy of the magistrate consists only in keeping it, if possible, still encreasing ; because, by that means, he keeps alive a spirit of industry

[1] These facts I give upon the authority of Mons. du TOT in his *Reflections politiques*, an author of reputation. Though I must confess, that the facts which he advances on other occasions, are often so suspicious, as to make his authority less in this matter. However, the general observation, that the augmenting of the money in FRANCE does not at first proportionably augment the prices, is certainly just.

By the by, this seems to be one of the best reasons which can be given, for a gradual and universal encrease of the denomination of money, though it has been entirely overlooked in all those volumes which have been written on that question by MELON, DU TOT, and PARIS DE VERNEY. Were all our money, for instance, recoined, and a penny's worth of silver taken from every shilling, the new shilling would probably purchase every thing that could have been bought by the old ; the prices of everything would thereby be insensibly diminished ; foreign trade enlivened ; and domestic industry, by the circulation of a great number of pounds and shillings, would receive some encrease and encouragement. In executing such a project, it would be better to make the new shilling pass for 24 halfpence, in order to preserve the illusion, and make it be taken for the same. *And as a recoinage of our silver begins to be requisite, by the continual wearing of our shillings and sixpences, it may be doubtful, whether we ought to imitate the example in KING WILLIAM's reign, when the clipt money was raised to the old standard.

* [*This sentence in Errata, A*].

in the nation, and encreases the stock of labour, in which consists all real power and riches.[1] A nation, whose money decreases, is actually, at that time, weaker and more miserable than another nation, which possesses no more money, but is on the encreasing hand. This will be easily accounted for, if we consider, that the alterations in the quantity of money, either on one side or the other, are not immediately attended with proportionable alterations in the price of commodities. There is always an interval before matters be adjusted to their new situation ; and this interval is as pernicious to industry, when gold and silver are diminishing, as it is advantageous when these metals are encreasing. The workman has not the same employment from the manufacturer and merchant ; though he pays the same price for everything in the market. The farmer cannot dispose of his corn and cattle ; though he must pay the same rent to his landlord. The poverty, and beggary, and sloth, which must ensue, are easily foreseen.

II. The second observation which I proposed to make with regard to money, may be explained after the following manner. There are some kingdoms, and many provinces in EUROPE, (and all of them were once in the same condition) where money is so scarce, that the landlord can get none at all from his tenants ; but is obliged to take his rent in kind, and either to consume it himself, or transport it to places where he may find a market. In those countries, the prince can levy few or no taxes, but in the same manner : And as he will receive small benefit from impositions so paid, it is evident that such a kingdom has little force even at home ; and cannot maintain fleets and armies to the same extent, as if every part of it abounded in gold and silver. There is surely a greater disproportion between the force of GERMANY, at present,

---

[1] [The relationship of this long-run and the preceding short-run analysis to Hume's acceptance of the quantity theory is discussed above, pp. lxiv–lxvii.—ED.]

and what it was three .centuries ago,[1] than there is in
its industry, people, and manufactures. The AUSTRIAN
dominions in the empire are in general well peopled and
well cultivated, and are of great extent ; but have not a
proportionable weight in the balance of EUROPE ; proceeding, as is commonly supposed, from the scarcity of
money. How do all these facts agree with that principle
of reason, that the quantity of gold and silver is in itself
altogether indifferent ? According to that principle wherever a sovereign has numbers of subjects, and these have
plenty of commodities, he should of course be great and
powerful, and they rich and happy, independent of the
greater or lesser abundance of the precious metals. These
admit of divisions and subdivisions to a great extent ; and
where the pieces might become so small as to be in danger
of being lost, it is easy to mix the gold or silver with a
baser metal, as is practised in some countries of EUROPE ;
and by that means raise the pieces to a bulk more sensible
and convenient. They still serve the same purposes of
exchange, whatever their number may be, or whatever
colour they may be supposed to have.

To these difficulties I answer, that the effect, here
supposed to flow from scarcity of money, really arises from
the manners and customs of the people ; and that we
mistake, as is too usual, a collateral effect for a cause.
The contradiction is only apparent ; but it requires some
thought and reflection to discover the principles, by which
we can reconcile *reason* to *experience*.

It seems a maxim almost self-evident, that the prices
of every thing depend on the proportion between commodities and money, and that any considerable alteration
on either has the same effect, either of heightening or
lowering the price. Encrease the commodities, they
become cheaper ; encrease the money, they rise in their

---

[1] The ITALIANS gave to the Emperor MAXIMILLIAN, the nickname of
POCCHI-DANARI. None of the enterprises of that prince ever succeeded,
for want of money.

value. As, on the other hand, a diminution of the former, and that of the latter, have contrary tendencies.

It is also evident, that the prices do not so much depend on the absolute quantity of commodities and that of money, which are in a nation, as on that of the commodities, which come or may come to market, and of the money which circulates. If the coin be locked up in chests, it is the same thing with regard to prices, as if it were annihilated ; if the commodities be hoarded in *magazines and granaries, a like effect follows. As the money and commodities, in these cases, never meet, they cannot affect each other. Were we, at any time, to form conjectures concerning the price of provisions, the corn, which the farmer·must reserve †for seed and for the maintenance of himself and family, ought never to enter into the estimation. It is only the overplus, compared to the demand, that determines the value.

To apply these principles, we must consider, that, in the first and more uncultivated ages of any state, ere fancy has confounded her wants with those of nature, men, content with the produce of their own fields, or with those rude improvements which they themselves can work upon them, have little occasion for exchange, at least for money, which, by agreement, is the common measure of exchange. The wool of the farmer's own flock, spun in his own family, and wrought by a neighbouring weaver, who receives his payment in corn or wool, suffices for furniture and cloathing. The carpenter, the smith, the mason, the tailor, are retained by wages of a like nature ; and the landlord himself, dwelling in the neighbourhood, is content to receive his rent in the commodities raised by the farmer. The greater part of these he consumes at home, in rustic hospitality : The rest, perhaps, he disposes of for money to the neighbouring town, whence he draws the few materials of his expence and luxury.

But after men begin to refine on all these enjoyments,

* magazines and [*not in A–G*].   † for seed and [*not in A–H*].

and live not always at home, nor are content with what can be raised in their neighbourhood, there is more exchange and commerce of all kinds, and more money enters into that exchange. The tradesmen will not be paid in corn ; because they want something more than barely to eat. The farmer goes beyond his own parish for the commodities he purchases, and cannot always carry his commodities to the merchant who supplies him. The landlord lives in the capital, or in a foreign country ; and demands his rent in gold and silver, which can easily be transported to him. Great undertakers, and manu-facturers, and merchants, arise in every commodity ; and these can conveniently deal in nothing but in specie. And consequently, in this situation of society, the coin enters into many more contracts, and by that means is much more employed than in the former.

The necessary effect is, that, provided the money encrease not in the nation, every thing must become much cheaper in times of industry and refinement, than in rude, uncultivated ages. It is the proportion between the circulating money, and the commodities in the market, which determines the prices. Goods, that are consumed at home, or exchanged with other goods in the neighbour-hood, never come to market ; they affect not in the least the current specie ; with regard to it they are as if totally annihilated ; and consequently this method of using them sinks the proportion on the side of the commodities, and encreases the prices. But after money enters into all contracts and sales, and is every where the measure of exchange, the same national cash has a much greater task to perform ; all commodities are then in the market ; the sphere of circulation is enlarged ; it is the same case as if that individual sum were to serve a larger kingdom ; and therefore, the proportion being here lessened on the side of the money, every thing must become cheaper, and the prices gradually fall.

By the most exact computations, that have been formed

all over EUROPE, after making allowance for the alteration
in the numerary value or the denomination, it is found,
that the prices of all things have only risen three, or at
most, four times, since the discovery of the WEST INDIES.
But will any one assert, that there is not much more than
four times the coin in EUROPE, that was in the fifteenth
century, and the centuries preceding it ? The SPANIARDS
and PORTUGUESE from their mines, the ENGLISH, FRENCH,
and DUTCH, by their AFRICAN trade, and by their inter-
lopers in the WEST INDIES, bring home about *six millions
a year, of which not above a third goes to the EAST INDIES.
This sum alone, in †ten years, would probably double
the ancient stock of money in EUROPE. And no other
satisfactory reason can be given, why all prices have not
risen to a much more exorbitant height, except that which
is derived from a change of customs and manners.
Besides that more commodities are produced by additional
industry, the same commodities come more to market,
after men depart from their ancient simplicity of manners.
And though this encrease has not been equal to that of
money, it has, however, been considerable, and has preserved the proportion between coin and commodities
nearer the ancient standard.

Were the question proposed, Which of these methods
of living in the people, the simple or refined, is the most
advantageous to the state or public ? I should, without
much scruple, prefer the latter, in a view to politics at
least ; and should produce this as an additional reason
for the encouragement of trade and manufactures.

While men live in the ancient simple manner, and
supply all their necessaries from domestic industry or from
the neighbourhood, the sovereign can levy no taxes in
money from a considerable part of his subjects ; and if
he will impose on them any burthens, he must take his
payment in commodities, with which alone they abound ;

* six millions . . . a third=seven millions . . . a tenth part [A–B].
† ten=five [A–B].

a method attended with such great and obvious inconveniencies, that they need not here be insisted on. All the money he can pretend to raise, must be from his principal cities, where alone it circulates ; and these, it is evident, cannot afford him so much as the whole state could, did gold and silver circulate throughout the whole. But besides this obvious diminution of the revenue, there is another cause of the poverty of the public in such a situation. Not only the sovereign receives less money, but the same money goes not so far as in times of industry and general commerce. Every thing is dearer, where the gold and silver are supposed equal ; and that because fewer commodities come to market, and the whole coin bears a higher proportion to what is to be purchased by it ; whence alone the prices of every thing are fixed and determined.[1]

Here then we may learn the fallacy of the remark, often to be met with in historians, and even in common conversation, that any particular state is weak, though fertile, populous, and well cultivated, merely because it wants money. It appears, that the want of money can never injure any state within itself : For men and commodities are the real strength of any community. It is the simple manner of living which here hurts the public, by confining the gold and silver to few hands, and preventing its universal diffusion and circulation. On the contrary, industry and refinements of all kinds incorporate it with the whole state, however small its quantity may be : They digest it into every vein, so to speak ; and make it enter into every transaction and contract. No hand is entirely empty of it. And as the prices of every thing fall by that means, the sovereign has a double advantage : He may draw money by his taxes from every part of the state ; and what he receives, goes farther in every purchase and payment.

We may infer, from a comparison of prices, that money

[1] [For critical comment, cf. above, pp. lxi–lxiii.—Ed.]

is not more plentiful in CHINA, than it was in EUROPE three centuries ago : But what immense power is that empire possessed of, if we may judge by the civil and military establishment maintained by it ? Polybius [1] tells us, that provisions were so cheap in ITALY during his time, that in some places the stated *price for a meal at the inns was a *semis* a head, little more than a farthing ! Yet the ROMAN power had even then subdued the whole known world. About a century before that period, the CARTHAGINIAN ambassador said, by way of raillery, that no people lived more sociably amongst themselves than the ROMANS ; for that, in every entertainment, which, as foreign ministers, they received, they still observed the same plate at every table.[2] The absolute quantity of the precious metals is a matter of great indifference. There are only two circumstances of any importance, namely, their gradual encrease, and their thorough concoction and circulation through the state ; and the influence of both these circumstances has here been explained.

In the following Essay we shall see an instance of a like fallacy as that above mentioned ; where a collateral effect is taken for a cause, and where a consequence is ascribed to the plenty of money ; though it be really owing to a change in the manners and customs of the people.

[1] Lib. ii. cap. 15.   [2] PLIN. lib. xxxiii. cap. 11.

* price for a meal=club [A–G].

Of Interest

NOTHING is esteemed a more certain sign of the flourishing condition of any nation than the lowness of interest : And with reason ; though I believe the cause is somewhat different from what is commonly apprehended. Lowness of interest is generally ascribed to plenty of money.[1] But money, however plentiful, has no other effect, *if fixed*, than to raise the price of labour. Silver is more common than gold ; and therefore you receive a greater quantity of it for the same commodities. But do you pay less interest for it ? Interest in BATAVIA and JAMAICA is at 10 *per cent.* in PORTUGAL at 6 ; though these places, as we may learn from the prices of every thing, abound more in gold and silver than either LONDON or AMSTERDAM.

Were all the gold in ENGLAND annihilated at once, and one and twenty shillings substituted in the place of every guinea, would money be more plentiful or interest lower ? No surely : We should only use silver instead of gold. Were gold rendered as common as silver, and silver as common as copper ; would money be more plentiful or interest lower ? We may assuredly give the same answer. Our shillings would then be yellow, and our halfpence white ; and we should have no guineas. No other difference would ever be observed ; no alteration on commerce, manufactures, navigation, or interest ; unless we imagine, that the colour of the metal is of any consequence.

Now, what is so visible in these greater variations of scarcity or abundance in the precious metals, must hold in all inferior changes. If the multiplying of gold and silver fifteen times makes no difference, much less can the

[1] [See above, pp. xiv-xvi, for material concerning the background of this essay.—ED.]

47

doubling or tripling them. All augmentation has no other effect than to heighten the price of labour and commodities ; and even this variation is little more than that of a name. In the progress towards these changes, the augmentation may have some influence, by exciting industry ; but after the prices are settled, suitably to the new abundance of gold and silver, it has no manner of influence.

An effect always holds proportion with its cause. Prices have risen near four times since the discovery of the INDIES ; and it is probable gold and silver have multiplied much more : But interest has not fallen much above half. The rate of interest, therefore, is not derived from the quantity of the precious metals.

Money having chiefly a fictitious *value, the greater or less plenty of it is of no consequence, if we consider a nation within itself ; and the quantity of specie, when once fixed, though ever so large, has no other effect, than to oblige every one to tell out a greater number of those shining bits of metal, for clothes, furniture or equipage, without encreasing any one convenience of life. If a man borrow money to build a house, he then carries home a greater load ; because the stone, timber, lead, glass, &c. with the labour of the masons and carpenters, are represented by a greater quantity of gold and silver. But as these metals are considered chiefly as representations, there can no alteration arise, from their bulk or quantity, their weight or colour, either upon their real value or their interest. The same interest, in all cases, bears the same proportion to the sum. And if you lent me so much labour and so many commodities ; by receiving five *per cent.* you always receive proportional labour and commodities, however represented, whether by yellow or white coin, whether by a pound or an ounce. It is in vain, therefore, to look for the cause of the fall or rise of interest

* value=value, arising from the agreement and convention of men [*A–G*].

in the greater or less quantity of gold and silver, which is fixed in any nation.

High interest arises from *three* circumstances : A great demand for borrowing ; little riches to supply that demand [1] ; and great profits arising from commerce : And these circumstances are a clear proof of the small advance of commerce and industry, not of the scarcity of gold and silver. Low interest, on the other hand, proceeds from the three opposite circumstances : A small demand for borrowing ; great riches to supply that demand ; and small profits arising from commerce : And these circumstances are all connected together, and proceed from the encrease of industry and commerce, not of gold and silver. We shall endeavour to prove these points ; and shall begin with the causes and the effects of a great or small demand for borrowing.

When a people have emerged ever so little from a savage state, and their numbers have encreased beyond the original multitude, there must immediately arise an inequality of property ; and while some possess large tracts of land, others are confined within narrow limits, and some are entirely without any landed property. Those who possess more land than they can labour, employ those who possess none, and agree to receive a determinate part of the product. Thus the *landed* interest is immediately established ; nor is there any settled government, however rude, in which affairs are not on this footing. Of these proprietors of land, some must presently discover themselves to be of different tempers from others ; and while one would willingly store up the produce of his land for futurity, another desires to consume

[1] [Though others before Hume had advanced a real-capital theory of interest (e.g. Massie and North), Adam Smith pointedly draws on Hume's statement (as well as his criticism of the mercantilist doctrine) in his own treatment of interest theory. Cf. *The Wealth of Nations*, ed. E. Cannan (New York 1937), p. 337. Smith's doctrine, however, was more advanced, in so far as, reflecting the further growth of capitalism, it gave more weight to borrowing for production as against consumption purposes.—ED.]

at present what should suffice for many years. But as the spending of a settled revenue is a way of life entirely without occupation ; men have so much need of somewhat to fix and engage them, that pleasures, such as they are, will be the pursuit of the greater part of the landholders, and the prodigals among them will always be more numerous than the misers. In a state, therefore, where there is nothing but a landed interest, as there is little frugality, the borrowers must be very numerous, and the rate of interest must hold proportion to it. The difference depends not on the quantity of money, but on the habits and manners which prevail. By this alone the demand for borrowing is encreased or diminished. Were money so plentiful as to make an egg be sold for sixpence ; so long as there are only landed gentry and peasants in the state, the borrowers must be numerous, and interest high. The rent for the same farm would be heavier and more bulky : But the same idleness of the landlord, with the higher price of commodities, would dissipate it in the same time, and produce the same necessity and demand for borrowing.*

Nor is the case different with regard to the *second* circumstance which we proposed to consider, namely, the great or little riches to supply the demand. This effect also depends on the habits and way of living of the people, not on the quantity of gold and silver. In order to have, in any state, a great number of lenders, it is not sufficient nor requisite, that there be great abundance of the precious metals. It is only requisite, that the property or command

---

* +I have been informed by a very eminent lawyer, and a man of great knowledge and observation, that it appears from antient papers and records, that, about four centuries ago, money in *Scotland*, and probably in other parts of [of = in (*B*)] *Europe*, was only at five per cent. and afterwards rose to ten before the discovery of the *West Indies*. This fact is curious ; but might easily be reconciled to the foregoing reasoning. Men, in that age, lived so much at home, and in so very simple and frugal a manner, that they had no occasion for money ; and though the lenders were then few, the borrowers were still fewer. The high rate of interest among the early *Romans* is accounted for by historians from the frequent losses sustained by the inroads of the enemy. [*A–E, as footnote.*]

of that quantity, which is in the state, whether great or small, should be collected in particular hands, so as to form considerable sums, or compose a great monied interest. This begets a number of lenders, and sinks the rate of usury ; and this I shall venture to affirm, depends not on the quantity of specie, but on particular manners and customs, which make the specie gather into separate sums or masses of considerable value.

For suppose, that, by miracle, every man in GREAT BRITAIN should have five pounds slipt into his pocket in one night ; this would much more than double the whole money that is at present in the kingdom ; yet there would not next day, nor for some time, be any more lenders, nor any variation in the interest. And were there nothing but landlords and peasants in the state, this money, however abundant, could never gather into sums ; and would only serve to encrease the prices of every thing, without any farther consequence. The prodigal landlord dissipates it, as fast as he receives it ; and the beggarly peasant has no means, nor view, nor ambition of obtaining above a bare livelihood. The overplus of borrowers above that of lenders continuing still the same, there will follow no reduction of interest. That depends upon another principle ; and must proceed from an encrease of industry and frugality, of arts and commerce.

Every thing useful to the life of man arises from the ground ; but few things arise in that condition which is requisite to render them useful. There must, therefore, beside the peasant and the proprietors of land, be another rank of men, who receiving from the former the rude materials, work them into their proper form, and retain part for their own use and subsistence. In the infancy of society, these contracts between the artisans and the peasants, and between one species of artisans and another are commonly entered into immediately by the persons themselves, who, being neighbours, are easily acquainted with each other's necessities, and can lend their mutual

51

assistance to supply them. But when men's industry encreases, and their views enlarge, it is found, that the most remote parts of the state can assist each other as well as the more contiguous, and that this intercourse of good offices may be carried on to the greatest extent and intricacy. Hence the origin of *merchants*, one of the most useful *races of men, who serve as agents between those parts of the state, that are wholly unacquainted, and are ignorant of each other's necessities. Here are in a city fifty workmen in silk and linen, and a thousand customers ; and these two ranks of men, so necessary to each other, can never rightly meet, till one man erects a shop, to which all the workmen and all the customers repair. In this province, grass rises in abundance : The inhabitants abound in cheese, and butter, and cattle ; but want bread and corn, which, in a neighbouring province, are in too great abundance for the use of the inhabitants. One man discovers this. He brings corn from the one province and returns with cattle ; and supplying the wants of both, he is, so far, a common benefactor. As the people encrease in numbers and industry, the difficulty of their intercourse encreases : The business of the agency or merchandize becomes more intricate ; and divides, subdivides, compounds, and mixes to a greater variety. In all these transactions, it is necessary, and reasonable, that a considerable part of the commodities and labour should belong to the merchant, to whom, in a great measure, they are owing. And these commodities he will sometimes preserve in kind, or more commonly convert into money, which is their common representation. If gold and silver have encreased in the state together with the industry, it will require a great quantity of these metals to represent a great quantity of commodities and labour. If industry alone has encreased, the prices of every thing must sink, and a small quantity of specie will serve as a representation.

* races of men = race of men in the whole society [*A-D*].

Of Interest

There is no craving or demand of the human mind
more constant and insatiable than that for exercise and
employment; and this desire seems the foundation of
most of our passions and pursuits. Deprive a man of all
business and serious occupation, he runs restless from one
amusement to another; and the weight and oppression,
which he feels from idleness, is so great, that he forgets
the ruin which must follow him from his immoderate
expences. Give him a more harmless way of employing
his mind or body, he is satisfied, and feels no longer that
insatiable thirst after pleasure. But if the employment
you give him be lucrative, especially if the profit be
attached to every particular exertion of industry, he has
gain so often in his eye, that he acquires, by degrees, a
passion for it, and knows no such pleasure as that of seeing
the daily encrease of his fortune. And this is the reason
why trade encreases frugality, and why, among merchants,
there is the same overplus of misers above prodigals, as,
among the possessors of land, there is the contrary.

Commerce encreases industry, by conveying it readily
from one member of the state to another, and allowing
none of it to perish or become useless. It encreases
frugality, by giving occupation to men, and employing
them in the arts of gain, which soon engage their affection,
and remove all relish for pleasure and expence. It is an
infallible consequence of all industrious professions, to
beget frugality, and make the love of gain prevail over
the love of pleasure. Among lawyers and physicians who
have any practice, there are many more who live within
their income, than who exceed it, or even live up to it.
But lawyers and physicians beget no industry; and it is
even at the expence of others they acquire their riches;
so that they are sure to diminish the possessions of some
of their fellow-citizens, as fast as they encrease their own.
Merchants, on the contrary, beget industry, by serving as
canals to convey it through every corner of the state:
And at the same time, by their frugality, they acquire

53

great power over that industry, and collect a large property in the labour and commodities, which they are the chief instruments in producing. There is no other profession, therefore, except merchandize, which can make the monied interest considerable, or, in other words, can encrease industry, and, by also encreasing frugality, give a great command of that industry to particular members of the society. Without commerce, the state must consist chiefly of landed gentry, whose prodigality and expence make a continual demand for borrowing ; and of peasants, who have no sums to supply that demand. The money never gathers into large stocks or sums, which can be lent at interest. It is dispersed into numberless hands, who either squander it in idle show and magnificence, or employ it in the purchase of the common necessaries of life. Commerce alone assembles it into considerable sums ; and this effect it has merely from the industry which it begets, and the frugality which it inspires, independent of that particular quantity of precious metal which may circulate in the state.

Thus an encrease of commerce, by a necessary consequence, raises a great number of lenders, and by that means produces lowness of interest. We must now consider how far this encrease of commerce diminishes the profits arising from that profession, and gives rise to the *third* circumstance requisite to produce lowness of interest.

It may be proper to observe on this head, that low interest and low profits of merchandize are two events, that mutually forward each other, and are both originally derived from that extensive commerce, which produces opulent merchants, and renders the monied interest considerable. Where merchants possess great stocks, whether represented by few or many pieces of metal, it must frequently happen, that, when they either become tired of business, or leave heirs unwilling or unfit to engage in commerce, a great proportion of these riches naturally seeks an annual and secure revenue. The plenty diminishes the price, and makes the lenders accept of a low interest. This consideration obliges many to keep their stock employed in trade, and rather be content with low profits than dispose of their money at an under-value. On the other hand, when commerce has become extensive, and employs large stocks, there must arise rivalships among the merchants, which diminish the profits of trade, at the same time that they encrease the trade itself. The low profits of merchandize induce the merchants to accept more willingly of a low interest, when they leave off business, and begin to indulge themselves in ease and indolence. It is needless, therefore, to enquire which of these circumstances, to wit, *low interest or low profits*, is the cause, and which the effect? They both arise from an extensive commerce, and mutually forward each other. No man will accept of low profits, where he can have high interest ; and no man will accept of low interest, where he can have high profits. An extensive commerce, by producing large stocks, diminishes both interest and profits ; and is always assisted, in its diminution of the one, by the proportional sinking of the other. I may add, that, as low profits arise from the encrease of commerce and industry, they serve in their turn to its farther encrease, by rendering the commodities cheaper, encouraging the consumption, and heightening the industry. And thus, if we consider the whole connexion of causes and effects, interest is the barometer of the state, and its lowness is a sign almost infallible of the flourishing condition of a people.[1] It proves the encrease of industry, and its prompt circulation through the whole state, little inferior to a demonstration. And though, perhaps, it may not be impossible but a sudden and a great check to commerce may have a momentary effect of the same kind,

[1] [In its treatment of interest as an effect rather than as a cause of the growth of commerce (the latter being the more common view), Hume's doctrine is most like Dudley North's. Cf. North's *Discourses upon Trade* (Baltimore 1907), p. 18.—ED.]

by throwing so many stocks out of trade ; it must be attended with such misery and want of employment in the poor, that, besides its short duration, it will not be possible to mistake the one case for the other.

Those who have asserted, that the plenty of money was the cause of low interest, seem to have taken a collateral effect for a cause ; since the same industry, which sinks the interest, commonly acquires great abundance of the precious metals. A variety of fine manufactures, with vigilant enterprising merchants, will soon draw money to a state, if it be any where to be found in the world. The same cause, by multiplying the conveniencies of life, and encreasing industry, collects great riches into the hands of persons, who are not proprietors of land, and produces, by that means, a lowness of interest. But though both these effects, plenty of money and low interest, naturally arise from commerce and industry, they are altogether independent of each other. For suppose a nation removed into the *Pacific* ocean, without any foreign commerce, or any knowledge of navigation : Suppose, that this nation possesses always the same stock of coin, but is continually encreasing in its numbers and industry : It is evident, that the price of every commodity must gradually diminish in that kingdom ; since it is the proportion between money and any species of goods, which fixes their mutual value ; and, upon the present supposition, the conveniencies of life become every day more abundant, without any alteration in the current specie. A less quantity of money, therefore, among this people, will make a rich man, during the times of industry, than would suffice to that purpose, in ignorant and slothful ages. Less money will build a house, portion a daughter, buy an estate, support a manufactory, or maintain a family and equipage. These are the uses for which men borrow money ; and therefore, the greater or less quantity of it in a state has no influence on the interest. But is is evident, that the greater or less stock of labour and commodities must have a great influence ; since we really and in effect borrow these, when we take money upon interest. It is true, when commerce is extended all over the globe, the most industrious nations always abound most with the precious metals : So that low interest and plenty of money are in fact almost inseparable. But still it is of consequence to know the principle whence any phenomenon arises, and to distinguish between a cause and a concomitant effect. Besides that the speculation is curious, it may frequently be of use in the conduct of public affairs At least, it must be owned, that nothing can be of more use than to improve, by practice, the method of reasoning on these subjects, which of all others are the most important ; though they are commonly treated in the loosest and most careless manner.

Another reason of this popular mistake with regard to the cause of low interest, seems to be the instance of some nations ; where, after a sudden acquisition of money or of the precious metals, by means of foreign conquest, the interest has fallen, not only among them, but in all the neighbouring states, as soon as that money was dispersed, and had insinuated itself into every corner. Thus, interest in Spain fell near a half immediately after the discovery of the West Indies, as we are informed by Garcilasso de la Vega : And it has been ever since gradually sinking in every kingdom of Europe. Interest in Rome, after the conquest of Egypt, fell from 6 to 4 *per cent.* as we learn from Dion.[1]

The causes of the sinking of interest, upon such an event, seem different in the conquering country and in the neighbouring states ; but in neither of them can we justly ascribe that effect merely to the encrease of gold and silver.

In the conquering country, it is natural to imagine, that this new acquisition of money will fall into a few hands, and be gathered into large sums, which seek a

[1] Lib. 51, 21.

secure revenue, either by the purchase of land or by
interest ; and consequently the same effect follows, for a
little time, as if there had been a great accession of
industry and commerce. The encrease of lenders above
the borrowers sinks the interest ; and so much the faster,
if those, who have acquired those large sums, find no
industry or commerce in the state, and no method of
employing their money but by lending it at interest. But
after this new mass of gold and silver has been digested,
and has circulated through the whole state, affairs will
soon return to their former situation ; while the landlords
and new money-holders, living idly, squander above their
income ; and the former daily contract debt, and the
latter encroach on their stock till its final extinction. The
whole money may still be in the state, and make itself
felt by the encrease of prices : But not being now collected into any large masses or stocks, the disproportion
between the borrowers and lenders is the same as formerly,
and consequently the high interest returns.[1]

Accordingly we find, in ROME, that, so early as
TIBERIUS's time, interest had again mounted to 6 *per cent.*[2]
though no accident had happened to drain the empire of
money. In TRAJAN's time, money lent on mortgages in
ITALY, bore 6 *per cent.* [3] ; on common securities in
BITHYNIA, 12.[4] And if interest in SPAIN has not risen to
its old pitch ; this can be ascribed to nothing but the
continuance of the same cause that sunk it, to wit, the
large fortunes continually made in the INDIES, which come
over to SPAIN from time to time, and supply the demand
of the borrowers. By this accidental and extraneous cause,
more money is to be lent in SPAIN, that is, more money is
collected into large sums than would otherwise be found
in a state, where there are so little commerce and industry.

---

[1] [See above, p. lxxii, for comment on the implications of this part of
Hume's analysis for the central portion of his interest theory.—ED.]
[2] COLUMELIA, lib. iii. cap. 3.   [3] PLINII epist. lib. vii. ep. 18.
[4] Id. lib. x. ep. 62.

Of Interest

As to the reduction of interest, which has followed in ENGLAND, FRANCE, and other kingdoms of EUROPE, that have no mines, it has been gradual ; and has not proceeded from the encrease of money, considered merely in itself ; but from that of industry, which is the natural effect of the former encrease, in that interval, before it raises the price of labour and provisions.[1] For to return to the foregoing supposition ; if the industry of ENGLAND had risen as much from other causes, (and that rise might easily have happened, though the stock of money had remained the same) must not all the same consequences have followed, which we observe at present ? The same people would, in that case, be found in the kingdom, the same commodities, the same industry, manufactures, and commerce ; and consequently the same merchants, with the same stocks, that is, with the same command over labour and commodities, only represented by a smaller number of white or yellow pieces ; which being a circumstance of no moment, would only affect the waggoner, porter, and trunk-maker. Luxury, therefore, manufactures, arts, industry, frugality, flourishing equally as at present, it is evident, that interest must also have been as low ; since that is the necessary result of all these circumstances ; so far as they determine the profits of commerce, and the proportion between the borrowers and lenders in any state.

[1] [See above, pp. lxx–lxxi.—ED.]

Of the Balance of Trade [1]

IT is very usual, in nations ignorant of the nature of commerce, to prohibit the exportation of commodities, and to preserve among themselves whatever they think valuable and useful. They do not consider, that, in this prohibition, they act directly contrary to their intention ; and that the more is exported of any commodity, the more will be raised at home, of which they themselves will always have the first offer.

It is well known to the learned, that the ancient laws of ATHENS rendered the exportation of figs criminal ; that being supposed a species of fruit so excellent in ATTICA, that the ATHENIANS deemed it too delicious for the palate of any foreigner. And in this ridiculous prohibition they were so much in earnest, that informers were thence called *sycophants* among them, from two GREEK words, which signify *figs* and *discoverer*.[2] *There are proofs in many old acts of parliament of the same ignorance in the nature of commerce, particularly in the reign of EDWARD III. And to this day, in †FRANCE, the exportation of corn is almost always prohibited ; in order, as they say, to prevent famines ; though it is evident, that nothing contributes more to the frequent famines, which so much distress that fertile country.

The same jealous fear, with regard to money, has also prevailed among several nations ; and it required both reason and experience to convince any people, that these

---

[1] [See above, pp. xiii–xvi, for relevant background material.—ED.
[2] PLUT. *De Curiositate.*

* There are proofs in many old acts of parliament of=I have been told, that many old acts of parliament show [A–D] ; There are proofs in many old acts of the SCOTCH parliament of [E].
† FRANCE=a neighbouring kingdom [A–D].

prohibitions serve to no other purpose than to raise the exchange against them, and produce a still greater exportation.

These errors, one may say, are gross and palpable : But there still prevails, even in nations well acquainted with commerce, a strong jealousy with regard to the balance of trade, and a fear, that all their gold and silver may be leaving them. This seems to me, almost in every case, a groundless apprehension ; and I should as soon dread, that all our springs and rivers should be exhausted, as that money should abandon a kingdom where there are people and industry. Let us carefully preserve these latter advantages ; and we need never be apprehensive of losing the former.

It is easy to observe, that all calculations concerning the balance of trade are founded on very uncertain facts and suppositions. The custom-house books are allowed to be an insufficient ground of reasoning ; nor is the rate of exchange much better ; unless we consider it with all nations, and know also the proportions of the several sums remitted ; which one may safely pronounce impossible. Every man, who has ever reasoned on this subject, has always proved his theory, whatever it was, by facts and calculations, and by an enumeration of all the commodities sent to all foreign kingdoms.[1]

The writings of Mr. Gee [2] struck the nation with an universal panic, when they saw it plainly demonstrated, by a detail of particulars, that the balance was against them for so considerable a sum as must leave them without a single shilling in five or six years. But luckily, twenty

[1] [Though often prompted by other considerations than Hume is concerned with here (e.g. the defence of the alleged unfavourable balance resulting from the East India Company's trade), others had already questioned the possibility of drawing up an accurate and meaningful balance of trade. Cf., for example, Nicholas Barbon, *A discourse concerning Coining the new Money lighter* (1696), p. 36.—ED.]

[2] [Joshua Gee, *The Trade and Navigation of Great Britain considered* (1729). —ED.]

years have since elapsed, with an expensive foreign war ; yet is it commonly supposed, that money is still more plentiful among us than in any former period.

Nothing can be more entertaining on this head than Dr. SWIFT ; an author *so quick in discerning the mistakes and absurdities of others. He says, in his *short view of the state of* IRELAND,[1] that the whole cash of that kingdom formerly amounted but to 500,000*l.* ; that out of this the IRISH remitted every year a neat million to ENGLAND, and had scarcely any other source from which they could compensate themselves, and little other foreign trade than the importation of FRENCH wines, for which they paid ready money. The consequence of this situation, which must be owned to be disadvantageous, was, that, in a course of three years, the current money of IRELAND, from 500,000*l.* was reduced to less than two. And at present, I suppose, in a course of 30 years it is absolutely nothing. Yet I know not how, that opinion of the advance of riches in IRELAND, which gave the Doctor so much indignation, seems still to continue, and gain ground with every body.

In short, this apprehension of the wrong balance of trade, appears of such a nature, that it discovers itself, wherever one is out of humour with the ministry, or is in low spirits ; and as it can never be refuted by a particular detail of all the exports, which counterbalance the imports, it may here be proper to form a general argument, that they may prove the impossibility of this event, as long as we preserve our people and our industry.

[2] Suppose four-fifths of all the money in GREAT BRITAIN

---

[1] [Published in 1728.—ED.]

[2] [Hume's first statement of the quantity-theory specie-flow doctrine appears in a letter to Montesquieu. Cf. below, p. 188. For Hume's discussion of the doctrine with James Oswald, cf. below, pp. 190 ff ; also above, p. lvi *n*.—ED.]

* so quick . . . others = who has more humour than knowledge, more taste than judgment, and more spleen, prejudice, and passion than any of these qualities [*A–B*].

to be annihilated in one night, and the nation reduced to the same condition, with regard to specie, as in the reigns of the HARRYS and EDWARDS, what would be the consequence ? Must not the price of all labour and commodities sink in proportion, and everything be sold as cheap as they were in those ages ? What nation could then dispute with us in any foreign market, or pretend to navigate or to sell manufactures at the same price, which to us would afford sufficient profit ? In how little time, therefore, must this bring back the money which we had lost, and raise us to the level of all the neighbouring nations ? Where, after we have arrived, we immediately lose the advantage of the cheapness of labour and commodities ; and the farther flowing in of money is stopped by our fulness and repletion.

Again, suppose, that all the money of GREAT BRITAIN were multiplied fivefold in a night, must not the contrary effect follow ? Must not all labour and commodities rise to such an exorbitant height, that no neighbouring nations could afford to buy from us ; while their commodities, on the other hand, became comparatively so cheap, that, in spite of all the laws which could be formed, they would be run in upon us, and our money flow out ; till we fall to a level with foreigners, and lose that great superiority of riches, which had laid us under such disadvantages ?

Now, it is evident, that the same causes, which would correct these exorbitant inequalities, were they to happen miraculously, must prevent their happening in the common course of nature, and must for ever, in all neighbouring nations, preserve money nearly proportionable to the art and industry of each nation. All water, wherever it communicates, remains always at a level. Ask naturalists the reason ; they tell you, that, were it to be raised in any one place, the superior gravity of that part not being balanced, must depress it, till it meet a counterpoise ; and that the same cause, which redresses the inequality when

63

it happens, must for ever prevent it, without some violent external operation.[1]

Can one imagine, that it had ever been possible, by any laws, or even by any art or industry, to have kept all the money in SPAIN, which the galleons have brought from the INDIES ? Or that all commodities could be sold in FRANCE for a tenth of the price which they would yield on the other side of the PYRENEES, without finding their way thither, and draining from that immense treasure ? What other reason, indeed, is there, why all nations, at present, gain in their trade with SPAIN and PORTUGAL ; but because it is impossible to heap up money, more than any fluid, beyond its proper level ? The sovereigns of these countries have shown, that they wanted not inclination to keep their gold and silver to themselves, had it been in any degree practicable.

But as any body of water may be raised above the level of the surrounding element, if the former has no communication with the latter ; so in money, if the communication be cut off, by any material or physical impediment, (for all laws alone are ineffectual) there may, in such a case, be a very great inequality of money. Thus the immense distance of CHINA, together with the monopolies of our INDIA companies, obstructing the communication, preserve in EUROPE the gold and silver, especially the latter, in much greater plenty than they are found in that kingdom. But, notwithstanding this great obstruction, the force of the causes abovementioned is still evident. The skill and ingenuity of EUROPE in general surpasses perhaps that of CHINA, with regard to manual arts and manufactures ; yet are we never able to trade

[1] There is another cause. though more limited in its operation, which checks the wrong balance of trade, to every particular nation to which the kingdom trades. When we import more goods than we export, the exchange turns against us, and this becomes a new encouragement to export ; as much as the charge of carriage and insurance of the money which becomes due would amount to. For the exchange can never rise but a little higher than that sum.

thither without great disadvantage. And were it not for
the continual recruits, which we receive from AMERICA,
money would soon sink in EUROPE, and rise in CHINA, till
it came nearly to a level in both places. Nor can any
reasonable man doubt, but that industrious nation, were
they as near us as POLAND or BARBARY, would drain us of
the overplus of our specie, and draw to themselves a larger
share of the WEST INDIAN treasures. We need not have
recourse to a physical attraction, in order to explain the
necessity of this operation. There is a moral attraction,
arising from the interests and passions of men, which is
full as potent and infallible.

How is the balance kept in the provinces of every
kingdom among themselves, but by the force of this
principle, which makes it impossible for money to lose its
level, and either to rise or sink beyond the proportion of
the labour and commodities which are in each province?
Did not long experience make people easy on this head,
what a fund of gloomy reflections might calculations afford
to a melancholy YORKSHIREMAN, while he computed and
magnified the sums drawn to LONDON by taxes, absentees,
commodities, and found on comparison the opposite articles
so much inferior? And no doubt, had the *Heptarchy*
subsisted in ENGLAND, the legislature of each state had
been continually alarmed by the fear of a wrong balance;
and as it is probable that the mutual hatred of these states
would have been extremely violent on account of their close
neighbourhood, they would have loaded and oppressed all
commerce, by a jealous and superfluous caution. Since
the union has removed the barriers between SCOTLAND
and ENGLAND, which of these nations gains from the other
by this free commerce? Or if the former kingdom has
received any encrease of riches, can it reasonably be
accounted for by any thing but the encrease of its art and
industry? It was a common apprehension in ENGLAND,
before the union, as we learn from L'ABBE DU BOS,[1] that

---

[1] *Les interets d'*ANGLETERRE *malentendus.*

65

SCOTLAND would soon drain them of their treasure, were an open trade allowed ; and on the other side the TWEED a contrary apprehension prevailed : With what justice in both, time has shown.

What happens in small portions of mankind, must take place in greater. The provinces of the ROMAN empire, no doubt, kept their balance with each other, and with ITALY, independent of the legislature ; as much as the several counties of GREAT BRITAIN, or the several parishes of each county. And any man who travels over EUROPE at this day, ·may see, by the prices of commodities, that money, in spite of the absurd jealousy of princes and states, has brought itself nearly to a level ; and that the difference between one kingdom and another is not greater in this respect, than it is often between different provinces of the same kingdom. Men naturally flock to capital cities, sea-ports, and navigable rivers. There we find more men, more industry, more commodities, and consequently more money ; but still the latter difference holds proportion with the former, and the level is preserved.[1]

Our jealousy and our hatred of FRANCE are without bounds ; and the former sentiment, at least, must be acknowledged reasonable and well-grounded. These passions have occasioned innumerable barriers and obstructions upon commerce, where we are accused of being commonly the aggressors. But what have we gained by the bargain ? We lost the FRENCH market for our woollen

---

[1] It must carefully be remarked, that throughout this discourse, wherever I speak of the level of money, I mean always its proportional level to the commodities, labour, industry, and skill, which is in the several states. And I assert, that where these advantages are double, triple, quadruple, to what they are in the neighbouring states, the money infallibly will also be double, triple, quadruple. The only circumstance that can obstruct the exactness of these proportions, is the expense of transporting the commodities from one place to another ; and this expense is sometimes unequal. Thus the corn, cattle, cheese, butter, of DERBYSHIRE, cannot draw the money of LONDON, so much as the manufactures of LONDON draw the money of DERBYSHIRE. But this objection is only a seeming one : For so far as the transport of commodities is expensive, so far is the communication between the places obstructed and imperfect.

manufactures, and transferred the commerce of wine to SPAIN and PORTUGAL, where we buy worse liquor at a higher price. There are few ENGLISHMEN who would not think their country absolutely ruined, were FRENCH wines sold in ENGLAND so cheap and in such abundance as to supplant, in some measure, all ale, and home-brewed liquors : But would we lay aside prejudice, it would not be difficult to prove, that nothing could be more innocent, perhaps advantageous. Each new acre of vineyard planted in FRANCE, in order to supply ENGLAND with wine, would make it requisite for the FRENCH to take the produce of an ENGLISH acre, sown in wheat or barley, in order to subsist themselves ; and it is evident, that we should thereby get command of the better commodity.

There are many edicts of the FRENCH king, prohibiting the planting of new vineyards, and ordering all those which are lately planted to be grubbed up : So sensible are they, in that country, of the superior value of corn, above every other product.

Mareschal VAUBAN complains often, and with reason, of the absurd duties which load the entry of those wines of LANGUEDOC, GUIENNE, and other southern provinces, that are imported into BRITANNY and NORMANDY. He entertained no doubt but these latter provinces could preserve their balance, notwithstanding the open commerce which he recommends. And it is evident, that a few leagues more navigation to ENGLAND would make no difference ; or if it did, that it must operate alike on the commodities of both kingdoms.

There is indeed one expedient by which it is possible to sink, and another by which we may raise money beyond its natural level in any kingdom ; but these cases, when examined, will be found to resolve into our general theory, and to bring additional authority to it.

I scarcely know any method of sinking money below its level, but those institutions of banks, funds, and paper-credit, *which are so much practised in this kingdom. These render paper equivalent to money, circulate it throughout the whole state, make it supply the place of gold and silver, raise proportionably the price of labour and commodities, and by that means either banish a great part of those precious metals, or prevent their farther encrease. What can be more short-sighted than our reasonings on this head ? We fancy, because an individual would be much richer, were his stock of money doubled, that the same good effect would follow were the money of every one encreased ; not considering, that this would raise as much the price of every commodity, and reduce every man, in time, to the same condition as before. It is only in our public negociations and transactions with foreigners, that a greater stock of money is advantageous ; and as our paper is there absolutely insignificant, we feel, by its means, all the ill effects arising from a great abundance of money, without reaping any of the advantages.[1]

Suppose that there are 12 millions of paper, which circulate in the kingdom as money, (for we are not to imagine, that all our enormous funds are employed in that shape) and suppose the real cash of the kingdom to be 18 millions : Here is a state which is found by experience to be able to hold a stock of 30 millions. I say, if it be able to hold it, it must of necessity have acquired it in gold and silver, had we not obstructed the entrance of these metals by this new invention of paper. *Whence would it have acquired that sum ?* From all the kingdoms of the world. *But why ?* Because, if you remove these 12 millions, money in this state is below its level, compared

---

[1] †We observed in Essay III ["Of Money"] that money, when encreasing, gives encouragement to industry, during the interval between the encrease of money and rise of the prices. A good effect of this nature may follow too from paper-credit ; but it is dangerous to precipitate matters, at the risk of losing all by the failing of that credit, as must happen upon any violent shock in public affairs.

* which . . . kingdom=with which we are in this kingdom so much infatuated [*A–E*].   † [*This footnote not in A*].

with our neighbours ; and we must immediately draw
from all of them, till we be full and saturate, so to speak,
and can hold no more. By our present politics, we are
as careful to stuff the nation with this fine commodity of
bank-bills and chequer-notes, as if we were afraid of being
overburthened with the precious metals.

It is not to be doubted, but the great plenty of bullion
in FRANCE is, in a great measure, owing to the want of
paper-credit. The FRENCH have no banks : Merchant
bills do not there circulate as with us : Usury or lending
on interest is not directly permitted ; so that many have
large sums in their coffers : Great quantities of plate are
used in private houses ; and all the churches are full of
it. By this means, provisions and labour still remain
cheaper among them, than in nations that are not half so
rich in gold and silver. The advantages of this situation,
in point of trade as well as in great public emergencies,
are too evident to be disputed.

The same fashion a few years ago prevailed in GENOA,
which still has place in ENGLAND and HOLLAND, of using
services of CHINA-ware instead of plate ; but the senate,
foreseeing the consequence, prohibited the use of that
brittle commodity beyond a certain extent ; while the
use of silver-plate was left unlimited. And I suppose, in
their late distresses, they felt the good effect of this
ordinance. *Our tax on plate is, perhaps, in this view,
somewhat impolitic.

Before the introduction of paper-money into our
colonies, they had gold and silver sufficient for their
circulation. Since the introduction of that commodity,
the least inconveniency that has followed is the total
banishment of the precious metals. And after the abolition
of paper, can it be doubted but money will return, while
these colonies possess manufactures and commodities, the
only thing valuable in commerce, and for whose sake alone
all men desire money.

* Our tax . . . impolitic [*A as footnote*].

What pity LYCURGUS did not think of paper-credit, when he wanted to banish gold and silver from SPARTA ! It would have served his purpose better than the lumps of iron he made use of as money ; and would also have prevented more effectually all commerce with strangers, as being of so much less real and intrinsic value.

*It must, however, be confessed, that, as all these questions of trade and money are extremely complicated, there are certain lights, in which this subject may be placed, so as to represent the advantages of paper-credit and banks to be superior to their disadvantages. That they banish specie and bullion from a state is undoubtedly true ; and whoever looks no farther than this circumstance does well to condemn them ; but specie and bullion are not of so great consequence as not to admit of a compensation, and even an overbalance from the encrease of industry and of credit, which may be promoted by the right use of paper-money. It is well known of what advantage it is to a merchant to be able to discount his bills upon occasion ; and every thing that facilitates this species of traffic is favourable to the general commerce of a state. But private bankers are enabled to give such credit by the credit they receive from the depositing of money in their shops ; and the bank of ENGLAND in the same manner, from the liberty it has to issue its notes in all payments. There was an invention of this kind, which was fallen upon some years ago by the banks of EDINBURGH ; and which, as it is one of the most ingenious ideas that has been executed in commerce, has also been thought advantageous to SCOTLAND. It is there called a BANK-CREDIT ; and is of this nature. A man goes to the bank and finds surety to the amount, we shall suppose, of a thousand pounds. This money, or any part of it, he has the liberty of drawing out whenever he pleases, and he pays only the ordinary interest for it, while it is in his hands. He may, when he pleases, repay any sum so small

* [*This and the following paragraph not in A–E*].

70

as twenty pounds, and the interest is discounted from the very day of the repayment. The advantages, resulting from this contrivance, are manifold. As a man may find surety nearly to the amount of his substance, and his bank-credit is equivalent to ready money, a merchant does hereby in a manner coin his houses, his household furniture, the goods in his warehouse, the foreign debts due to him, his ships at sea ; and can, upon occasion, employ them in all payments, as if they were the current money of the country. If a man borrow a thousand pounds from a private hand, besides that it is not always to be found when required, he pays interest for it, whether he be using it or not : His bank-credit costs him nothing except during the very moment in which it is of service to him : And this circumstance is of equal advantage as if he had borrowed money at much lower interest. Merchants, likewise from this invention, acquire a great facility in supporting each other's credit, which is a considerable security against bankruptcies. A man, when his own bank-credit is exhausted, goes to any of his neighbours who is not in the same condition ; and he gets the money, which he replaces at his convenience.

After this practice had taken place during some years at EDINBURGH, several companies of merchants at GLASGOW carried the matter farther. They associated themselves into different banks, and issued notes so low as ten shillings, which they used in all payments for goods, manufactures, tradesmen's labour of all kinds ; and these notes, from the established credit of the companies, passed as money in all payments throughout the country. By this means, a stock of five thousand pounds was able to perform the same operations as if it were six or seven ; and merchants were thereby enabled to trade to a greater extent, and to require less profit in all their transactions.[1] But whatever other advantages result from these inventions,

[1] [In "Of Public Credit" Hume links the fall in the rate of profit to economic development. Cf. below, pp. 93-4.—ED.]

it must still be allowed that, besides giving too great facility to credit, which is dangerous, they banish the precious metals : and nothing can be a more evident proof of it, than a comparison of the past and present condition of SCOTLAND in that particular. It was found, upon the recoinage made after the union, that there was near a million of specie in that country : But notwithstanding the great encrease of riches, commerce and manufactures of all kinds, it is thought, that, even where there is no extraordinary drain made by ENGLAND, the current specie will not now amount to a third of that sum.

*But as our projects of paper-credit are almost the only expedient, by which we can sink money below its level ; so, in my opinion, the only expedient, by which we can raise money above it, is a practice which we should all exclaim against as destructive, namely, the gathering of large sums into a public treasure, locking them up, and absolutely preventing their circulation. The fluid, not communicating with the neighbouring element, may, by such an artifice, be raised to what height we please. To prove this, we need only return to our first supposition, of annihilating the half or any part of our cash ; where we found, that the immediate consequence of such an event would be the attraction of an equal sum from all the neighbouring kingdoms. Nor does there seem to be any necessary bounds set, by the nature of things, to this practice of hoarding. A small city, like GENEVA, continuing this policy for ages, might engross nine tenths of the money of EUROPE. There seems, indeed, in the nature of man, an invincible obstacle to that immense growth of riches. A weak state, with an enormous treasure, will soon become a prey to some of its poorer, but more powerful neighbours. A great state would dissipate its wealth in dangerous and ill-concerted projects ; and probably destroy, with it, what is much more valuable, the industry,

* But . . . are=But as our darling projects of paper credit are pernicious, being [A-E].

morals, and numbers of its people. The fluid, in this
case, raised to too great a height, bursts and destroys the
vessel that contains it ; and mixing itself with the surrounding element, soon falls to its proper level.

So little are we commonly acquainted with this
principle, that, though all historians agree in relating
uniformly so recent an event, as the immense treasure
amassed by HARRY VII. (which they make amount to
*2,700,000 pounds,) we rather reject their concurring
testimony, than admit of a fact, which agrees so ill with
our inveterate prejudices. It is indeed probable, that this
sum might be three-fourths of all the money in ENGLAND.
But where is the difficulty in conceiving, that such a sum
might be amassed in twenty years, by a cunning, rapacious,
frugal, and almost absolute monarch ? Nor is it probable,
that the diminution of circulating money was ever sensibly
felt by the people, or ever did them any prejudice. The
sinking of the prices of all commodities would immediately replace it, by giving ENGLAND the advantage in its
commerce with the neighbouring kingdoms.

Have we not an instance in the small republic of
ATHENS with its allies, who, in about fifty years, between
the MEDIAN and PELOPONNESIAN wars, amassed a sum
†not much inferior to that of HARRY VII. ?‡ For all the
GREEK historians [1] and orators [2] agree, that the ATHENIANS
collected in the citadel more than 10,000 talents, which
they afterwards dissipated in their own ruin, in rash and
imprudent enterprises. But when this money was set a
running, and began to communicate with the surrounding
fluid ; what was the consequence ? Did it remain in the
state ? No. For we find, by the memorable *census* men-

---

[1] THUCYDIDES, lib. ii. 13 and DIOD. SIC. lib. xii. 40.
[2] *Vid.* AESCHINIS (p. 688) *et* DEMOSTHENIS *Epist.*

* 2,700,000 = 1,700,000 [A–G].
† not much inferior to = greater than [A–G].
‡ +There were about eight ounces of silver in a pound *Sterling* in
Harry the VII.'s time [A–G, *as footnote*].

tioned by DEMOSTHENES [1] and POLYBIUS,[2] that, in about fifty years afterwards, the whole value of the republic, comprehending lands, houses, commodities, slaves, and money, was less than 6,000 talents.

What an ambitious high-spirited people was this, to collect and keep in their treasury, with a view to conquests, a sum, which it was every day in the power of the citizens, by a single vote, to distribute among themselves, and which would have gone near to triple the riches of every individual ! For we must observe, that the numbers and private riches of the ATHENIANS are said, by ancient writers, to have been no greater at the beginning of the PELOPONNESIAN war, than at the beginning of the MACEDONIAN.

Money was little more plentiful in GREECE during the age of PHILIP and PERSEUS, than in ENGLAND during that of HARRY VII. : Yet these two monarchs in thirty years [3] collected from the small kingdom of MACEDON, a larger treasure than that of the ENGLISH monarch. PAULUS ÆMILIUS brought to ROME about 1,700,000 pounds *Sterling*.[4] PLINY says, 2,400,000.[5] And that was but a part of the MACEDONIAN treasure. The rest was dissipated by the resistance and flight of PERSEUS.[6]

We may learn from STANIAN, that the canton of BERNE had 300,000 pounds lent at interest, and had above six times as much in their treasury. Here then is a sum hoarded of 1,800,000 pounds *Sterling*, which is at least quadruple what should naturally circulate in such a petty state ; and yet no one, who travels in the PAIS DE VAUX, or any part of that canton, observes any want of money more than could be supposed in a country of that extent, soil, and situation. On the contrary, there are scarce any inland provinces in the continent of FRANCE or GERMANY, where the inhabitants are at this time so opulent, though

[1] Περὶ Συμμορίας, 183.
[2] Lib. ii. cap. 62.
[3] Titi Livii, lib. xlv. cap. 40.
[4] VEL. PATERC. lib. i. cap. 9.
[5] LIB. xxxiii. cap. 3.
[6] Titi Livii, *ibid*.

that canton has vastly encreased its treasure since 1714, the time when STANIAN wrote his judicious account of SWITZERLAND.[1]

The account given by APPIAN [2] of the treasure of the PTOLEMIES, is so prodigious, that one cannot admit of it ; and so much the less, because the historian says, that the other successors of ALEXANDER were also frugal, and had many of them treasures not much inferior. For this saving humour of the neighbouring princes must necessarily have checked the frugality of the EGYPTIAN monarchs, according to the foregoing theory. The sum he mentions is 740,000 talents, or 191,166,666 pounds 13 shillings and 4 pence, according to Dr. ARBUTHNOT's computation. And yet APPIAN says, that he extracted his account from the public records ; and he was himself a native of ALEXANDRIA.

From these principles we may learn what judgment we ought to form of those numberless bars, obstructions, and imposts, which all nations of Europe, and none more than ENGLAND, have put upon trade ; from an exorbitant desire of amassing money, which never will heap up beyond its level, while it circulates ; or from an ill-grounded apprehension of losing their specie, which never will sink below it. Could any thing scatter our riches, it would be such impolitic contrivances. But this general ill effect, however, results from them, that they deprive neighbouring nations of that free communication and exchange which the Author of the world has intended, by giving them soils, climates, and geniuses, so different from each other.

Our modern politics embrace the only method of banishing money, the using of paper-credit ; they reject the only method of amassing it, the practice of hoarding ; and they adopt a hundred contrivances, which serve to no purpose but to check industry, and rob ourselves

[1] The poverty which STANIAN speaks of is only to be seen in the most mountainous cantons, where there is no commodity to bring money. And even there the people are not poorer than in the diocese of SALTSBURGH on the one hand, or SAVOY on the other.

[2] *Proem.* 10.

and our neighbours of the common benefits of art and nature.

All taxes, however, upon foreign commodities, are not to be regarded as prejudicial or useless, but those only which are founded on the jealousy above-mentioned. A tax on German linen encourages home manufactures, and thereby multiplies our people and industry. A tax on brandy encreases the sale of rum, and supports our southern colonies.[1] And as it is necessary, that imposts should be levied, for the support of government, it may be thought more convenient to lay them on foreign commodities, which can easily be intercepted at the port, and subjected to the impost. We ought, however, always to remember the maxim of Dr. Swift, That, in the arithmetic of the customs, two and two make not four, but often make only one. It can scarcely be doubted, but if the duties on wine were lowered to a third, they would yield much more to the government than at present : Our people might thereby afford to drink commonly a better and more wholesome liquor ; and no prejudice would ensue to the balance of trade, of which we are so jealous. The manufacture of ale beyond the agriculture is but inconsiderable, and gives employment to few hands. The transport of wine and corn would not be much inferior.

But are there not frequent instances, you will say, of states and kingdoms, which were formerly rich and opulent, and are now poor and beggarly ? Has not the money left them, with which they formerly abounded ? I answer, If they lose their trade, industry, and people, they cannot expect to keep their gold and silver : For these precious metals will hold proportion to the former advantages. When Lisbon and Amsterdam got the East-India trade from Venice and Genoa, they also got the

---

[1] [Though it is the logical outgrowth of a phase of Hume's thinking (the law of growth and decay presented in the essay "Of Money", p. 34), this appears to be his only major concession to the case for tariff-protection. It is pointedly repudiated in the next essay.—Ed.]

profits and money which arose from it. Where the seat
of government is transferred, where expensive armies are
maintained at a distance, where great funds are possessed
by foreigners ; there naturally follows from these causes
a diminution of the specie. But these, we may observe,
are violent and forcible methods of carrying away money,
and are in time commonly attended with the transport of
people and industry. But where these remain, and the
drain is not continued, the money always finds its way
back again, by a hundred canals, of which we have no
notion or suspicion. What immense treasures have been
spent, by so many nations, in FLANDERS, since the revolution, in the course of three long wars ! More money
perhaps than the half of what is at present in EUROPE.
But what has now become of it ? Is it in the narrow
compass of the AUSTRIAN provinces ? No, surely : It has
most of it returned to the several countries whence it
came, and has followed that art and industry, by which
at first it was acquired. *For above a thousand years,
the money of EUROPE has been flowing to ROME, by an
open and sensible current ; but it has been emptied by
many secret and insensible canals : And the want of
industry and commerce renders at present the papal
dominions the poorest territory in all ITALY.

In short, a government has great reason to preserve
with care its people and its manufactures. Its money, it
may safely trust to the course of human affairs, without
fear or jealousy. Or if it ever give attention to this latter
circumstance, it ought only to be so far as it affects the
former.[1]

[1] [For comment on this passage see above, pp. lxv–lxvi.—ED.]

* [*This sentence not in A–B*]

*Of the Jealousy of Trade

HAVING endeavoured to remove one species of ill-founded jealousy, which is so prevalent among commercial nations, it may not be amiss to mention another, which seems equally groundless. Nothing is more usual, among states which have made some advances in commerce, than to look on the progress of their neighbours with a suspicious eye, to consider all trading states as their rivals, and to suppose that it is impossible for any of them to flourish, but at their expence. In opposition to this narrow and malignant opinion, I will venture to assert, that the encrease of riches and commerce in any one nation, instead of hurting, commonly promotes the riches and commerce of all its neighbours ; and that a state can scarcely carry its trade and industry very far, where all the surrounding states are buried in ignorance, sloth, and barbarism.

It is obvious, that the domestic industry of a people cannot be hurt by the greatest prosperity of their neighbours ; and as this branch of commerce is undoubtedly the most important in any extensive kingdom, we are so far removed from all reason of jealousy. But I go farther, and observe, that where an open communication is preserved among nations, it is impossible but the domestic industry of every one must receive an encrease from the improvements of the others. Compare the situation of GREAT BRITAIN at present, with what it was two centuries ago. All the arts both of agriculture and manufactures were then extremely rude and imperfect. Every improvement, which we have since made, has arisen from our imitation of foreigners ; and we ought so far to esteem it happy, that they had previously made advances in arts and ingenuity. But this intercourse is still upheld to our great advantage : Notwithstanding the advanced state of

* [*This essay first appeared in D (1758)*].
78

our manufactures, we daily adopt, in every art, the inventions and improvements of our neighbours. The commodity is first imported from abroad, to our great discontent, while we imagine that it drains us of our money : Afterwards, the art itself is gradually imported, to our visible advantage : Yet we continue still to repine, that our neighbours should possess any art, industry, and invention ; forgetting that, had they not first instructed us, we should have been at present barbarians ; and did they not still continue their instructions, the arts must fall into a state of languor, and lose that emulation and novelty, which contribute so much to their advancement.

The encrease of domestic industry lays the foundation of foreign commerce. Where a great number of commodities are raised and perfected for the home market, there will always be found some which can be exported with advantage. But if our neighbours have no art or cultivation, they cannot take them ; because they will have nothing to give in exchange. In this respect, states are in the same condition as individuals. A single man can scarcely be industrious, where all his fellow-citizens are idle. The riches of the several members of a community contribute to encrease my riches, whatever profession I may follow. They consume the produce of my industry, and afford me the produce of theirs in return.

Nor needs any state entertain apprehensions, that their neighbours will improve to such a degree in every art and manufacture, as to have no demand from them. Nature, by giving a diversity of geniuses, climates, and soils, to different nations, has secured their mutual intercourse and commerce, as long as they all remain industrious and civilized.[1] Nay, the more the arts encrease in any state, the more will be its demands from its industrious neighbours. The inhabitants, having become opulent and skilful, desire to have every commodity in the utmost

[1] [For the relation of this and the point of the preceding paragraph to Hume's discussion with Josiah Tucker see below, p. 204*n*.—ED.]

perfection ; and as they have plenty of commodities to give in exchange, they make large importations from every foreign country. The industry of the nations, from whom they import, receives encouragement : Their own is also encreased, by the sale of the commodities which they give in exchange.

But what if a nation has any staple commodity, such as the woollen manufacture is in ENGLAND ? Must not the interfering of our neighbours in that manufacture be a loss to us ? I answer, that, when any commodity is denominated the staple of a kingdom, it is supposed that this kingdom has some peculiar and natural advantages for raising the commodity ; and if, notwithstanding these advantages, they lose such a manufacture, they ought to blame their own idleness, or bad government, not the industry of their neighbours. It ought also to be considered, that, by the encrease of industry among the neighbouring nations, the consumption of every particular species of commodity is also encreased ; and though foreign manufactures interfere with them in the market, the demand for their product may still continue, or even encrease. And should it diminish, ought the consequence to be esteemed so fatal ? If the spirit of industry be preserved, it may easily be diverted from one branch to another ; and the manufacturers of wool, for instance, be employed in linen, silk, iron, or any other commodities, for which there appears to be a demand.[1] We need not apprehend, that all the objects of industry will be exhausted, or that our manufacturers, while they remain on an equal footing with those of our neighbours, will be in danger of wanting employment. The emulation among rival nations serves rather to keep industry alive in all of them : And any people is happier who possess a variety

[1] [In the context the resource-diversion referred to seems to contemplate some production for export. Elsewhere (cf. above, p. 14), Hume argues that in a fully developed economy home demand alone would suffice to maintain employment. Cf. also above, p. cviii *n*, on Adam Smith's treatment of this issue.—ED.]

of manufactures, than if they enjoyed one single great manufacture, in which they are all employed. Their situation is less precarious ; and they will feel less sensibly those revolutions and uncertainties, to which every particular branch of commerce will always be exposed.

The only commercial state, that ought to dread the improvements and industry of their neighbours, is such a one as the DUTCH, who enjoying no extent of land, nor possessing any number of native commodities, flourish only by their being the brokers, and factors, and carriers of others. Such a people may naturally apprehend, that, as soon as the neighbouring states come to know and pursue their interest, they will take into their own hands the management of their affairs, and deprive their brokers of that profit, which they formerly reaped from it. But though this consequence may naturally be dreaded, it is very long before it takes place ; and by art and industry it may be warded off for many generations, if not wholly eluded. The advantage of superior stocks and correspondence is so great, that it is not easily overcome ; and as all the transactions encrease by the encrease of industry in the neighbouring states, even a people whose commerce stands on this precarious basis, may at first reap a considerable profit from the flourishing condition of their neighbours. The DUTCH, having mortgaged all their revenues, make not such a figure in political transactions as formerly ; but their commerce is surely equal to what it was in the middle of the last century, when they were reckoned among the great powers of EUROPE.

Were our narrow and malignant politics to meet with success, we should reduce all our neighbouring nations to the same state of sloth and ignorance that prevails in MOROCCO and the coast of BARBARY. But what would be the consequence ? They could send us no commodities : They could take none from us : Our domestic commerce itself would languish for want of emulation, example and instruction : And we ourselves should soon fall into the same abject condition, to which we had reduced them. I shall therefore venture to acknowledge, that, not only as a man, but as a BRITISH subject, I pray for the flourishing commerce of GERMANY, SPAIN, ITALY, and even FRANCE itself. I am at least certain, that GREAT BRITAIN, and all those nations, would flourish more, did their sovereigns and ministers adopt such enlarged and benevolent sentiments towards each other.

Of Taxes

THERE is a prevailing maxim, among *some reasoners, *that every new tax creates a new ability in the subject to bear it, and that each encrease of public burdens encreases proportionably the industry of the people.* This maxim is of such a nature as is most likely to be †abused ; and is so much the more dangerous, as its truth cannot be altogether denied : but it must be owned, when kept within certain bounds, to have some foundation in reason and experience.

When a tax is laid upon commodities, which are consumed by the common people, the necessary consequence may seem to be, either that the poor must retrench something from their way of living, or raise their wages, so as to make the burden of the tax fall entirely upon the rich. But there is a third consequence, which often follows upon taxes, namely, that the poor encrease their industry, perform more work, and live as well as before, without demanding more for their labour.[1] Where taxes are moderate, are laid on gradually, and affect not the necessaries of life, this consequence naturally follows ; and it is certain, that such difficulties often serve to excite the industry of a people, and render them more opulent and laborious, than others, who enjoy the greatest advantages. For we may observe, as a parallel instance, that the most commercial nations have not always possessed the greatest extent of fertile land ; but, on the contrary, that they have laboured under many natural disadvantages. TYRE, ATHENS, CARTHAGE, RHODES, GENOA, VENICE, HOLLAND,

[1] [Each of these effects had already been noted in the literature. Because Hume regards all as potential consequences of an excise, his tax theory has been classified as "eclectic". Cf. E. R. A. Seligman, *The Shifting and Incidence of Taxation* (New York 1921), pp. 116–17.—ED.]

* Some reasoners = those whom in this country we call *ways and means men*, and who are denominated *Financiers* and *Maltotiers* in France [A–G].
† abused = extremely abused [A–D].

are strong examples to this purpose. And in all history, we find only three instances of large and fertile countries, which have possessed much trade ; the NETHERLANDS, ENGLAND, and FRANCE. The two former seem to have been allured by the advantages of their maritime situation, and the necessity they lay under of frequenting foreign ports, in order to procure what their own climate refused them. And as to FRANCE, trade has come late into that kingdom, and seems to have been the effect of reflection and observation in an ingenious and enterprizing people, who remarked the riches acquired by such of the neighbouring nations as cultivated navigation and commerce.

The places mentioned by CICERO,[1] as possessed of the greatest commerce in his time, are ALEXANDRIA, COLCHUS, TYRE, SIDON, ANDROS, CYPRUS, PAMPHYLIA, LYCIA, RHODES, CHIOS, BYZANTIUM, LESBOS, SMYRNA, MILETUM, Coos. All these, except ALEXANDRIA, were either small islands, or narrow territories. And that city owed its trade entirely to the happiness of its situation.

Since therefore some natural necessities or disadvantages may be thought favourable to industry, why may not artificial burdens have the same effect ? Sir WILLIAM TEMPLE,[2] we may observe, ascribes the industry of the DUTCH entirely to necessity, proceeding from their natural disadvantages ; and illustrates his doctrine by a striking comparison with IRELAND ; "where", says he, "by the largeness and plenty of the soil, and scarcity of people, all things necessary to life are so cheap, that an industrious man, by two days labour, may gain enough to feed him the rest of the week. Which I take to be a very plain ground of the laziness attributed to the people. For men naturally prefer ease before labour, and will not take pains if they can live idle ; though when, by necessity, they have been inured to it, they cannot leave it, being grown a custom necessary to their health, and to their

[1] Epist. ad ATT. lib. ix. ep. ii.
[2] Account of the NETHERLANDS, chap. 6.

84

very entertainment. Nor perhaps is the change harder, from constant ease to labour, than from constant labour to ease". After which the author proceeds to confirm his doctrine, by enumerating, as above, the places where trade has most flourished, in ancient and modern times ; and which are commonly observed to be such narrow confined territories, as beget a necessity for industry.*

The best taxes are †such as are levied upon consumptions, especially those of luxury ; because such taxes are ‡least felt by the people. They §seem, in some measure, voluntary ; since a man may chuse how far he will use the commodity which is taxed : ‖They are paid gradually, and insensibly : They naturally produce sobriety and frugality, if judiciously imposed : And being confounded with the natural price of the commodity, they are scarcely perceived by the consumers. Their only disadvantage is, that they are expensive in the levying.

Taxes upon possessions are levied without expence ; but have every other disadvantage. Most states, however, are obliged to have recourse to them, in order to supply the deficiencies of the other.

---

* †'Tis always observed, in years of scarcity, if it be not extreme, that the poor labour more, and really live better, than in years of great plenty, when they indulge themselves in idleness and riot. I have been told, by a considerable manufacturer, that in the year 1740, when bread and provisions of all kinds were very dear, his workmen not only made a shift to live, but paid debts, which they had contracted in former years, that were much more favourable and abundant.[1]

This doctrine, therefore, with regard to taxes, may be admitted in some degree : But beware of the abuse. Exorbitant taxes, like extreme necessity, destroy industry, by producing despair ; and even before they reach this pitch, they raise the wages of the labourer and manufacturer, and heighten the price of all commodities. An attentive disinterested legislature, will observe the point when the emolument ceases, and the prejudice begins : But as the contrary character is much more common, 'tis to be feared that taxes, all over *Europe*, are multiplying to such a degree, as will intirely crush all art and industry ; tho', perhaps, their first increase, together with other circumstances, might have contributed to the growth of these advantages. [*A–G*].

† such as = those which [*A–B*].   ‡ least = less [*A–B*].
§ seem = seem to be [*A–B*].   ‖ [*This clause not in A–G*].

[1] To this purpose see also Essay I [:"Of Commerce"] at the end.

But the most pernicious of all taxes are *the arbitrary. They are commonly converted, by their management, into punishments on industry ; and also, by their unavoidable inequality, are more grievous, than by the real burden which they impose. It is surprising, therefore, to see them have place among any civilized people.

In general, all poll-taxes, even when not arbitrary, which they commonly are, may be esteemed dangerous : Because it is so easy for the sovereign to add a little more, and a little more, to the sum demanded, that these taxes are apt to become altogether oppressive and intolerable. On the other hand, a duty upon commodities checks itself; and a prince will soon find, that an encrease of the impost is no encrease of his revenue. It is not easy, therefore, for a people to be altogether ruined by such taxes.

Historians inform us, that one of the chief causes of the destruction of the ROMAN state, was the alteration, which CONSTANTINE introduced into the finances, by substituting an universal poll-tax, in lieu of almost all the tithes, customs, and excises, which formerly composed the revenue of the *empire*. The people, in all the provinces, were so grinded and oppressed by the *publicans*, that they were glad to take refuge under the conquering arms of the barbarians ; whose dominion, as they had fewer necessities and less art, was found preferable to the refined tyranny of the ROMANS.

¹ †It is an opinion, zealously promoted by some politi-

---

¹ [The arguments presented here, are repeated and somewhat elaborated in a discussion which Hume had with Turgot on the physiocratic position on taxes. See below, pp. 208–9.—ED.]

* the = those which are [*A–B*].

† It is an opinion . . . yields in foreign markets = There is a prevailing opinion, that all taxes, however levied, fall upon the land at last. Such an opinion may be useful in *Britain*, by checking the landed gentlemen, in whose hands our legislature is chiefly lodged, and making them preserve great regard for trade and industry. But I must confess, that this principle, tho' first advanced by a celebrated writer, has so little appearance of reason, that, were it not for his authority, it had never been received by anybody [*A–G*].

cal writers, that, since all taxes, as they pretend, fall ultimately upon land, it were better to lay them originally there, and abolish every duty upon consumptions. But it is denied, that all taxes fall ultimately upon land. If a duty be laid upon any commodity, consumed by an artisan, he has two obvious expedients for paying it ; he may retrench somewhat of his expence, or he may encrease his labour. Both these resources are more easy and natural, than that of heightening his wages. We see, that, in years of scarcity, the weaver either consumes less or labours more, or employs both these expedients of frugality and industry, by which he is enabled to reach the end of the year. It is but just, that he should subject himself to the same hardships, if they deserve the name, for the sake of the publick, which gives him protection. By what contrivance can he raise the price of his labour ? The manufacturer who employs him, will not give him more : Neither can he, because the merchant, who exports the cloth, cannot raise its price, being limited by the price which it yields in foreign markets. Every man, to be sure, is desirous of pushing off from himself the burden of any tax, which is imposed, and of laying it upon others : But as every man has the same inclination, and is upon the defensive ; no set of men can be supposed to prevail altogether in this contest.[1] And why the landed gentle-

---

[1] [It will be noted that Hume fails to see the necessity of reconciling his doctrine here (which would now be classified as a diffusion theory of incidence) with his preceding contention that the necessity of meeting the world price prevents the entrepreneur from allowing labour to shift the excise through a wage-increase. The former assumes that profits contain a surplus ; the latter assumes they do not. The two would be compatible if this latter were assumed to apply only to a single or relatively minor sector of the economy. That is, from this viewpoint a given rate of profit may be wholly "necessary", but in terms of the supply price of entrepreneurship to the economy as a whole (which is what is involved in the former case) may contain a surplus. It will also be noted that the argument that the world price prohibits any shifting implicitly supposes that within the effective range of output foreign supply or foreign demand and domestic supply are perfectly elastic at the prevailing price. Tacit suppositions of this character were common during the period.—ED.]

man should be the victim of the whole, and should not be able to defend himself, as well as others are, I cannot readily imagine. All tradesmen, indeed, would willingly prey upon him, and divide him among them, if they could : But this inclination they always have, though no taxes were levied ; and the same methods, by which he guards against the imposition of tradesmen before taxes, will serve him afterwards, and make them share the burden with him. *They must be very heavy taxes, indeed, and very injudiciously levied, which the artizan will not, of himself, be enabled to pay, by superior industry and frugality, without raising the price of his labour.

I shall conclude this subject with observing, that we have, with regard to taxes, an instance of what frequently happens in political institutions, that the consequences of things are diametrically opposite to what we should expect on the first appearance. It is regarded as a fundamental maxim of the TURKISH government, that the *Grand Signior*, though absolute master of the lives and fortunes of each individual, has no authority to impose a new tax ; and every OTTOMAN prince, who has made such an attempt, either has been obliged to retract, or has found the fatal effects of his perseverance. One would imagine, that this prejudice or established opinion were the firmest barrier in the world against oppression ; yet it is certain, that its effect is quite contrary. The emperor, having no regular method of encreasing his revenue, must allow all the bashaws and governors to oppress and abuse the subjects : And these he squeezes after their return from their government. Whereas, if he could impose a new tax, like our

* They must . . . his labour [*not in A-F*] ;=No labour in any commodities, that are exported, can be very considerably raised in the price, without losing the foreign market ; and as some part of almost every manufactory is exported, this circumstance keeps the price of most species of labour nearly the same after the imposition of taxes. I may add, that it has this effect upon the whole : For were any kind of labour paid beyond its proportion, all hands would flock to it, and would soon sink it to a level with the rest [G].

EUROPEAN princes, his interest would so far be united with that of his people, that he would immediately feel the bad effects of these disorderly levies of money, and would find, that a pound, raised by a general imposition, would have less pernicious effects, than a shilling taken in so unequal and arbitrary a manner.

Of Public Credit

It appears to have been the common practice of antiquity, to make provision, during peace, for the necessities of war, and to hoard up treasures before-hand, as the instruments either of conquest or defence ; without trusting to extraordinary impositions, much less to borrowing, in times of disorder and confusion. Besides the immense sums above mentioned,[1] which were amassed by Athens, and by the Ptolemies, and other successors of Alexander ; we learn from Plato,[2] that the frugal Lacedemonians had also collected a great treasure ; and Arrian[3] and Plutarch[4] take notice of the riches which Alexander got possession of on the conquest of Susa and Ecbatana, and which were reserved, some of them, from the time of Cyrus. If I remember right, the scripture also mentions the treasure of Hezekiah and the Jewish princes ; as profane history does that of Philip and Perseus, kings of Macedon. The ancient republics of Gaul had commonly large sums in reserve.[5] Every one knows the treasure seized in Rome by Julius Cæsar, during the civil wars : and we find afterwards, that the wiser emperors, Augustus, Tiberius, Vespasian, Severus, &c. always discovered the prudent foresight, of saving great sums against any public exigency.

On the contrary, our modern expedient, which has become very general, is to mortgage the public revenues, and to trust that posterity will pay off the incumbrances contracted by their ancestors[6] : And they, having before

[1] Essay V ["Of the Balance of Trade"].
[2] Alcib. i. p. 123.   [3] Lib. iii. 16 and 19.
[4] Plut. *in vita* Alex. 36, 37. He makes these treasures amount to 80,000 talents, or about 15 millions sterl. Quintus Curtius (lib. v. cap. 2.) says, that Alexander found in Susa above 50,000 talents.
[5] Strabo, lib. iv. p. 188.
[6] [Cf. above, pp. lxxxv-lxxxvi for comment on the background of the essay.—Ed.]

their eyes, so good an example of their wise fathers, have the same prudent reliance on *their* posterity ; who, at last, from necessity more than choice, are obliged to place the same confidence in a new posterity. But not to waste time in declaiming against a practice which appears ruinous, beyond all controversy ; it seems pretty apparent, that the ancient maxims are, in this respect, more prudent than the modern ; even though the latter had been confined within some reasonable bounds, and had ever, in any instance, been attended with such frugality, in time of peace, as to discharge the debts incurred by an expensive war. For why should the case be so different between the public and an individual, as to make us establish different maxims of conduct for each ? If the funds of the former be greater, its necessary expences are proportionably larger ; if its resources be more numerous, they are not infinite ; and as its frame should be calculated for a much longer duration than the date of a single life, or even of a family, it should embrace maxims, large, durable, and generous, agreeably to the supposed extent of its existence. To trust to chances and temporary expedients, is, indeed, what the necessity of human affairs frequently renders unavoidable : but whoever voluntarily depend on such resources, have not necessity, but their own folly, to accuse for their misfortunes, when any such befal them.

If the abuses of treasures be dangerous, either by engaging the state in rash enterprizes, or making it neglect military discipline, in confidence of its riches ; the abuses of mortgaging are more certain and inevitable ; poverty, impotence, and subjection to foreign powers.

According to modern policy war is attended with every destructive circumstance ; loss of men, encrease of taxes, decay of commerce, dissipation of money, devastation by sea and land. According to ancient maxims, the opening of the public treasure, as it produced an uncommon affluence of gold and silver, served as a temporary encouragement to industry, and atoned, in some degree, for the inevitable calamities of war.

*It is very tempting to a minister to employ such an expedient, as enables him to make a great figure during his administration, without overburthening the people with taxes, or exciting any immediate clamours against himself. The practice, therefore, of contracting debt will almost infallibly be abused, in every government. It would scarcely be more imprudent to give a prodigal son a credit in every banker's shop in London, than to impower a statesman to draw bills, in this manner, upon posterity.

What then shall we say to the new paradox, that public incumbrances are, of themselves, advantageous, independent of the necessity of contracting them ; and that any state, even though it were not pressed by a foreign enemy, could not possibly have embraced a wiser expedient for promoting commerce and riches, than to create funds, and debts, and taxes, without limitation ? Reasonings, such as these, might naturally have passed for trials of wit among rhetoricians, like the panegyrics on folly and a fever, on BUSIRIS and NERO, had we not seen such absurd maxims patronized by great ministers, and by a whole party among us.†

Let us examine the consequences of public debts, both in our domestic management, by their influence on commerce and industry ; and in our foreign transactions, by their effect on wars and negociations.‡

---

* [*This paragraph not in A–G*].

† +And these puzzling arguments (for they deserve not the name of specious) tho' they could not be the foundation of *Lord Oxford's* conduct, for he had more sense ; served at least to keep his partizans in countenance, and perplex the understanding of the nation [*A–G*].

‡ +There is a word, which is here in the mouth of every body, and which, I find, has also got abroad, and is much employed by foreign writers,[1] in imitation of the *English* ; and that is CIRCULATION. This word serves as an account of every thing ; and tho' I confess, that I have sought for its meaning in the present subject, ever since I was a school-boy, I have never yet been able to discover it. What possible advantage is there which the

Of Public Credit

Public securities are with us become a kind of money, and pass as readily at the current price as gold or silver. Wherever any profitable undertaking offers itself, how expensive soever, there are never wanting hands enow to embrace it ; nor need a trader, who has sums in the public stocks, fear to launch out into the most extensive trade ; since he is possessed of funds, which will answer the most sudden demand that can be made upon him. No merchant thinks it necessary to keep by him any considerable cash. Bank-stock, or India-bonds, especially the latter, serve all the same purposes ; because he can dispose of them, or pledge them to a banker, in a quarter of an hour ; and at the same time they are not idle, even when in his scritoire, but brings him in a constant revenue. In short, our national debts furnish merchants with a species of money, that is continually multiplying in their hands, and produces sure gain, besides the profits of their commerce. This must enable them to trade upon less profit. The small profit of the merchant renders the commodity cheaper, causes a greater consumption, quickens

---

nation can reap by the easy transference of stock from hand to hand ? Or is there any parallel to be drawn from the circulation of other commodities, to that of chequer-notes and *India* bonds ? Where a manufacturer has a quick sale of his goods to the merchant, the merchant to the shopkeeper, the shopkeeper to his customers ; this enlivens industry, and gives new encouragement to the first dealer or the manufacturer and all his tradesmen, and makes them produce more and better commodities of the same species. A stagnation is here pernicious, wherever it happens ; because it operates backwards, and stops or benumbs the industrious hand in its production of what is useful to human life. But what production we owe to *Change-alley,* or even what consumption, except that of coffee, and pen, ink, and paper, I have not yet learned ; nor can one forsee the loss or decay of any one beneficial commerce or commodity, though that place and all its inhabitants were for ever buried in the ocean.

But though this term has never been explained by those who insist so much on the advantages that result from a circulation, there seems, however, to be some benefit of a similar kind, arising from our incumbrances : As indeed, what human evil is there, which is not attended with some advantage ? This we shall endeavour to explain, that we may estimate the weight which we ought to allow it [A–G].

[1] *Melon, Du Tot, Law,* in the pamphlets published in *France.*

the labour of the common people, and helps to spread arts and industry throughout the whole society.[1]

There are also, we may observe, in ENGLAND and in all states, which have both commerce and public debts, a set of men, who are half merchants, half stock-holders, and may be supposed willing to trade for small profits ; because commerce is not their principal or sole support, and their revenues in the funds are a sure resource for themselves and their families. Were there no funds, great merchants would have no expedient for realizing or securing any part of their profit, but by making purchases of lands ; and land has many disadvantages in comparison of funds. Requiring more care and inspection, it divides the time and attention of the merchant ; upon any tempting offer or extraordinary accident in trade, it is not so easily converted into money ; and as it attracts too much, both by the many natural pleasures it affords, and the authority it gives, it soon converts the citizen into the country gentleman. More men, therefore, with large stocks and incomes, may naturally be supposed to continue in trade, where there are public debts ; and this, it must be owned, is of some advantage to commerce, by diminishing its profits, promoting circulation, and encouraging industry.*

But, in opposition to these two favourable circumstances, perhaps of no very great importance, weigh the many disadvantages which attend our public debts, in the whole *interior* œconomy of the state : You will find no comparison between the ill and the good which result from them.

---

[1] [For the relation of this and other points to the views of others see above, pp. lxxxiv *n*, lxxxv *n*.—ED.]

* +On this head, I shall observe, without interrupting the thread of the argument, that the multiplicity of our public debts serves rather to sink the interest, and that the more the government borrows, the cheaper may they expect to borrow ; contrary to first appearance, and contrary to common opinion. The profits of trade have an influence on interest. See Essay IV ["Of Interest"]. [*A–F, as foo'note*].

94

First, It is certain, that national debts cause a mighty confluence of people and riches to the capital, by the great sums, levied in the provinces to pay the interest ; and perhaps, too, by the advantages in trade above mentioned, which they give the merchants in the capital above the rest of the kingdom. The question is, whether, in our case, it be for the public interest, that so many privileges should be conferred on LONDON, which has already arrived at such an enormous size, and seems still encreasing ? Some men are apprehensive of the consequences. For my own part, I cannot forbear thinking, that, though the head is undoubtedly too large for the body, yet that great city is so happily situated, that its excessive bulk causes less inconvenience than even a smaller capital to a greater kingdom. There is more difference between the prices of all provisions in PARIS and LANGUEDOC, than between those in LONDON and YORKSHIRE. *The immense greatness, indeed, of LONDON, under a government which admits not of discretionary power, renders the people factious, mutinous, seditious, and even perhaps rebellious. But to this evil the national debts themselves tend to provide a remedy. The first visible eruption, or even immediate danger, of public disorders must alarm all the stockholders, whose property is the most precarious of any ; and will make them fly to the support of government, whether menaced by Jacobitish violence or democratical frenzy.

Secondly, Public stocks, being a kind of paper-credit, have all the disadvantages attending that species of money. They banish gold and silver from the most considerable commerce of the state, reduce them to common circulation, and by that means render all provisions and labour dearer than otherwise they would be.†

* [*The rest of this paragraph not in A–G*].

† +We may also remark, that this increase of prices, derived from paper credit, has a more durable and a more dangerous influence than when it arises from a great increase of gold and silver : where an accidental overflow of money raises the price of labor and commodities, the evil

Thirdly, The taxes, which are levied to pay the interests of these debts, *are apt either to heighten the price of labour, or be an oppression on the poorer sort.

Fourthly, As foreigners possess a great share of our national funds, they render the public, in a manner, tributary to them, and may in time occasion the transport of our people and our industry.

Fifthly, The greater part of the public stock being always in the hands of idle people, who live on their revenue, our funds, in that view, give great encouragement to an useless and unactive life.

But though the injury, that arises to commerce and industry from our public funds, will appear, upon balancing the whole, not inconsiderable, it is trivial, in comparison of the prejudice that results to the state considered as a body politic, which must support itself in the society of nations, and have various transactions with other states in wars and negociations. The ill, there, is pure and unmixed, without any favourable circumstance to atone for it ; and it is an ill too of a nature the highest and most important.

We have, indeed, been told, that the public is no weaker upon account of its debts ; since they are mostly due among ourselves, and bring as much property to one as they take from another. It is like transferring money from the right hand to the left ; which leaves the person neither richer nor poorer than before.[1] Such loose reasonings and specious comparisons will always pass, where we judge not upon principles. I ask, Is it possible, in the nature of things, to overburthen a nation with taxes, even

[1] [This view had been stated by Jean François Melon in his *Essai Politique sur le Commerce* (1736), chap. xxiii, esp. p. 296.—ED.]

* are apt . . . poorer sort = are a check upon industry, heighten the price of labour, and are an oppression on the poorer sort [*A–E*].

remedies itself in a little time : The money soon flows out into all the neighbouring nations : The prices fall to a level : And industry may be continued as before ; a relief, which cannot be expected, where the circulating specie consists chiefly of paper, and has no intrinsic value [*G only*].

where the sovereign resides among them? The very doubt seems extravagant ; since it is requisite, in every community, that there be a certain proportion observed between the laborious and the idle part of it. But if all our present taxes be mortgaged, must we not invent new ones? And may not this matter be carried to a length that is ruinous and destructive?

In every nation, there are always some methods of levying money more easy than others, agreeably to the way of living of the people, and the commodities they make use of. In GREAT BRITAIN, the excise upon malt and beer afford a large revenue ; because the operations of malting and brewing are tedious, and are impossible to be concealed ; and at the same time, these commodities are not so absolutely necessary to life, as that the raising of their price would very much affect the poorer sort. These taxes being all mortgaged, what difficulty to find new ones! what vexation and ruin of the poor!

Duties upon consumption are more equal and easy than those upon possessions. What a loss to the public, that the former are all exhausted, and that we must have recourse to the more grevious method of levying taxes!

Were all the proprietors of land only stewards to the public, must not necessity force them to practise all the arts of oppression used by stewards ; where the absence or negligence of the proprietor render them secure against enquiry?

It will scarcely be asserted, that no bounds ought ever to be set to national debts ; and that the public would be no weaker, were twelve or fifteen shillings in the pound, land-tax, mortgaged, with all the present customs and excises. There is something, therefore, in the case, beside the mere transferring of property from the one hand to another. In 500 years, the posterity of those now in the coaches, and of those upon the boxes, will probably have changed places, without affecting the public by these revolutions.

*Suppose the public once fairly brought to that condition, to which it is hastening with such amazing rapidity ; suppose the land to be taxed eighteen or nineteen shillings in the pound ; for it can never bear the whole twenty ; suppose all the excises and customs to be screwed up to the utmost which the nation can bear, without entirely losing its commerce and industry ; and suppose that all those funds are mortgaged to perpetuity, and that the invention and wit of all our projectors can find no new imposition, which may serve as the foundation of a new loan ; and let us consider the necessary consequences of this situation. Though the imperfect state of our political knowledge, and the narrow capacities of men, make it difficult to foretel the effects which will result from any untried measure, the seeds of ruin are here scattered with such profusion as not to escape the eye of the most careless observer.

In this unnatural state of society, the only persons, who possess any revenue beyond the immediate effects of their industry, are the stock-holders, who draw almost all the rent of the land and houses, besides the produce of all the customs and excises. These are men, who have no connexions with the state, who can enjoy their revenue in any part of the globe in which they chuse to reside, who will naturally bury themselves in the capital or in great cities, and who will sink into the lethargy of a stupid and pampered luxury, without spirit, ambition, or enjoyment. Adieu to all ideas of nobility, gentry, and family. The stocks can be transferred in an instant, and being in such a fluctuating state, will seldom be transmitted during three generations from father to son. Or were they to remain ever so long in one family, they convey no hereditary authority or credit to the possessor ; and by this means, the several ranks of men, which form a kind of independent magistracy in a state, instituted by the hand of nature, are entirely lost ; and every man in authority derives his

* [*This and the following five paragraphs not in A–E*].

influence from the commission alone of the sovereign. No expedient remains for preventing or suppressing insurrections, but mercenary armies : No expedient at all remains for resisting tyranny : Elections are swayed by bribery and corruption alone : And the middle power between king and people being totally removed, a grievous despotism must infallibly prevail.[1] The landholders, despised for their poverty, and hated for their oppressions, will be utterly unable to make any opposition to it.

Though a resolution should be formed by the legislature never to impose any tax which hurts commerce and discourages industry, it will be impossible for men, in subjects of such extreme delicacy, to reason so justly as never to be mistaken, or amidst difficulties so urgent, never to be seduced from their resolution. The continual fluctuations in commerce require continual alterations in the nature of the taxes ; which exposes the legislature every moment to the danger both of wilful and involuntary error. And any great blow given to trade, whether by injudicious taxes or by other accidents, throws the whole system of government into confusion.

But what expedient can the public now employ, even supposing trade to continue in the most flourishing condition, in order to support its foreign wars and enterprizes, and to defend its own honour and interests, or those of its allies ? I do not ask how the public is to exert such a prodigious power as it has maintained during our late wars ; where we have so much exceeded, not only our own natural strength, but even that of the greatest empires. This extravagance is the abuse complained of, as the source of all the dangers, to which we are at present exposed. But since we must still suppose great commerce and opulence to remain, even after every fund is mortgaged ;

[1] [Elsewhere Hume calls attention to the central importance for liberty and parliamentary government of a prosperous middle class, in particular the merchant class. Cf. above, pp. 28–9. It is not clear there, as it is here, that he believed that, like the landowners, such a class should have "hereditary authority".—ED.]

99

these riches must be defended by proportional power ; and whence is the public to derive the revenue which supports it ? It must plainly be from a continual taxation of their annuitants, or, which is the same thing, from mortgaging anew, on every exigency, a certain part of their annuities ; and thus making them contribute to their own defence, and to that of the nation. But the difficulties, attending this system of policy, will easily appear, whether we suppose the king to have become absolute master, or to be still controuled by national councils, in which the annuitants themselves must necessarily bear the principal sway.

If the prince has become absolute, as may naturally be expected from this situation of affairs, it is so easy for him to encrease his exactions upon the annuitants, which amount only to the retaining money in his own hands, that this species of property would soon lose all its credit, and the whole income of every individual in the state must lie entirely at the mercy of the sovereign : A degree of despotism, which no oriental monarchy has ever yet attained. If, on the contrary, the consent of the annuitants be requisite for every taxation, they will never be persuaded to contribute sufficiently even to the support of government ; as the diminution of their revenue must in that case be very sensible, would not be disguised under the appearance of a branch of excise or customs, and would not be shared by any other order of the state, who are already supposed to be taxed to the utmost. There are instances, in some republics, of a hundredth penny, and sometimes of the fiftieth, being given to the support of the state ; but this is always an extraordinary exertion of power, and can never become the foundation of a constant national defence. We have always found, where a government has mortgaged all its revenues, that it necessarily sinks into a state of languor, inactivity, and impotence.

Such are the inconveniencies, which may reasonably

be foreseen, of this situation, to which GREAT BRITAIN is visibly tending. Not to mention, the numberless inconveniencies, which cannot be foreseen, and which must result from so monstrous a situation as that of making the public the chief or sole proprietor of land, besides investing it with every branch of customs and excise, which the fertile imagination of ministers and projectors have been able to invent.

I must confess, that there is a strange supineness, from long custom, creeped into all ranks of men, with regard to public debts, not unlike what divines so vehemently complain of with regard to their religious doctrines. We all own, that the most sanguine imagination cannot hope, either that this or any future ministry will be possessed of such rigid and steady frugality, as to make a considerable progress in the payment of our debts ; or that the situation of foreign affairs will, for any long time, allow them leisure and tranquillity for such an undertaking.* *What then is to become of us ?* Were we ever so good Christians, and ever so resigned to Providence ; this, methinks, were a curious question, even considered as a speculative one, and what it might not be altogether impossible to form some conjectural solution of. The events here will depend little upon the contingencies of battles, negociations, intrigues, and factions. There seems to be a natural progress of things, which may guide our reasoning. As it would have required but a moderate share of prudence, when we first began this practice of mortgaging, to have foretold, from the nature of men and of ministers, that

* +In times of peace and security, when alone it is possible to pay debt, the monied interest are averse to receive partial payments, which they know not how to dispose of to advantage ; and the landed interest are averse to continue the taxes requisite for that purpose. Why therefore should a minister persevere in a measure so disagreeable to all parties ? For the sake, I suppose, of a posterity, which he will never see, or of a few reasonable reflecting people, whose united interest, perhaps, will not be able to secure him the smallest burrough in *England.* 'Tis not likely we shall ever find any minister so bad a politician. With regard to these narrow destructive maxims of politics, all ministers are expert enough [*A–G, as footnote*].

things would necessarily be carried to the length we see ; so now, that they have at last happily reached it, it may not be difficult to guess at the consequences. It must, indeed, be one of these two events ; either the nation must destroy public credit, or public credit will destroy the nation. It is impossible that they can both subsist, after the manner they have been hitherto managed, in this, as well as in some other countries.

There was, indeed, a scheme for the payment of our debts, which was proposed by an excellent citizen, Mr. HUTCHINSON,[1] above thirty years ago, and which was much approved of by some men of sense, but never was likely to take effect. He asserted, that there was a fallacy in imagining that the public owed this debt ; for that really every individual owed a proportional share of it, and paid, in his taxes, a proportional share of the interest, beside the expence of levying these taxes. Had we not better, then, says he, make a distribution of the debt among ourselves, and each of us contribute a sum suitable to his property, and by that means discharge at once all our funds and public mortgages ? He seems not to have considered, that the laborious poor pay a con-siderable part of the taxes by their annual consumptions, though they could not advance, at once, a proportional part of the sum required. Not to mention, that property in money and stock in trade might easily be concealed or disguised ; and that visible property in lands and houses would really at last answer for the whole : An inequality and oppression, which never would be submitted to. But though this project is not likely to take place ; it is not altogether improbable, that, when the nation becomes heartily sick of their debts, and is cruelly oppressed by them, some daring projector may arise with visionary schemes for their discharge. And as public credit will begin, by that time, to be a little frail, the least touch will

[1] [Archibald Hutchinson, *A Collection of Treatises relating to the Public Debt and the Discharge of Same* (1721).—ED.]

destroy it, as happened in FRANCE during the regency ;
and in this manner it will *die of the doctor.**

But it is more probable, that the breach of national
faith will be the necessary effect of wars, defeats, misfortunes, and public calamities, or even perhaps of victories
and conquests. I must confess, when I see princes and
states fighting and quarrelling, amidst their debts, funds,
and public mortgages, it always brings to my mind a
match of cudgel-playing fought in a *China* shop. How
can it be expected, that sovereigns will spare a species of
property, which is pernicious to themselves and to the
public, when they have so little compassion on lives and
properties, that are useful to both ? Let the time come
(and surely it will come) when the new funds, created
for the exigencies of the year, are not subscribed to, and
raise not the money projected. Suppose, either that the
cash of the nation is exhausted ; or that our faith, which
has hitherto been so ample, begins to fail us. Suppose,
that, in this distress, the nation is threatened with an
invasion ; a rebellion is suspected or broken out at home ;
a squadron cannot be equipped for want of pay, victuals,
or repairs ; or even a foreign subsidy cannot be advanced.
What must a prince or minister do in such an emergence ?
The right of self-preservation is unalienable in every
individual, much more in every community. And the
folly of our statesmen must then be greater than the folly

* +Some neighbouring states practise an easy expedient, by which
they lighten their public debts. The French have a custom (as the Romans
formerly had) of augmenting their money ; and this the nation has been
so much familiarised to, that it hurts not public credit, though it be really
cutting off at once, by an edict, so much of their debts. The Dutch diminish
the interest without the consent of their creditors, or, which is the same thing,
they arbitrarily tax the funds, as well as other property. Could we practise
either of these methods, we need never be oppressed by the national debt ;
and it is not impossible but one of these, or some other method, may, at
all adventures, be tried, on the augmentation of our incumbrances and
difficulties. But people in this country are so good reasoners upon whatever
regards their interests, that such a practice will deceive nobody ; and
public credit will probably tumble at once, by so dangerous a trial [*A–G,
as footnote*].

of those who first contracted debt, or, what is more, than that of those who trusted or continue to trust this security, if these statesmen have the means of safety in their hands, and do not employ them. The funds, created and mortgaged, will, by that time, bring in a large yearly revenue, sufficient for the defence and security of the nation : Money is perhaps lying in the exchequer, ready for the discharge of the quarterly interest : Necessity calls, fear urges, reason exhorts, compassion alone exclaims : The money will immediately be seized for the current service, under the most solemn protestations, perhaps, of being immediately replaced. But no more is requisite. The whole fabric, already tottering, falls to the ground, and buries thousands in its ruins. And this, I think, may be called the *natural death* of public credit : For to this period it tends as naturally as an animal body to its dissolution and destruction.

*So great dupes are the generality of mankind, that, notwithstanding such a violent shock to public credit, as a voluntary bankruptcy in ENGLAND would occasion, it would not probably be long ere credit would again revive in as flourishing a condition as before. The present king of FRANCE, during the late war, borrowed money at lower interest than ever his grandfather did ; and as low as the BRITISH parliament, comparing the natural rate of interest in both kingdoms. And though men are commonly more governed by what they have seen, than by what they foresee, with whatever certainty ; yet promises, protestations, fair appearances, with the allurements of present interest, have such powerful influence as few are able to resist. Mankind are, in all ages, caught by the same baits : The same tricks, played over and over again, still trepan them. The heights of popularity and patriotism are still the beaten road to power and tyranny ; flattery to treachery ; standing armies to arbitrary government ; and the glory of God to the temporal interest of the clergy.

* [*This paragraph as footnote A–G*].

The fear of an everlasting destruction of credit, allowing it to be an evil, is a needless bugbear. A prudent man, in reality, would rather lend to the public immediately after we had taken a spunge to our debts, than at present ; as much as an opulent knave, even though one could not force him to pay, is a preferable debtor to an honest bankrupt : For the former, in order to carry on business, may find it his interest to discharge his debts, where they are not exorbitant : The latter has it not in his power. The reasoning of TACITUS,[1] as it is eternally true, is very applicable to our present case. *Sed vulgus ad magnitudinem beneficiorum aderat : Stultissimus quisque pecuniis mercabatur : Apud sapientes cassa habebantur, quæ neque dari neque accipi, salva republica, poterant.* The public is a debtor, whom no man can oblige to pay. The only check which the creditors have upon her, is the interest of preserving credit ; an interest, which may easily be overbalanced by a great debt, and by a difficult and extraordinary emergence, even supposing that credit irrecoverable. Not to mention, that a present necessity often forces states into measures, which are, strictly speaking, against their interest.

These two events, supposed above, are calamitous, but not the most calamitous. Thousands are thereby sacrificed to the safety of millions. But we are not without danger, that the contrary event may take place, and that millions may be sacrificed for ever to the temporary safety of thousands.[2] Our popular government, perhaps, will render it difficult or dangerous for a minister to venture

[1] *Hist. lib.* iii. 55.

[2] I have heard it has been computed, that all the creditors of the public, natives and foreigners, amount only to 17,000. These make a figure at present on their income ; but, in case of a public bankruptcy, would, in an instant, become the lowest, as well as the most wretched of the people. The dignity and authority of the landed gentry and nobility is much better rooted ; and would render the contention very unequal, if ever we come to that extremity. One would incline to assign to this event a very near period, such as half a century, had not our father's prophecies of this kind been already found fallacious, by the duration of our public credit, so much beyond all reasonable expectation. When the astrologers in FRANCE were every year foretelling the death of HENRY IV,

on so desperate an expedient, as that of a voluntary bankruptcy. And though the house of Lords be altogether composed of proprietors of land, and the house of Commons chiefly ; and consequently neither of them can be supposed to have great property in the funds ; yet the connections of the members may be so great with the proprietors, as to render them more tenacious of public faith, than prudence, policy, or even justice, strictly speaking, requires.[1] And perhaps too, our foreign *enemies may be so politic as to discover, that our safety lies in despair, and may not, therefore, show the danger, open and barefaced, till it be inevitable. The balance of power in EUROPE, our grandfathers, our fathers, and we, have all deemed too unequal to be preserved without our attention and assistance. But our children, weary of the struggle, and fettered with incumbrances, may sit down secure, and see their neighbours oppressed and conquered ; till, at last, they themselves and their creditors lie both at the mercy of the conqueror. And this may properly enough be denominated the *violent death* of our public credit.[2]

These seem to be the events, which are not very remote, and which reason foresees as clearly almost as she can do

---

[1] [Since, as a debtor, the landowner's interest would conflict with that of the security holder, it is difficult to see why the two would join forces to maintain public solvency. Indeed, elsewhere Hume more consistently and accurately treats a growing debt as potentially the chief source of conflict between the "landed" and the "trading" interest. Cf. "Of Parties in General", *Phil. Wks.*, III, 130.—ED.]

[2] [Adam Smith likewise spoke of "the ruinous expedient of perpetual funding" (*Wealth of Nations*, ed. Cannan, p. 873) and was plainly concerned over the rise of England's national debt. However, as in Hume's footnote on p. 105, he too voices the view that perhaps England's capacity to bear debt would continue to rise sufficiently to avoid the danger of bankruptcy. *Op. cit.*, p. 882.—ED.]

* enemies may=enemies, or rather enemy (for we have but one to dread) may [A–G].

These fellows, says he, *must be right at last*. We shall, therefore, be more cautious than to assign any precise date ; and shall content ourselves with pointing out the event in general.

any thing that lies in the womb of time. And though the ancients maintained, that in order to reach the gift of prophecy, a certain divine fury or madness was requisite, one may safely affirm, that, in order to deliver such prophecies as these, no more is necessary, than merely to be in one's senses, free from the influence of popular madness and delusion.

Of the Populousness of Ancient Nations*

THERE is very little ground, either from reason or observation, to conclude the world eternal or incorruptible. The continual and rapid motion of matter, the violent revolutions with which every part is agitated, the changes remarked in the heavens, the plain traces as well as tradition of an universal deluge, or general convulsion of the elements ; all these prove strongly the mortality of this fabric of the world, and its passage, by corruption or dissolution, from one state or order to another. It must therefore, as well as each individual form which it contains, have its infancy, youth, manhood, and old age ; and it is probable, that, in all these variations, man, equally with every animal and vegetable, will partake.

* + (1) An eminent clergyman in *Edinburgh,* having wrote, some years ago, a discourse on the same question with this, of the populousness of antient nations, was pleas'd lately to communicate it to the author. [The reference here is to Robert Wallace, whose *Dissertation on the Numbers of Mankind in Ancient and Modern Times* was published in 1753.—ED.] It maintain'd the opposite side of the argument, to what is here insisted on, and contained much erudition and good reasoning. The author acknowledges to have borrow'd, with some variations, from that discourse, two computations, that with regard to the numbers of inhabitants in *Belgium,* and that with regard to those in *Epirus.* If this learned gentleman be prevailed on to publish his dissertation, it will serve to give light into the present question, the most curious and important of all questions of erudition [*A–B, as footnote*] ; (2) An ingenious writer has honoured this discourse with an answer, full of politeness, erudition, and good sense. So learned a refutation would have made the author suspect that his reasonings were entirely over thrown, had he not used the precaution, from the beginning, to keep himself on the sceptical side ; and having taken this advantage of the ground, he was enabled, tho' with much inferior forces, to preserve himself from total defeat. That Reverend gentleman will always find where his antagonist is so entrenched that it will be very difficult to force him. Vano, in such a situation, could defend himself against Hannibal, Pharnaces against Caesar. The author, however, very willingly acknowledges, that his antagonist has detected many mistakes both in his authorities and reasonings : and it was owing entirely to that gentleman's indulgence, that many more errors were not remarked. In this edition, advantage has been taken of his learned animadversions, and the discourse has been rendered less imperfect than formerly [*C–G, as footnote.* See also *Additional Note, below, p. 184.*-ED.]

In the flourishing age of the world, it may be expected, that the human species should possess greater vigour both of mind and body, more prosperous health, higher spirits, longer life, and a stronger inclination and power of generation. But if the general system of things, and human society of course, have any such gradual revolutions, they are too slow to be discernible in that short period which is comprehended by history and tradition. Stature and force of body, length of life, even courage and extent of genius, seem hitherto to have been naturally, in all ages, pretty much the same. The arts and sciences, indeed, have flourished in one period, and have decayed in another : But we may observe, that, at the time when they rose to greatest perfection among one people, they were perhaps totally unknown to all the neighbouring nations ; and though they universally decayed in one age, yet in a succeeding generation they again revived, and diffused themselves over the world. As far, therefore, as observation reaches, there is no universal difference discernible in the human species ; and though it were allowed, that the universe, like an animal body, had a natural progress from infancy to old age ; yet as it must still be uncertain, whether, at present, it be advancing to its point of perfection, or declining from it, we cannot thence presuppose any decay in human nature.[1] To prove, therefore, or account for that superior populousness of antiquity, which is commonly supposed, by the imaginary youth or vigour of the world, will scarcely be admitted by any just reasoner. These *general physical* causes ought entirely to be excluded from this question.

There are indeed some more *particular physical* causes

[1] Columella says, lib. iii. cap. 8., that in Egypt and Africa the bearing of twins was frequent, and even customary ; *gemini partus familiares, ac poene solennes sunt*. If this was true, there is a physical difference both in countries and ages. For travellers make no such remarks on these countries at present. On the contrary, we are apt to suppose the northern nations more prolific. As those two countries were provinces of the Roman empire, it is difficult, though not altogether absurd, to suppose that such a man as Columella might be mistaken with regard to them.

of importance. Diseases are mentioned in antiquity, which are almost unknown to modern medicine ; and new diseases have arisen and propagated themselves, of which there are no traces in ancient history. In this particular we may observe, upon comparison, that the disadvantage is much on the side of the moderns. Not to mention some others of less moment ; the small-pox commits such ravages, as would almost alone account for the great superiority ascribed to ancient times. The tenth or the twelfth part of mankind, destroyed every generation, should make a vast difference, it may be thought, in the numbers of the people ; and when joined to venereal distempers, a new plague diffused every where, this disease is perhaps equivalent, by its constant operation, to the three great scourges of mankind, war, pestilence, and famine. Were it certain, therefore, that ancient times were more populous than the present, and could no moral causes be assigned for so great a change ; these physical causes alone, in the opinion of many, would be sufficient to give us satisfaction on that head.

But is it certain, that antiquity was so much more populous, as is pretended ? The extravagancies of Vossius, with regard to this subject, are well known. But an author of much greater genius and discernment has ventured to affirm, that, according to the best computations which these subjects will admit of, there are not now, on the face of the earth, the fiftieth part of mankind, which existed in the time of Julius Cæsar.[1] It may easily be observed, that the comparison, in this case, must be imperfect, even though we confine ourselves to the scene of ancient history ; Europe, and the nations round the Mediterranean. We know not exactly the numbers of any European kingdom, or even city, at present : How can we pretend to calculate those of ancient cities and states, where historians have left us such imperfect traces ? For my part, the matter appears to me so uncertain, that,

[1] *Lettres* Persanes. See also *L'Esprit des Loix*, liv. xxiii. cap. 17, 18, 19.

as I intend to throw together some reflections on that head, I shall intermingle the enquiry concerning *causes* with that concerning *facts* ; which ought never to be admitted, where the facts can be ascertained with any tolerable assurance. We shall, *first*, consider whether it be probable, from what we know of the situation of society in both periods, that antiquity must have been more populous ; *secondly*, whether in reality it was so. If I can make it appear, that the conclusion is not so certain as is pretended, in favour of antiquity, it is all I aspire to.

In general, we may observe, that the question, with regard to the comparative populousness of ages or kingdoms, implies important consequences, and commonly determines concerning the preference of their whole police, their manners, and the constitution of their government. For as there is in all men, both male and female, a desire and power of generation, more active than is ever universally exerted, the restraints, which they lie under, must proceed from some difficulties in their situation, which it belongs to a wise legislature carefully to observe and remove. Almost every man who thinks he can maintain a family will have one ; and the human species, at this rate of propagation, would more than double every generation.* How fast do mankind multiply in every colony or new settlement ; where it is an easy matter to provide for a family ; and where men are nowise straitened or confined, as in long established governments ? History tells us frequently of plagues, which have swept away the third or fourth part of a people : Yet in a generation or two, the destruction was not perceived ; and the society had again acquired their former number. The lands which were cultivated, the houses built, the commodities raised, the riches acquired, enabled the people, who escaped, immediately to marry, and to rear families, which supplied the place of those who had

* +were every one coupled as soon as he comes to the age of puberty [*A–D*].

perished.[1] And for a like reason, every wise, just, and
mild government, by rendering the condition of its subjects
easy and secure, will always abound most in people, as
well as in commodities and riches. A country, indeed,
whose climate and soil are fitted for vines, will naturally
be more populous than one which produces corn only,
and that more populous than one which is only fitted for
pasturage. *In general, warm climates, as the necessities
of the inhabitants are there fewer, and vegetation more
powerful, are likely to be most populous : But if everything else be equal, it seems natural to expect, that,
wherever there are most happiness and virtue, and the
wisest institutions, there will also be most people.

The question, therefore, concerning the populousness
of ancient and modern times, being allowed of great
importance, it will be requisite, if we would bring it to
some determination, to compare both the *domestic* and
political situation of these two periods, in order to judge
of the facts by their moral causes ; which is the *first* view
in which we proposed to consider them.

The chief difference between the *domestic* œconomy of
the ancients and that of the moderns consists in the
practice of slavery, which prevailed among the former,
and which has been abolished for some centuries throughout the greater part of EUROPE. Some passionate admirers
of the ancients, and zealous partizans of civil liberty, (for
these sentiments, as they are, both of them, in the main,
extremely just, are found to be almost inseparable) cannot
forbear regretting the loss of this institution ; and whilst
they brand all submission to the government of a single
person with the harsh denomination of slavery, they would

---

[1] This too is a good reason why the small-pox does not depopulate
countries so much as may at first sight be imagined. Where there is room
for more people, they will always arise, even without the assistance of
naturalization bills. It is remarked by DON GERONIMO DE USTARIZ, that
the provinces of SPAIN, which send most people to the INDIES, are most
populous ; which proceeds from their superior riches.

* In general . . . populous : [*not in A–G*].

gladly reduce the greater part of mankind to real slavery and subjection. But to one who considers coolly on the subject it will appear, that human nature, in general, really enjoys more liberty at present, in the most arbitrary government of EUROPE, than it ever did during the most flourishing period of ancient times. As much as submission to a petty prince, whose dominions extend not beyond a single city, is more grievous than obedience to a great monarch ; so much is domestic slavery more cruel and oppressive than any civil subjection whatsoever. The more the master is removed from us in place and rank, the greater liberty we enjoy ; the less are our actions inspected and controled ; and the fainter that cruel comparison becomes between our own subjection, and the freedom, and even dominion of another. The remains which are found of domestic slavery, in the AMERICAN colonies, and among some EUROPEAN nations, would never surely create a desire of rendering it more universal. The little humanity, commonly observed in persons, accustomed, from their infancy, to exercise so great authority over their fellow-creatures, and to trample upon human nature, were sufficient alone to disgust us with that unbounded dominion. Nor can a more probable reason be assigned for the severe, I might say, barbarous manners of ancient times, than the practice of domestic slavery ; by which every man of rank was rendered a petty tyrant, and educated amidst the flattery, submission, and low debasement of his slaves.

According to ancient practice, all checks were on the inferior, to restrain him to the duty of submission ; none on the superior, to engage him to the reciprocal duties of gentleness and humanity. In modern times, a bad servant finds not easily a good master, nor a bad master a good servant ; and the checks are mutual, suitably to the inviolable and eternal laws of reason and equity.

The custom of exposing old, useless, or sick slaves in an island of the TYBER, there to starve, seems to have been pretty common in ROME ; and whoever recovered, after having been so exposed, had his liberty given him, by an edict of the emperor CLAUDIUS ; in which it was likewise forbidden to kill any slave merely for old age or sickness.[1] But supposing that this edict was strictly obeyed, would it better the domestic treatment of slaves, or render their lives much more comfortable ? We may imagine what others would practise, when it was the professed maxim of the elder CATO, to sell his superannuated slaves for any price, rather than maintain what he esteemed a useless burden.[2]

The *ergastula,* or dungeons, where slaves in chains were forced to work, were very common all over ITALY. COLUMELLA [3] advises, that they be always built under ground ; and recommends [4] it as the duty of a careful overseer, to call over every day the names of these slaves, like the mustering of a regiment or ship's company, in order to know presently when any of them had deserted. A proof of the frequency of these *ergastula,* and of the great number of slaves usually confined in them.*

A chained slave for a porter, was usual in ROME, as appears from OVID,[5] and other authors.[6] Had not these people shaken off all sense of compassion towards that unhappy part of their species, would they have presented their friends, at the first entrance, with such an image of the severity of the master, and misery of the slave ?

Nothing so common in all trials, even of civil causes, as to call for the evidence of slaves ; which was always extorted by the most exquisite torments. DEMOSTHENES says,[7] that, where it was possible to produce, for the same fact, either freemen or slaves, as witnesses, the judges

---

[1] SUETONIUS in vita CLAUDII, 25.
[2] PLUT. in vita CATONIS, 4.   [3] Lib. i. cap. 6.
[4] Id. lib. xi. cap. 1.   [5] Amor. lib. i. eleg. 6.
[6] SUETON, *de claris rhetor.* 3. So also the ancient poet, *Janitoris tintinnire impedimenta audio.*
[7] *In Onetor, orat.* 1. 874.

* + *Partem Italiæ ergastula a solitudine vindicant,* says *Livy [A–B].*

always preferred the torturing of slaves, as a more certain evidence.[1]

SENECA draws a picture of that disorderly luxury, which changes day into night, and night into day, and inverts every stated hour of every office in life. Among other circumstances, such as displacing the meals and times of bathing, he mentions, that, regularly about the third hour of the night, the neighbours of one, who indulges this false refinement, hear the noise of whips and lashes ; and, upon enquiry, find that he is then taking an account of the conduct of his servants, and giving them due correction and discipline. This is not remarked as an instance of cruelty, but only of disorder, which even in actions the most usual and methodical, changes the fixed hours that an established custom had assigned for them.[2]

But our present business is only to consider the influence of slavery on the populousness of a state. It is pretended, that, in this particular, the ancient practice had infinitely the advantage, and was the chief cause of that extreme populousness, which is supposed in those times. At present, all masters discourage the marrying of their male servants, and admit not by any means the

[1] The same practice was very common in ROME ; but CICERO seems not to think this evidence so certain as the testimony of free-citizens. *Pro Cælio*, 28.

[2] *Epist.* 122. The inhuman sports exhibited at ROME, may justly be considered too as an effect of the people's contempt for slaves, and was also a great cause of the general inhumanity of their princes and rulers. Who can read the accounts of the amphitheatrical entertainments without horror ? Or who is surprized, that the emperors should treat that people in the same way the people treated their inferiors ? One's humanity, on that occasion, is apt to renew the barbarous wish of CALIGULA, that the people had but one neck. A man could almost be pleased, by a single blow, to put an end to such a race of monsters. You may thank GOD, says the author above cited (*epist.* 7) addressing himself to the ROMAN people, that you have a master (*viz.* the mild and merciful NERO) who is incapable of learning cruelty from your example. This was spoke in the beginning of his reign : But he fitted them very well afterwards ; and no doubt was considerably improved by the sight of the barbarous objects, to which he had, from his infancy, been accustomed.

marriage of the female, who are then supposed altogether incapacitated for their service. But where the property of the servants is lodged in the master, their marriage forms his riches, and brings him a succession of slaves that supply the place of those whom age and infirmity have disabled. He encourages, therefore, their propagation as much as that of his cattle ; rears the young with the same care ; and educates them to some art or calling, which may render them more useful or valuable to him. The opulent are, by this policy, interested in the being at least, though not in the well-being of the poor ; and enrich themselves, by encreasing the number and industry of those who are subjected to them. Each man, being a sovereign in his own family, has the same interest with regard to it, as the prince with regard to the state ; and has not, like the prince, any opposite motives of ambition or vainglory, which may lead him to depopulate his little sovereignty. All of it is, at all times, under his eye ; and he has leisure to inspect the most minute detail of the marriage and education of his subjects.[1]

Such are the consequences of domestic slavery, according to the first aspect and appearance of things : But if we enter more deeply into the subject, we shall perhaps find reason to retract our hasty determinations. The comparison is shocking between the management of human creatures and that of cattle ; but being extremely just, when applied to the present subject, it may be proper to trace the consequences of it. At the capital, near all great cities, in all populous, rich, industrious provinces, few cattle are bred. Provisions, lodging, attendance, labour are there dear ; and men find their account better in buying the cattle, after they come to a certain age, from

[1] We may here observe, that if domestic slavery really encreased populousness, it would be an exception to the general rule, that the happiness of any society and its populousness are necessary attendants. A master, from humour or interest, may make his slaves very unhappy, yet be careful, from interest, to increase their number. Their marriage is not a matter of choice with them, more than any other action of their life.

the remoter and cheaper countries. These are consequently the only breeding countries for cattle ; and by a parity of reason, for men too, when the latter are put on the same footing with the former. To rear a child in LONDON, till he could be serviceable, would cost much dearer, than to buy one of the same age from SCOTLAND or IRELAND ; where he had been bred in a cottage, covered with rags, and fed on oatmeal or potatoes. Those who had slaves, therefore, in all the richer and more populous countries, would discourage the pregnancy of the females, and either prevent or destroy the birth. The human species would perish in those places where it ought to encrease the fastest ; and a perpetual recruit be wanted from the poorer and more desert provinces. Such a continued drain would tend mightily to depopulate the state, and render great cities ten times more destructive than with us ; where every man is master of himself, and provides for his children from the powerful instinct of nature, not the calculations of sordid interest. If LONDON, at present, without much encreasing, needs a yearly recruit from the country, of 5000 people, as is usually computed, what must it require, if the greater part of the tradesmen and common people were slaves, and were hindered from breeding by their avaricious masters ?

All ancient authors tell us, that there was a perpetual flux of slaves to ITALY from the remoter provinces, particularly SYRIA, CILICIA,[1] CAPPADOCIA, and the Lesser ASIA, THRACE, and ÆGYPT : Yet the number of people did not encrease in ITALY ; and writers complain of the continual decay of industry and agriculture.[2] Where then is that extreme fertility of the ROMAN slaves, which is commonly supposed ? So far from multiplying, they could not, it seems, so much as keep up the stock, without

---

[1] Ten thousand slaves in a day have often been sold for the use of the ROMANS, at DELUS in CILICIA. STRABO, lib. xiv., 668.

[2] COLUMELLA, lib. i. *proœm.* et cap. 2, et. 7. VARRO, lib. iii. cap. i. HORACE, lib. ii. od. 15. TACIT. *annal.* lib. iii. cap. 54. SUETON. *in vita* AUG. cap. xlii. PLIN. lib. xviii, cap. 13.

immense recruits. And though great numbers were continually manumitted and converted into ROMAN citizens, the numbers even of these did not encrease,[1] till the freedom of the city was communicated to foreign provinces.

The term for a slave, born and bred in the family, was *verna* [2] ; and these slaves seem to have been entitled by custom to privileges and indulgences beyond others ; a sufficient reason why the masters would not be fond of rearing many of that kind.[3] Whoever is acquainted with the maxims of our planters, will acknowledge the justness of this observation.[4]

[1] *Minore indies plebe ingenua*, says TACITUS, *ann.* lib. iv. cap. 27.

[2] As *servus* was the name of the genus, and *verna* of the species, without any correlative, this forms a strong presumption, that the latter were by far the least numerous. It is an universal observation which we may form upon language, that where two related parts of a whole bear any proportion to each other, in numbers, rank or consideration, there are always correlative terms invented, which answer to both the parts, and express their mutual relation. If they bear no proportion to each other, the term is only invented for the less, and marks its distinction from the whole. Thus *man* and *woman*, *master* and *servant*, *father* and *son*, *prince* and *subject*, *stranger* and *citizen* are correlative terms. But the words, *seaman*, *carpenter*, *smith*, *tailor*, &c. have no correspondent terms, which express those who are no seamen, or carpenters, &c. Languages differ very much with regard to the particular words where this distinction obtains ; and may thence afford very strong inferences, concerning the manners and customs of different nations. The military government of the ROMAN emperors had exalted the soldiery so high, that they balanced all the other orders of the state : Hence *miles* and *paganus* became relative terms ; a thing, till then, unknown to ancient, and still so, to modern languages. Modern superstition exalted the clergy so high, that they overbalanced the whole state : Hence *clergy* and *laity* are terms opposed in all modern languages ; and in these alone. And from the same principles I infer, that if the number of slaves bought by the ROMANS from foreign countries, had not extremely exceeded those which were bred at home, *verna* would have had a correlative, which would have expressed the former species of slaves. But these, it would seem, composed the main body of the ancient slaves, and the latter were but a few exceptions.

[3] *Verna* is used by ROMAN writers as a word equivalent to *scurra*, on account of the petulance and impudence of those slaves. MART. lib. i. ep. 42. HORACE also mentions the *vernae procaces* ; and PETRONIUS, cap. 24. *vernula urbanitas.* SENECA, *de provid.* cap. 1. *vernularum licentia.*

[4] It is computed in the WEST INDIES, that a stock of slaves grow worse five *per cent.* every year, unless new slaves be bought to recruit them. They are not able to keep up their number, even in those warm countries, where cloaths and provisions are so easily got. How much more must this happen in EUROPEAN countries, and in or near great cities ? *I shall add, that, from the experience of our planters, slavery is as little advantageous to the

Of the Populousness of Ancient Nations

ATTICUS is much praised by his historian for the care, which he took in recruiting his family from the slaves born in it [1] : May we not thence infer, that this practice was not then very common ?

The names of slaves in the GREEK comedies, SYRUS, MYSUS, GETA, THRAX, DAVUS, LYDUS, PHRYX, &c. afford a presumption, that, at ATHENS at least, most of the slaves were imported from foreign countries. The ATHENIANS, says STRABO,[2] gave to their slaves, either the names of the nations whence they were bought, as LYDUS, SYRUS ; or the names that were most common among those nations, as MANES or MIDAS to a PHRYGIAN, TIBIAS to a PAPHLAGONIAN.

DEMOSTHENES, having mentioned a law which forbad any man to strike the slave of another, praises the humanity of this law ; and adds, that, if the barbarians from whom the slaves were bought, had information, that their countrymen met with such gentle treatment, they would entertain a great esteem for the ATHENIANS.[3] ISOCRATES [4] too insinuates, that the slaves of the GREEKS were generally or very commonly barbarians. *ARISTOTLE in his Politics [5] plainly supposes, that a slave is always a foreigner. The ancient comic writers represented the slaves as speaking a barbarous language.[6] This was an imitation of nature.

---

[1] CORN. NEPOS *in vita* ATTICI. We may remark, that ATTICUS's estate lay chiefly in EPIRUS, which, being a remote, desolate place, would render it profitable for him to rear slaves there.

[2] Lib. vii., 304.   [3] *In* MIDIAM, p. 221, *ex edit.* ALDI.

[4] *Panegyr.*   [5] Lib. vii. cap. 10, sub fin.

[6] ARISTOPH. *Equites.* 1. 17. The ancient scholiast remarks on this passage βαρβαρίζει ὡς δοῦλος.

* [*The rest of this paragraph not in A–C*].

---

master as to the slave, wherever hired servants can be procured. A man is obliged to cloath and feed his slave ; and he does no more for his servant ; The price of the first purchase is, therefore, so much loss to him : not to mention, that the fear of punishment will never draw so much labour from a slave, as the dread of being turned off and not getting another service, will from a freeman.

* [*The rest of this note not in A–H*].

It is well known that DEMOSTHENES, in his nonage, had been defrauded of a large fortune by his tutors, and that afterwards he recovered, by a prosecution at law, the value of his patrimony. His orations, on that occasion, still remain, and contain an exact detail of the whole substance left by his father,[1] in money, merchandise, houses, and slaves, together with the value of each particular. Among the rest were 52 slaves, handicraftsmen, namely, 32 sword-cutlers, and 20 cabinet-makers [2]; all males ; not a word of any wives, children or family, which they certainly would have had, had it been a common practice at ATHENS to breed from the slaves : And the value of the whole must have much depended on that circumstance. No female slaves are even so much as mentioned, except some house-maids, who belonged to his mother. This argument has great force, if it be not altogether conclusive.

Consider this passage of PLUTARCH,[3] speaking of the Elder CATO. "He had a great number of slaves, whom "he took care to buy at the sales of prisoners of war ; "and he chose them young, that they might easily be "accustomed to any diet or manner of life, and be "instructed in any business or labour, as men teach any "thing to young dogs or horses.——And esteeming love "the chief source of all disorders, he allowed the male "slaves to have a commerce with the female in his family, "upon paying a certain sum for this privilege : But he "strictly prohibited all intrigues out of his family". Are there any symptoms in this narration of that care which is supposed in the ancients, of the marriage and propagation of their slaves ? If that was a common practice, founded on general interest, it would surely have been embraced by Cato, who was a great œconomist, and lived

---

[1] *In Aphobum orat.* 1. 816.

[2] κλινοποιοί, makers of those beds which the ancients lay upon at meals.

[3] *In vita* CATONIS, 21.

in times when the ancient frugality and simplicity of manners were still in credit and reputation.

It is expressly remarked by the writers of the ROMAN law, that scarcely any ever purchase slaves with a view of breeding from them.[1]

Our lackeys and house-maids, I own, do not serve much to multiply their species : But the ancients, besides those who attended on their person, had almost all their labour performed, *and even manufactures executed, by slaves, who lived, many of them, in their family ; and some great men possessed to the number of 10,000. If there be any suspicion, therefore, that this institution was unfavourable to propagation, (and the same reason, at least in part, holds with regard to ancient slaves as modern servants) how destructive must slavery have proved ?

History mentions a ROMAN nobleman, who had 400 slaves under the same roof with him : And having been assassinated at home by the furious revenge of one of them, the law was executed with rigour, and all without exception were put to death.[2] Many other ROMAN

---

[1] "Non temere ancillae ejus rei causa comparantur ut pariant". *Digest.* lib. 5. tit. 3. *de haered. petit. lex* 27. The following texts are to the same purpose. "Spadonem morbosum non esse, neque vitiosum, verius mihi videtur ; sed sanum esse, sicuti illum qui unum testiculum habet, qui etiam generare potest". *Digest.* lib. 9. tit. 1. *de aedilitio edicto, lex,* 6.§2. "Sin autem quis ita spado sit, ut tam necessaria pars corporis penitus absit, morbosus est". *Id. lex* 7. His impotence, it seems, was only regarded so far as his health or life might be affected by it. In other respects, he was full as valuable. The same reasoning is employed with regard to female slaves. "Quaeritur de ea muliere quae semper mortuos parit, an morbosa sit ? et ait Sabinus, si vulvae vitio hoc contingit, morbosam esse". *Id. lex* 14. It has even been doubted, whether a woman pregnant was morbid or vitiated ; and it is determined, that she is sound, not on account of the value of her offspring, but because it is the natural part or office of women to bear children. "Si mulier praegnans venerit, inter omnes convenit sanam eam esse. Maximum enim ac praecipuum munus foeminarum accipere ac tueri conceptum. Puerperam quoque sanam esse ; si modo nihil extrinsecus accedit, quod corpus ejus in aliquam valetudinem immitteret. De sterili Caelius distinguere Trebatium dicit, ut si natura sterilis sit, sana sit ; si vitio corporis, contra". *Id.*

[2] TACIT. *ann.* lib. xiv. cap. 43.

* and . . . executed, [*not in A–G*].

noblemen had families equally, or more numerous ; and I believe every one will allow, that this would scarcely be practicable, were we to suppose all the slaves married, and the females to be breeders.[1]

So early as the poet HESIOD,[2] married slaves, whether male or female, were esteemed inconvenient. How much more, where families had encreased to such an enormous size as in ROME, and where the ancient simplicity of manners was banished from all ranks of people ?

XENOPHON in his Oeconomics, where he gives directions for the management of a farm, recommends a strict care and attention of laying the male and the female slaves at a distance from each other. He seems not to suppose that they are ever married. The only slaves among the GREEKS that appear to have continued their own race, were the HELOTES, who had houses apart, and were more the slaves of the public than of individuals.[3]

*The same author [4] tells us that NICIAS's overseer, by agreement with his master, was obliged to pay him an obolus a day for each slave ; besides maintaining them, and keeping up the number. Had the ancient slaves been all breeders, this last circumstance of the contract had been superfluous.

The ancients talk so frequently of a fixed, stated portion of provisions assigned to each slave,[5] that we are naturally led to conclude, that slaves lived almost all single, and received that portion as a kind of board-wages.

The practice, indeed, of marrying slaves seems not to have been very common, even among the country-

---

[1] The slaves in the great houses had little rooms assigned to them, called *cellae*. Whence the name of cell was transferred to the monk's room in a convent. See farther on this head, JUST. LIPSIUS, *Saturn.* i. cap. 14. These form strong presumptions against the marriage and propagation of the family slaves.

[2] *Opera et Dies,* 405, also 602.

[3] STRABO, lib. viii. 365. [4] *De ratione redituum,* 4, 14.

[5] See CATO *de re rustica,* cap. 56. DONATUS *in Phormion,* 1.1, 9. SENECAE *epist.* 80.

* [*This paragraph not in A–B*].

labourers, where it is more naturally to be expected. CATO,[1] enumerating the slaves requisite to labour a vineyard of a hundred acres, makes them amount to 15 ; the overseer and his wife, *villicus* and *villica*, and 13 male slaves ; for an olive plantation of 240 acres, the overseer and his wife, and 11 male slaves ; and so in proportion to a greater or less plantation or vineyard.

VARRO,[2] quoting this passage of CATO, allows his computation to be just in every respect, except the last. For as it is requisite, says he, to have an overseer and his wife, whether the vineyard or plantation be great or small, this must alter the exactness of the proportion. Had CATO's computation been erroneous in any other respect, it had certainly been corrected by VARRO, who seems fond of discovering so trivial an error.

The same author,[3] as well as COLUMELLA,[4] recommends it as requisite to give a wife to the overseer, in order to attach him the more strongly to his master's service. This was therefore a peculiar indulgence granted to a slave, in whom so great confidence was reposed.

In the same place, VARRO mentions it as an useful precaution, not to buy too many slaves from the same nation, lest they beget factions and seditions in the family : A presumption, that in ITALY, the greater part, even of the country labouring slaves, (for he speaks of no other) were bought from the remoter provinces. All the world knows, that the family slaves in ROME, who were instruments of show and luxury, were commonly imported from the east. *Hoc profecere,* says PLINY, speaking of the jealous care of masters, *mancipiorum legiones, et in domo turba externa, ac servorum quoque causa nomenclator adhibendus.*[5]

It is indeed recommended by VARRO,[6] to propagate

---

[1] *De re rust.* cap. 10. 11. [2] Lib. i. cap. 18.
[3] Lib. i. cap. 17. [4] Lib. i. cap. 18.
[5] Lib. xxxiii. cap. 1. *So likewise TACITUS, *annal.* lib. xiv. cap. 44.
[6] Lib. ii. cap. 10.

* [*Not in A–B*].

young shepherds in the family from the old ones. For as grasing farms were commonly in remote and cheap places, and each shepherd lived in a cottage apart, his marriage and encrease were not liable to the same inconveniencies as in dearer places, and where many servants lived in the family ; which was universally the case in such of the ROMAN farms as produced wine or corn. If we consider this exception with regard to shepherds, and weigh the reasons of it, it will serve for a strong confirmation of all our foregoing suspicions.[1]

COLUMELLA,[2] I own, advises the master to give a reward, and even liberty to a female slave, that had reared him above three children : A proof that sometimes the ancients propagated from their slaves ; which, indeed, cannot be denied. Were it otherwise, the practice of slavery, being so common in antiquity, must have been destructive to a degree which no expedient could repair. All I pretend to infer from these reasonings is, that slavery is in general disadvantageous both to the happiness and populousness of mankind, and that its place is much better supplied by the practice of hired servants.

The laws, or, as some writers call them, the seditions of the GRACCHI, were occasioned by their observing the encrease of slaves all over ITALY, and the diminution of free citizens. APPIAN [3] ascribes this encrease to the propagation of the slaves : PLUTARCH [4] to the purchasing of barbarians, who were chained and imprisoned, βαρβαρικα δεσμωτηρια.[5] It is to be presumed that both causes concurred.

---

[1] *Pastoris duri est hic filius, ille bubulci.* JUVEN. *sat.* 11, 151.
[2] Lib. i. cap. 8.
[3] *De bel. civ.* lib. i. 7.
[4] *In vita* TIB. & C. GRACCHI.
[5] To the same purpose is that passage of the elder SENECA, *ex controversia* 5, lib. v. "Arata quondam populis rura, singulorum ergastulorum sunt ; latiusque nunc villici, quam olim reges, imperant. At nunc eadem", says PLINY, "vincti pedes, damnatae manus, inscripti vultus exercent". Lib. xciii. cap. 3. So also MARTIAL.
"Et sonet innumera compede Thuscus ager". Lib. ix. ep. 23.

Of the Populousness of Ancient Nations

SICILY, says FLORUS,[1] was full of *ergastula*, and was cultivated by labourers in chains. EUNUS and ATHENIO excited the servile war, by breaking up these monstrous prisons, and giving liberty to 60,000 slaves. The younger POMPEY augmented his army in SPAIN by the same expedient.[2] If the country labourers, throughout the ROMAN empire, were so generally in this situation, and if it was difficult or impossible to find separate lodgings for the families of the city servants, how unfavourable to propagation, as well as to humanity, must the institution of domestic slavery be esteemed?

CONSTANTINOPLE, at present, requires the same recruits of slaves from all the provinces, that ROME did of old; and these provinces are of consequence far from being populous.

EGYPT, according to Mons. MAILLET, sends continual colonies of black slaves to the other parts of the TURKISH empire; and receives annually an equal return of white: The one brought from the inland parts of AFRICA; the other from MINGRELIA, CIRCASSIA, and TARTARY.

Our modern convents are, no doubt, bad institutions: But there is reason to suspect, that anciently every great family in Italy, and probably in other parts of the world, was a species of convent. And though we have reason to condemn all those popish institutions, as nurseries of *superstition, burthensome to the public, and oppressive to the poor prisoners, male as well as female; yet may it be questioned whether they be so destructive to the

[1] Lib. iii. cap. 19.   [2] Id. lib. iv. cap. 8.

* superstition = the most abject superstition [A–G].

And LUCAN.
> "Tum longos jungere fines
> Agrorum, et quondam duro sulcata Camilli
> Vomere, et antiquas Curiorum passa ligones
> Longa sub ignotis estendere rura colonis". Lib. i. 167.
>   "Vincto fossore coluntur
> Hesperiae segetes.——" Lib. vii. 402.

populousness of a state, as is commonly imagined. Were the land, which belongs to a convent, bestowed on a nobleman, he would spend its revenue on dogs, horses, grooms, footmen, cooks, and house-maids ; and his family would not furnish many more citizens than the convent.

The common reason, why any parent thrusts his daughters into nunneries, is, that he may not be over-burthened with too numerous a family ; but the ancients had a method almost as innocent, and more effectual to that purpose, to wit, exposing their children in early infancy. This practice was very common ; and is not spoken of by any author of those times with the horror it deserves, or scarcely [1] even with disapprobation. PLU-TARCH, the humane, good-natured PLUTARCH,[2] mentions it as a merit in ATTALUS, king of PERGAMUS, that he murdered, or, if you will, exposed all his own children, in order to leave his crown to the son of his brother, EUMENES ; signalizing in this manner his gratitude and affection to EUMENES, who had left him his heir preferably to that son. It was SOLON, the most celebrated of the sages of GREECE, that gave parents permission by law to kill their children.[3]

Shall we then allow these two circumstances to compensate each other, to wit, monastic vows, and the exposing of children, and to be unfavourable, in equal degrees, to the propagation of mankind ? I doubt the advantage is here on the side of antiquity. Perhaps, by an odd connexion of causes, the barbarous practice of the ancients might rather render those times more populous. By removing the terrors of too numerous a family it would engage many people in marriage ; and such is the force of natural affection, that very few, in comparison, would

---

[1] TACITUS blames it. *De morib. Germ.* 19.

[2] *De fraterno amore.* SENECA also approves of the exposing of sickly infirm children. *De ira,* lib. i. cap. 15.

[3] SEXT. EMP. lib. iii. cap. 24.

have resolution enough, when it came to the push, to carry into execution their former intentions.

CHINA, the only country where this practice of exposing children prevails at present, is the most populous country we know of ; and every man is married before he is twenty. Such early marriages could scarcely be general, had not men the prospect of so easy a method of getting rid of their children. I own that PLUTARCH [1] speaks of it as a very general maxim of the poor to expose their children ; and as the rich were then averse to marriage, on account of the courtship they met with from those who expected legacies from them, the public must have been in a bad situation between them.[2]

Of all sciences there is none, where first appearances are more deceitful than in politics. Hospitals for foundlings seem favourable to the encrease of numbers ; and perhaps, may be so, when kept under proper restrictions. But when they open the door to every one, without distinction, they have probably a contrary effect, and are pernicious to the state. It is computed, that every ninth child born at PARIS, is sent to the hospital ; though it seems certain, according to the common course of human affairs, that it is not a hundredth child whose parents are altogether incapacitated to rear and educate him. The *great difference, for health, industry, and morals, between an education in an hospital and that in a private family,

[1] *De amore prolis.*

[2] The practice of leaving great sums of money to friends, tho' one had near relations, was common in GREECE as well as ROME ; as we may gather from LUCIAN. This practice prevails much less in modern times ; and BEN. JOHNSON's VOLPONE is therefore almost entirely extracted from antient authors, and suits better the manners of those times.

It may justly be thought, that the liberty of divorces in Rome was another discouragement to marriage. Such a practice prevents not quarrels from *humour*, but rather increases them ; and occasions also those from *interest*, which are much more dangerous and destructive. See farther on this head, Essays moral, political and literary, Part I. essay XIX. Perhaps too the unnatural lusts of the antients ought to be taken into consideration, as of some moment.

* great=infinite [*A–G*].

should induce us not to make the entrance into the former too easy and engaging. To kill one's own child is shocking to nature, and must therefore be somewhat unusual ; but to turn over the care of him upon others, is very tempting to the natural indolence of mankind.

Having considered the domestic life and manners of the ancients, compared to those of the moderns ; where, in the main, we seem rather superior, so far as the present question is concerned ; we shall now examine the *political* customs and institutions of both ages, and weigh their influence in retarding or forwarding the propagation of mankind.

Before the encrease of the ROMAN power, or rather till its full establishment, almost all the nations, which are the scene of ancient history, were divided into small territories or petty commonwealths, where of course a great equality of fortune prevailed, and the center of the government was always very near its frontiers.

This was the situation of affairs not only in GREECE and ITALY, but also in SPAIN, GAUL, GERMANY, AFRIC, and a great part of the Lesser ASIA : And it must be owned, that no institution could be more favourable to the propagation of mankind. For, though a man of an overgrown fortune, not being able to consume more than another, must share it with those who serve and attend him ; yet their possession being precarious, they have not the same encouragement to marry, as if each had a small fortune, secure and independent. Enormous cities are, besides, destructive to society, beget vice and disorder of all kinds, starve the remoter provinces, and even starve themselves, by the prices to which they raise all provisions. Where each man had his little house and field to himself, and each county had its capital, free and independent ; what a happy situation of mankind ! How favourable to industry and agriculture ; to marriage and propagation ! The prolific virtue of men, were it to act in its full extent, without that restraint which poverty and necessity imposes on it, would double the number every generation : And nothing surely can give it more liberty, than such small commonwealths, and such an equality of fortune among the citizens. All small states naturally produce equality of fortune, because they afford no opportunities of great encrease ; but small commonwealths much more, by that division of power and authority which is essential to them.

When XENOPHON [1] returned after the famous expedition with CYRUS, he hired himself and 6000 of the GREEKS into the service of SEUTHES, a prince of THRACE ; and the articles of his agreement were, that each soldier should receive a *daric* a month, each captain two *darics*, and he himself, as general, four : A regulation of pay which would not a little surprise our modern officers.

DEMOSTHENES and ÆSCHINES, with eight more, were sent ambassadors to PHILIP of MACEDON, and their appointments for above four months were a thousand *drachmas*, which is less than a *drachma* a day for each ambassador.[2] But a *drachma* a day, nay sometimes two,[3] was the pay of a common foot-soldier.

A centurion among the ROMANS had only double pay to a private man, in POLYBIUS's time,[4] and we accordingly find the gratuities after a triumph regulated by that proportion.[5] But MARK ANTHONY and the triumvirate gave the centurions five times the reward of the other.[6] So much had the encrease of the commonwealth encreased the inequality among the citizens.[7]

It must be owned, that the situation of affairs in modern times, with regard to civil liberty, as well as

---

[1] *De exp.* CYR. lib. vii. 6.
[2] DEMOST. *de falsa leg.* 390. He calls it a considerable sum.
[3] THUCYD. lib. iii. 17.   [4] Lib. vi. cap. 37.
[5] TIT. LIV. lib. xli. cap. 7, 13 *& alibi passim.*
[6] APPIAN. *De bell civ.* lib. iv., 20.
[7] CÆSAR gave the centurions ten times the gratuity of the common soldiers, *De bello Gallico*, lib. viii. 4. In the RHODIAN cartel, mentioned afterwards, no distinction in the ransom was made on account of ranks in the army.

equality of fortune, is not near so favourable, either to the propagation or happiness of mankind. EUROPE is shared out mostly into great monarchies ; and such parts of it as are divided into small territories, are commonly governed by absolute princes, who ruin their people by a mimicry of the greater monarchs, in the splendor of their court and number of their forces. SWISSERLAND alone and HOLLAND resemble the ancient republics ; and though the former is far from possessing any advantage either of soil, climate, or commerce, yet the numbers of people, with which it abounds, notwithstanding their enlisting themselves into every service in Europe, prove sufficiently the advantages of their political institutions.

The ancient republics derived their chief or only security from the numbers of their citizens. The TRACHINIANS having lost great numbers of their people, the remainder, instead of enriching themselves by the inheritance of their fellow-citizens, applied to SPARTA, their metropolis, for a new stock of inhabitants. The SPARTANS immediately collected ten thousand men ; among whom the old citizens divided the lands of which the former proprietors had perished.[1]

After TIMOLEON had banished DIONYSIUS from SYRA-CUSE, and had settled the affairs of SICILY, finding the cities of SYRACUSE and SELLINUNTIUM extremely depopulated by tyranny, war, and faction, he invited over from GREECE some new inhabitants to repeople them.[2] Immediately forty thousand men (PLUTARCH [3] says sixty thousand) offered themselves ; and he distributed so many lots of land among them, to the great satisfaction of the ancient inhabitants : A proof at once of the maxims of ancient policy, which affected populousness more than riches ; and of the good effects of these maxims, in the extreme populousness of that small country, GREECE, which could at once supply so great a colony. The case

---

[1] DIOD. SIC. lib. xii. 59.   THUCYD. lib. iii. 92.
[2] DIOD. SIC. lib. xvi. 82.   ʃ   [3] *In vita* TIMOL. 23.

was not much different with the ROMANS in early times. He is a pernicious citizen, said M. CURIUS, who cannot be content with seven acres.[1] Such ideas of equality could not fail of producing great numbers of people.

We must now consider what disadvantages the ancients lay under with regard to populousness, and what checks they received from their political maxims and institutions. There are commonly compensations in every human condition : and though these compensations be not always perfectly equal, yet they serve, at least, to restrain the prevailing principle. To compare them and estimate their influence, is indeed difficult, even where they take place in the same age, and in neighbouring countries : But where several ages have intervened, and only scattered lights are afforded us by ancient authors ; what can we do but amuse ourselves by talking *pro* and *con*, on an interesting subject, and thereby correcting all hasty and violent determinations ?

First, We may observe, that the ancient republics were almost in perpetual war, a natural effect of their martial spirit, their love of liberty, their mutual emulation, and that hatred which generally prevails among nations that live in close neighbourhood. Now, war in a small state is much more destructive than in a great one ; both because all the inhabitants, in the former case, must serve in the armies ; and because the whole state is frontier, and is all exposed to the inroads of the enemy.

The maxims of ancient war were much more destructive than those of modern ; chiefly by that distribution of plunder, in which the soldiers were indulged. The

---

[1] PLIN. lib. 18. cap. 3. The same author, in cap. 6, says, *Verumque fatentibus latifundia perdidere* ITALIAM ; *jam vero et provincias. Sex domi semissem* AFRICAE *possidebant, cum interfecit eos* NERO *princeps*. In this view, the barbarous butchery committed by the first ROMAN emperors, was not, perhaps, so destructive to the public as we may imagine. These never ceased till they had extinguished all the illustrious families, which had enjoyed the plunder of the world, during the latter ages of the republic. The new nobles who rose in their place, were less splendid, as we learn from TACIT. *ann.* lib. 3. cap. 55.

private men in our armies are such a low set of people, that we find any abundance, beyond their simple pay, breeds confusion and disorder among them, and a total dissolution of discipline. The very wretchedness and meanness of those, who fill the modern armies, render them less destructive to the countries which they invade : One instance, among many, of the deceitfulness of first appearances in all political reasonings.[1]

Ancient battles were much more bloody, by the very nature of the weapons employed in them. The ancients drew up their men 16 or 20, sometimes 50 men deep, which made a narrow front ; and it was not difficult to find a field, in which both armies might be marshalled, and might engage with each other. Even where any body of the troops was kept off by hedges, hillocks, woods, or hollow ways, the battle was not so soon decided between the contending parties, but that the others had time to overcome the difficulties which opposed them, and take part in the engagement. And as the whole army was thus engaged, and each man closely buckled to his antagonist, the battles were commonly very bloody, and great slaughter was made on both sides, especially on the vanquished. The long thin lines, required by fire-arms, and the quick decision of the fray, render our modern engagements but partial rencounters, and enable the general, who is foiled in the beginning of the day, to draw off the greater part of his army, sound and entire.*

The battles of antiquity, both by their duration, and

---

[1] The ancient soldiers, being free citizens, above the lowest rank, were all married. Our modern soldiers are either forced to live unmarried, or their marriages turn to small account towards the encrease of mankind. A circumstance which ought, perhaps, to be taken into consideration, as of some consequence in favour of the ancients.

* +Could Folard's project of the column take place (which seems impracticable) [1] it would render modern battles as destructive as the antient [A–G].

[1] What is the advantage of the column after it has broke the enemy's line ? only, that it then takes them in flank, and dissipates whatever stands near it by a fire from all sides. But till it has broke them, does it not present a flank to the enemy, and that exposed to their musquetry, and, what is much worse, to their cannon ?

their resemblance to single combats, were wrought up to a degree of fury quite unknown to later ages. Nothing could then engage the combatants to give quarter, but the hopes of profit, by making slaves of their prisoners. In civil wars, as we learn from TACITUS,[1] the battles were the most bloody, because the prisoners were not slaves.

What a stout resistance must be made, where the vanquished expected so hard a fate ! How inveterate the rage, where the maxims of war were, in every respect, so bloody and severe !

Instances are frequent, in ancient history, of cities besieged, whose inhabitants, rather than open their gates, murdered their wives and children, and rushed themselves on a voluntary death, sweetened perhaps by a little prospect of revenge upon the enemy. GREEKS,[2] as well as BARBARIANS, have often been wrought up to this degree of fury. And the same determined spirit and cruelty must, in other instances less remarkable, have been destructive to human society, in those petty commonwealths, which lived in close neighbourhood, and were engaged in perpetual wars and contentions.

Sometimes the wars in GREECE, says PLUTARCH,[3] were carried on entirely by inroads, and robberies, and piracies. Such a method of war must be more destructive in small states, than the bloodiest battles and sieges.

By the laws of the twelve tables, possession during two years formed a prescription for land ; one year for moveables [4] : An indication, that there was not in ITALY, at that time, much more order, tranquillity, and settled police, than there is at present among the TARTARS.

[1] Hist. lib. ii. cap. 44.
[2] As ABYDUS, mentioned by LIVY, lib. xxxi. cap. 17, 18, and POLYB. lib. xvi. 34. As also the XANTHIANS, APPIAN. *de bell. civil.* lib. iv. 80.
[3] *In vita* ARATI, 6.   [4] INST. lib. ii. cap. 6.*

* +'Tis true, the same law seems to have continued till the time of *Justinian.* But abuses, introduced by barbarism, are not always corrected by civility [A–G].

The only cartel I remember in ancient history, is that between DEMETRIUS POLIORCETES and the RHODIANS ; when it was agreed, that a free citizen should be restored for 1000 *drachmas*, a slave bearing arms for 500.[1]

But, *secondly*, it appears that ancient manners were more unfavourable than the modern, not only in times of war, but also in those of peace ; and that too in every respect, except the love of civil liberty and of equality, which is, I own, of considerable importance. To exclude faction from a free government, is very difficult, if not altogether impracticable ; but such inveterate rage between the factions, and such bloody maxims, are found, in modern times amongst religious parties alone.* In ancient history, we may always observe, where one party prevailed, whether the nobles or people (for I can observe no difference in this respect [2]) that they immediately butchered all of the opposite party who fell into their hands, and banished such as had been so fortunate as to escape their fury. No form of process, no law, no trial, no pardon. A fourth, a third, perhaps near half of the city was slaughtered, or expelled, every revolution ; and the exiles always joined foreign enemies, and did all the mischief possible to their fellow-citizens ; till fortune put it in their power to take full revenge by a new revolution. And as these were frequent in such violent governments, the disorder, diffidence, jealousy, enmity, which must prevail, are not easy for us to imagine in this age of the world.

There are only two revolutions I can recollect in ancient history, which passed without great severity, and great effusion of blood in massacres and assassinations, namely, the restoration of the ATHENIAN Democracy by

[1] DIOD. SICUL. lib. xx. 84.

[2] LYSIAS, who was himself of the popular faction, and very narrowly escaped from the thirty tyrants, says, that the Democracy was as violent a government as the Oligarchy. *Orat.* 25, *de statu popul.*

* +where bigotted priests are the accusers, judges, and executioners [*A–G*].

THRASYBULUS, and the subduing of the ROMAN republic
by CÆSAR. We learn from ancient history, that THRA-
SYBULUS passed a general amnesty for all past offences ;
and first introduced that word, as well as practice, into
GREECE.[1] It appears, however, from many orations of
LYSIAS,[2] that the chief, and even some of the subaltern
offenders, in the preceding tyranny, were tried and
capitally punished.* And as to CÆSAR's clemency, though
much celebrated, it would not gain great applause in the
present age. He butchered, for instance, all CATO's
senate, when he became master of UTICA[3] ; and these,
we may readily believe, were not the most worthless of
the party. All those who had borne arms against that
usurper, were attainted ; and, by HIRTIUS's law, declared
incapable of all public offices.

These people were extremely fond of liberty ; but
seem not to have understood it very well. When the thirty
tyrants first established their dominion at ATHENS, they
began with seizing all the sycophants and informers, who
had been so troublesome during the Democracy, and
putting them to death by an arbitrary sentence and
execution. *Every man*, says SALLUST[4] and LYSIAS,[5] *was
rejoiced at these punishments ;* not considering, that liberty
was from that moment annihilated.

The utmost energy of the nervous style of THUCYDIDES,
and the copiousness and expression of the GREEK language,
seem to sink under that historian, when he attempts to
describe the disorders, which arose from faction throughout all the GRECIAN commonwealths. You would imagine,

[1] CICERO, PHILIP. I, I.

[2] As *orat.* 12. *contra* ERATOST. *orat.* 13. *contra.* AGORAT. *orat.* 16, *pro*
MANTITH.

[3] APPIAN, *de bell. civ.* lib. ii. 100.

[4] See CÆSAR's speech *de bell. Catil.* c. 51.

[5] *Orat.* 25, 173. And in *orat.* 30, 184, he mentions the factious spirit of
the popular assemblies as the only cause why these illegal punishments
should displease.

* +This is a difficulty not cleared up, and even not observed by
antiquarians and historians [*A-H*].

135

that he still labours with a thought greater than he can find words to communicate. And he concludes his pathetic description with an observation, which is at once refined and solid. "In these contests", says he, "those who were the dullest, and most stupid, and had the least foresight, commonly prevailed. For being conscious of this weakness, and dreading to be over-reached by those of greater penetration, they went to work hastily, without premeditation, by the sword and poinard, and thereby got the start of their antagonists, who were forming fine schemes and projects for their destruction".[1]

Not to mention Dionysius [2] the elder, who is computed to have butchered in cool blood above 10,000 of his fellow-citizens ; or Agathocles,[3] Nabis,[4] and others, still more bloody than he ; the transactions, even in free governments, were extremely violent and destructive. At Athens, the thirty tyrants and the nobles, in a twelve-month, murdered, without trial, about 1200 of the people, and banished above the half of the citizens that remained.[5] In Argos, near the same time, the people killed 1200 of the nobles ; and afterwards their own demagogues, because they had refused to carry their prosecutions farther.[6] The people also in Corcyra killed 1500 of the

---

[1] Lib. iii.*
[2] Plut. *de virt. & fort.* Alex.
[3] Diod. Sic. lib. xviii, xix.
[4] Tit. Liv. xxxi. xxxiii. xxxiv.
[5] Diod. Sic. lib. xiv, 5. Isocrates says there were only 5000 banished. He makes the number of those killed amount to 1500. Areop. 153. Aeschines *contra*. Ctesiph. 455 assigns precisely the same number. Seneca (*de tranq. anim.* cap. 5.) says 1300.
[6] Diod. Sic. lib. xv. c. 58.

* +The country in *Europe*, wherein I have observ'd the factions to be most violent and party hatred the strongest, is *Ireland*. This goes so far as to cut off even the most common intercourse of civilities betwixt the Protestants and Catholics. Their cruel insurrections, and the severe revenges which they have taken of each other, are the causes of this mutual ill will, which is the chief source of the disorder, poverty, and depopulation of that country. The *Greek* factions, I imagine, to have been inflamed still to a higher degree of rage ; The revolutions being commonly more frequent, and the maxims of assassination much more avow'd and acknowledg'd [*A-G*].

nobles, and banished a thousand.[1] These numbers will appear the more surprising, if we consider the extreme smallness of these states. But all ancient history is full of such instances.[2]

When ALEXANDER ordered all the exiles to be restored throughout all the cities ; it was found, that the whole amounted to 20,000 men [3] ; the remains probably of still greater slaughters and massacres. What an astonishing multitude in so narrow a country as ancient GREECE ! And what domestic confusion, jealousy, partiality, revenge, heart-burnings, must tear those cities, where factions were wrought up to such a degree of fury and despair.

[1] DIOD. SIC. lib. xiii. c. 48.

[2] We shall mention from DIODORUS SICULUS alone a few massacres, which passed in the course of sixty years, during the most shining age of GREECE. There were banished from SYBARIS 500 of the nobles and their partizans ; lib. xii. p. 77, *ex edit.* RHODOMANNI. Of CHIANS, 600 citizens banished ; lib. xiii. p. 189. At EPHESUS, 349 killed, 1000 banished ; lib. xiii. p. 223. Of CYRENIANS, 500 nobles killed, all the rest banished ; lib. xiv. p. 263. The CORINTHIANS killed 120, banished 500 ; lib. xiv. p. 304. PHAEBIDAS the SPARTAN banished 300 BŒOTIANS ; lib. xv. p. 342. Upon the fall of the LACEDÆMONIANS, Democracies were restored in many cities, and severe vengeance taken of the nobles, after the GREEK manner. But matters did not end there. For the banished nobles, returning in many places, butchered their adversaries at PHIALAE, in CORINTH, in MEGARA, in PHLIASIA. In this last place they killed 300 of the people ; but these again revolting, killed above 600 of the nobles, and banished the rest ; lib. xv. p. 357. In ARCADIA 1400 banished, besides many killed. The banished retired to SPARTA and to PALLANTIUM : The latter were delivered up to their countrymen, and all killed ; lib. xv. p. 373. Of the banished from ARGOS and THEBES, there were 509 in the SPARTAN army ; *id.* p. 374. Here is a detail of the most remarkable of AGATHOCLES's cruelties from the same author. The people before his usurpation had banished 600 nobles ; lib. xix. p. 655. Afterwards that tyrant, in concurrence with the people, killed 4000 nobles, and banished 6000 ; *id.* p. 647. He killed 4000 people at GELA ; *id.* p. 741. By AGATHOCLES's brother 8000 banished from SYRACUSE ; lib. xx. p. 757. The inhabitants of ÆGESTA, to the number of 40,000, were killed, man, woman, and child ; and with tortures, for the sake of their money ; *id.* p. 802. All the relations, to wit, father, brother, children, grandfather, of his LIBYAN army, killed ; *id.* p. 803. He killed 7000 exiles after capitulation ; *id.* p. 816. It is to be remarked, that AGATHOCLES was a man of great sense and courage, *and is not to be suspected of wanton cruelty, contrary to the maxims of his age.

[3] DIOD. SIC. lib. xviii, c. 8.

* and . . . age [*not in A–F*] ;=His violent tyranny, therefore, is a stronger proof of the measures of the age [*G*].

It would be easier, says Isocrates to Philip, to raise an army in Greece at present from the vagabonds than from the cities.

Even when affairs came not to such extremities (which they failed not to do almost in every city twice or thrice every century) property was rendered very precarious by the maxims of ancient government. Xenophon, in the Banquet of Socrates, gives us a natural unaffected description of the tyranny of the Athenian people. "In my poverty", says Charmides, "I am much more happy than I ever was while possessed of riches : as much as it is happier to be in security than in terrors, free than a slave, to receive than to pay court, to be trusted than suspected. Formerly I was obliged to caress every informer ; some imposition was continually laid upon me ; and it was never allowed me to travel, or be absent from the city. At present, when I am poor I look big, and threaten others. The rich are afraid of me, and show me every kind of civility and respect ; and I am become a kind of tyrant in the city".[1]

In one of the pleadings of Lysias,[2] the orator very coolly speaks of it, by the by, as a maxim of the Athenian people, that, whenever they wanted money, they put to death some of the rich citizens as well as strangers, for the sake of the forfeiture. In mentioning this, he seems not to have any intention of blaming them ; still less of provoking them, who were his audience and judges.

Whether a man was a citizen or a stranger among that people, it seems indeed requisite, either that he should impoverish himself, or that the people would impoverish him, and perhaps kill him into the bargain. The orator last mentioned gives a pleasant account of an estate laid out in the public service [3] ; that is, above the third of it in raree-shows and figured dances.

---

[1] Pag. 885. *ex edit.* Leunclav.   [2] *Orat.* 29. *in* Nicom. 185.
[3] In order to recommend his client to the favour of the people, he enumerates all the sums he had expended. When χορηγὸς, 30 minas :

I need not insist on the GREEK tyrannies, which were altogether horrible. Even the mixed monarchies, by which most of the ancient states of GREECE were governed, before the introduction of republics, were very unsettled. Scarcely any city, but ATHENS, says ISOCRATES, could show a succession of kings for four or five generations.[1]

Besides many other obvious reasons for the instability of ancient monarchies, the equal division of property among the brothers in private families, must, by a necessary consequence, contribute to unsettle and disturb the state. The universal preference given to the elder by modern laws, though it encreases the inequality of fortunes, has, however, this good effect, that it accustoms men to the same idea in public succession, and cuts off all claim and pretension of the younger.

The new settled colony of HERACLEA, falling immediately into faction, applied to SPARTA, who sent HERIPIDAS with full authority to quiet their dissentions. This man, not provoked by any opposition, not inflamed by party

[1] *Panath.* 258.

Upon a chorus of men 20 minas ; εἰς πυρριχιστὰς, 8 minas ; ἀνδράσι χορηγῶν, 50 minas ; κυκλικῷ χορῷ, 3 minas ; Seven times trierarch, where he spent 6 talents : Taxes, once 30 minas, another time 40 ; γυμνασιαρχῶν, 12 minas ; χορηγὸς παιδικῷ χορῷ, 15 minas ; κωμωδοῖς χορηγῶν, 18 minas ; πυρριχισταῖς ἀγενείοις, 7 minas ; τριήρει ἁμιλλώμενος, 15 minas ; ἀρχιθέωρος, 30 minas : In the whole ten talents 38 minas. An immense sum for an ATHENIAN fortune, and what alone would be esteemed great riches, *Orat.* 21. 161. 'Tis true, he says, the law did not oblige him absolutely to be at so much expence, not above a fourth. But without the favour of the people, no body was so much as safe ; and this was the only way to gain it. See farther, *orat.* 25. *de pop. statu.* In another place, he introduces a speaker, who says that he had spent his whole fortune, and an immense one, eighty talents, for the people. *Orat.* 26 *de prob.* EVANDRI. The μέτοικοι, or strangers, find, says he, if they do not contribute largely enough to the people's fancy, that they have reason to repent. *Orat.* 31 *contra* PHIL. You may see with what care DEMOSTHENES displays his expences of this nature, when he pleads for himself *de corona* ; and how he exaggerates MIDIAS's stinginess in this particular, in his accusation of that criminal. All this, by the by, is a mark of a very iniquitous judicature : And yet the ATHENIANS valued themselves on having the most legal and regular administration of any people in GREECE.

rage, knew no better expedient than immediately putting
to death about 500 of the citizens.[1] A strong proof how
deeply rooted these violent maxims of government were
throughout all GREECE.

If such was the disposition of men's minds among that
refined people, what may be expected in the commonwealths of ITALY, AFRIC, SPAIN, and GAUL, which were
denominated barbarous ? Why otherwise did the GREEKS
so much value themselves on their humanity, gentleness,
and moderation, above all other nations ? This reasoning seems very natural. But unluckily the history of the
ROMAN commonwealth, in its earlier times, if we give
credit to the received accounts, presents an opposite
conclusion. No blood was ever shed in any sedition at
ROME, till the murder of the GRACCHI. DIONYSIUS
HALICARNASSÆUS,[2] observing the singular humanity of
the ROMAN people in this particular, makes use of it
as an argument that they were originally of GRECIAN
extraction : Whence we may conclude, that the factions and revolutions in the barbarous republics were
usually more violent than even those of GREECE above-
mentioned.

If the ROMANS were so late in coming to blows, they
made ample compensation, after they had once entered
upon the bloody scene ; and APPIAN's history of their
civil wars contains the most frightful picture of massacres,
proscriptions, and forfeitures, that ever was presented to
the world. What pleases most, in that historian, is that
he seems to feel a proper resentment of these barbarous
proceedings ; and talks not with that provoking coolness
and indifference, which custom had produced in many
of the GREEK historians.[3]

---

[1] DIOD. SIC. lib. xiv. 38.   [2] Lib. i. 89.

[3] The authorities cited above, are all historians, orators, and philosophers
whose testimony is unquestioned. 'Tis dangerous to rely upon writers who
deal in ridicule and satyr. What will posterity, for instance, infer from
this passage of Dr. SWIFT ? "I told him, that in the kingdom of TRIBNIA
(BRITAIN) by the natives called LANGDON (LONDON) where I had sojourned

The maxims of ancient politics contain, in general, so little humanity and moderation, that it seems superfluous to give any particular reason for the acts of violence committed at any particular period. Yet I cannot forbear observing, that the laws, in the later period of the ROMAN commonwealth, were so absurdly contrived, that they obliged the heads of parties to have recourse to these extremities. All capital punishments were abolished : However criminal, or, what is more, however dangerous any citizen might be, he could not regularly be punished otherwise than by banishment : And it became necessary, in the revolutions of party, to draw the sword of private vengeance ; nor was it easy, when laws were once violated, to set bounds to these sanguinary proceedings. Had BRUTUS himself prevailed over the *triumvirate*, could he, in common prudence have allowed OCTAVIUS and ANTHONY, to live, and have contented himself with banishing them to RHODES or MARSEILLES, where they might still have plotted new commotions and rebellions ? His executing C. ANTONIUS, brother to the *triumvir*, shows evidently his sense of the matter. Did not CICERO, with the approbation of all the wise and virtuous of ROME, arbitrarily put to death CATILINE's accomplices, contrary to law, and without any trial or form of process ? And if he moderated his executions, did it not proceed, either from the clemency of his temper, or the conjunctures of the times ? A

---

some time in my travels, the bulk of the people consist, in a manner, wholly of discoverers, witnesses, informers, accusers, prosecutors, evidences, swearers, together with their several subservient and subaltern instruments, all under the colours, the conduct, and pay of ministers of state and their deputies. The plots in that kingdom are usually the workmanship of those persons", &c. GULLIVER's *travels*. Such a representation might suit the government of ATHENS ; but not that of ENGLAND, which is a prodigy even in modern times, for humanity, justice and liberty. Yet the Doctor's satyr, tho' carried to extremes, as is usual with him, even beyond other satyrical writers, did not altogether want an object. The Bishop of ROCHESTER, who was his friend, and of the same party, had been banished a little before by a bill of attainder, with great justice, but without such a proof as was legal, or according to strict forms of common law.

wretched security in a government which pretends to laws and liberty !

Thus, one extreme produces another. In the same manner as excessive severity in the laws is apt to beget great relaxation in their execution ; so their excessive lenity naturally produces cruelty and barbarity. It is dangerous to force us, in any case, to pass their sacred boundaries.

One general cause of the disorders, so frequent in all ancient governments, seems to have consisted in the great difficulty of establishing any Aristocracy in those ages, and the perpetual discontents and seditions of the people, whenever even the meanest and most beggarly were excluded from the legislature and from public offices. The very quality of *freemen* gave such a rank, being opposed to that of slave, that it seemed to entitle the possessor to every power and privilege of the commonwealth. SOLON's [1] laws excluded no freeman from votes or elections, but confined some magistracies to a particular *census* ; yet were the people never satisfied till those laws were repealed. By the treaty with ANTIPATER,[2] no ATHENIAN was allowed a vote whose *census* was less than 2000 *drachmas* (about 60*l. Sterling*). And though such a government would to us appear sufficiently democratical, it was so disagreeable to that people, that above two-thirds of them immediately left their country.[3] CASSANDER reduced that *census* to the half [4] ; yet still the government was considered as an oligarchical tyranny, and the effect of foreign violence.

SERVIUS TULLIUS's [5] laws seem equal and reasonable, by fixing the power in proportion to the property : Yet the ROMAN people could never be brought quietly to submit to them.

In those days there was no medium between a severe, jealous Aristocracy, ruling over discontented subjects ;

---

[1] PLUTARCHUS *in vita* SOLON, 18.   [2] DIOD. SIC. lib. xviii. 18.
[3] Id. ibid.   [4] Id. ibid. 74.   [5] TIT. LIV. lib. i. cap. 43.

and a turbulent, factious, tyrannical Democracy. *At present, there is not one republic in EUROPE, from one extremity of it to the other, that is not remarkable for justice, lenity, and stability, equal to, or even beyond MARSEILLES, RHODES, or the most celebrated in antiquity. Almost all of them are well-tempered Aristocracies.

But *thirdly*, there are many other circumstances, in which ancient nations seem inferior to the modern, both for the happiness and encrease of mankind. Trade, manufactures, industry, were no where, in former ages, so flourishing as they are at present in EUROPE. The only garb of the ancients, both for males and females, seems to have been a kind of flannel, which they wore commonly white or grey, and which they scoured as often as it became dirty. TYRE, which carried on, after CARTHAGE, the greatest commerce of any city in the MEDITERRANEAN, before it was destroyed by ALEXANDER, was no mighty city, if we credit ARRIAN's account of its inhabitants.[1] ATHENS is commonly supposed to have been a trading city : But it was as populous before the MEDIAN war as at any time after it, according to HERODOTUS[2] ; yet its commerce, at that time, was so inconsiderable, that, as the same historian observes,[3] even the neighbouring coasts of ASIA were as little frequented by the GREEK as the pillars of HERCULES : For beyond these he conceived nothing.

Great interest of money, and great profits of trade, are an infallible indication, that industry and commerce are but in their infancy. We read in LYSIAS[4] of 100 *per cent.* profit made on a cargo of two talents, sent to no greater distance than from ATHENS to the ADRIATIC : Nor is

---

[1] Lib. ii. 24. There were 8,000 killed during the siege ; and the captives amounted to 30,000. DIODORUS SICULUS, lib. xvii. 46, says only 13,000 : But he accounts for this small number, by saying that the TYRIANS had sent away before-hand part of their wives and children to CARTHAGE.

[2] Lib. v. 97, he makes the number of the citizens amount to 30,000.

[3] Ib. viii. 132.   [4] *Orat.* 32, 908 *advers.* DIOGIT.

* [*The rest of this paragraph not in A–H*].

this mentioned as an instance of extraordinary profit. ANTIDORUS, says DEMOSTHENES,[1] paid three talents and a half for a house which he let at a talent a year : And the orator blames his own tutors for not employing his money to like advantage. My fortune, says he, in eleven years minority, ought to have been tripled. The value of 20 of the slaves left by his father, he computes at 40 minas, and the yearly profit of their labour at 12.[2] The most moderate interest at ATHENS, (for there was higher [3] often paid) was 12 *per cent.*,[4] and that paid monthly. Not to insist upon the high interest, to which the vast sums distributed in elections had raised money [5] at ROME, we find, that VERRES, before that factious period, stated 24 *per cent.* for money which he left in the hands of the publicans : And though CICERO exclaims against this article, it is not on account of the extravagant usury ; but because it had never been customary to state any interest on such occasions.[6] Interest, indeed, sunk at Rome, after the settlement of the empire : But it never remained any considerable time so low, as in the commercial states of modern times.[7]

Among the other inconveniencies, which the ATHENIANS felt from the fortifying of DECELIA by the LACEDEMONIANS, it is represented by THUCYDIDES,[8] as one of the most considerable, that they could not bring over their corn from EUBEA by land, passing by OROPUS ; but were obliged to embark it, and to sail round the promontory of SUNIUM. A surprising instance of the imperfection of ancient navigation ! For the water-carriage is not here above double the land.

I do not remember a passage in any ancient author, where the growth of a city is ascribed to the establishment of a manufacture. The commerce, which is said to

[1] *Contra* APHOB. p. 25. *ex edit.* ALDI.
[2] Id. p. 19. [3] Id. ibid.
[4] Id. ibid. and AESCHINES *contra* CTESIPH. 104.
[5] *Epist. ad.* ATTIC. lib. iv. epist. 15. [6] *Contra* VERR. *orat.* 3, 71.
[7] See Essay IV ["Of Interest"]. [8] Lib. vii. 28.

flourish, is chiefly the exchange of those commodities, for which different soils and climates were suited. The sale of wine and oil into AFRICA, according to DIODORUS SICULUS,[1] was the foundation of the riches of AGRIGENTUM. The situation of the city of SYBARIS, according to the same author,[2] was the cause of its immense populousness ; being built near the two rivers CRATHYS and SYBARIS. But these two rivers, we may observe, are not navigable ; and could only produce some fertile vallies, for agriculture and tillage ; an advantage so inconsiderable, that a modern writer would scarcely have taken notice of it.

The barbarity of the ancient tyrants, together with the extreme love of liberty, which animated those ages, must have banished every merchant and manufacturer, and have quite depopulated the state, had it subsisted upon industry and commerce. While the cruel and suspicious DIONYSIUS was carrying on his butcheries, who, that was not detained by his landed property, and could have carried with him any art or skill to procure a subsistence in other countries, would have remained exposed to such implacable barbarity ? The persecutions of PHILIP II. and LEWIS XIV. filled all EUROPE with the manufacturers of FLANDERS and of FRANCE.

I grant, that agriculture is the species of industry chiefly requisite to the subsistence of multitudes ; and it is possible, that this industry may flourish, even where manufactures and other arts are unknown and neglected. SWISSERLAND is at present a remarkable instance where, we find, at once, the most skilful husbandmen, and the most bungling tradesmen, that are to be met with in EUROPE. That agriculture flourished in GREECE and ITALY, at least in some parts of them, and at some periods, we have reason to presume : And whether the mechanical arts had reached the same degree of perfection, may not be esteemed so material ; especially, if we consider the great equality of riches in the ancient republics, where

[1] Lib. xiii. 81.   [2] Lib. xii. 9.

each family was obliged to cultivate, with the greatest care and industry, its own little field, in order to its subsistence.

But is it just reasoning, because agriculture may, in some instances, flourish without trade or manufactures, to conclude, that, in any great extent of country, and for any great tract of time, it would subsist alone? The most natural way, surely, of encouraging husbandry, is, first, to excite other kinds of industry, and thereby afford the labourer a ready market for his commodities, and a return of such goods as may contribute to his pleasure and enjoyment. This method is infallible and universal; and, as it prevails more in modern government than in the ancient, it affords a presumption of the superior populousness of the former.

Every man, says XENOPHON,[1] may be a farmer: No art or skill is requisite: All consists in industry, and in attention to the execution. A strong proof, as COLUMELLA hints, that agriculture was but little known in the age of XENOPHON.

All our later improvements and refinements, have they done nothing towards the easy subsistence of men, and consequently towards their propagation and encrease? Our superior skill in mechanics; the discovery of new worlds, by which commerce has been so much enlarged; the establishment of posts; and the use of bills of exchange: These seem all extremely useful to the encouragement of art, industry, and populousness. Were we to strike off these, what a check should we give to every kind of business and labour, and what multitudes of families would immediately perish from want and hunger? And it seems not probable, that we could supply the place of these new inventions by any other regulation or institution.

Have we reason to think, that the police of ancient states was any wise comparable to that of modern, or that

[1] *Oecon.* 15, 10.

men had then equal security, either at home, or in their journies by land or water ? I question not, but every impartial examiner would give us the preference in this particular.[1]

Thus, upon comparing the whole, it seems impossible to assign any just reason, why the world should have been more populous in ancient than in modern times. The equality of property among the ancients, liberty, and the small divisions of their states, were indeed circumstances favourable to the propagation of mankind : But their wars were more bloody and destructive, their governments more factious and unsettled, commerce and manufactures more feeble and languishing, and the general police more loose and irregular. These latter disadvantages seem to form a sufficient counter-balance to the former advantages ; and rather favour the opposite opinion to that which commonly prevails with regard to this subject.

But there is no reasoning, it may be said, against matter of fact. If it appear that the world was then more populous than ,at present, we may be assured that our conjectures are false, and that we have overlooked some material circumstance in the comparison. This I readily own : All our preceding reasonings, I acknowledge to be mere trifling, or, at least, small skirmishes and frivolous rencounters, which decide nothing. But unluckily the main combat, where we compare facts, cannot be rendered much more decisive. The facts, delivered by ancient authors, are either so uncertain or so imperfect as to afford us nothing positive in this matter. How indeed could it be otherwise ? The very facts, which we must oppose to them, in computing the populousness of modern states, are far from being either certain or complete. Many grounds of calculation proceeded on by celebrated writers, are little better than those of the Emperor HELIOGABALUS, who formed an estimate of the immense greatness of

[1] See Part I. Essay XI ["Of the Dignity or Meanness of Human Nature"].

ROME, from ten thousand pound weight of cobwebs which had been found in that city.[1]

It is to be remarked, that all kinds of numbers are uncertain in ancient manuscripts, and have been subject to much greater corruptions than any other part of the text ; and that for an obvious reason. Any alteration, in other places, commonly affects the sense or grammar, and is more readily perceived by the reader and transcriber.

Few enumerations of inhabitants have been made of any tract of country by any ancient author of good authority, so as to afford us a large enough view for comparison.

It is probable, that there was formerly a good foundation for the number of citizens assigned to any free city ; because they entered for a share in the government, and there were exact registers kept of them. But as the number of slaves is seldom mentioned, this leaves us in as great uncertainty as ever, with regard to the populousness even of single cities.

The first page of THUCYDIDES is, in my opinion, the commencement of real history. All preceding narrations are so intermixed with fable, that philosophers ought to abandon them, in a great measure, to the embellishment of poets and orators.[2]

With regard to remote times, the numbers of people assigned are often ridiculous, and lose all credit and authority. The free citizens of SYBARIS, able to bear

[1] AELII LAMPRID. *in vita* HELIOGAB. cap. 26.

[2] In general, there is more candour and sincerity in ancient historians, but less exactness and care, than in the moderns. Our speculative factions, especially those of religion, throw such an illusion over our minds, that men seem to regard impartiality to their adversaries and to heretics, as a vice or weakness : But the commonness of books, by means of printing, has obliged modern historians to be more careful in avoiding contradictions and incongruities. DIODORUS SICULUS is a good writer, but it is with pain I see his narration contradict, in so many particulars, the two most authentic pieces of all GREEK history, to wit, XENOPHON's expedition, and DEMOSTHENES's orations. PLUTARCH and APPIAN seem scarce ever to have read CICERO's epistles.

arms, and actually drawn out in battle, were 300,000.
They encountered at SIAGRA with 100,000 citizens of
CROTONA, another GREEK city contiguous to them ; and
were defeated. This is DIODORUS SICULUS's [1] account ;
and is very seriously insisted on by that historian.[2]
STRABO also mentions the same number of SYBARITES.

DIODORUS SICULUS,[3] enumerating the inhabitants of
AGRIGENTUM, when it was destroyed by the CARTHA-
GINIANS, says, that they amounted to 20,000 citizens,
200,000 strangers, besides slaves, who, in so opulent a
city as he represents it, would probably be, at least, as
numerous. We must remark, that the women and the
children are not included ; and that, therefore, upon the
whole, this city must have contained near two millions
of inhabitants.[4] And what was the reason of so immense
an encrease ! They were industrious in cultivating the
neighbouring fields, not exceeding a small ENGLISH county ;
and they traded with their wine and oil to AFRICA, which,
at that time, produced none of these commodities.

PTOLEMY, says THEOCRITUS,[5] commands 33,339 cities.
I suppose the singularity of the number was the reason of
assigning it. DIODORUS SICULUS [6] assigns three millions
of inhabitants to ÆGYPT, a small number : But then he
makes the number of cities amount to 18,000 : An evident contradiction.

He says,[7] the people were formerly seven millions.
Thus remote times are always most envied and admired.

That XERXES's army was extremely numerous, I can
readily believe ; both from the great extent of his empire,
and from the practice among the eastern nations, of
encumbering their camp with a superfluous multitude :
But will any rational man cite HERODOTUS's wonderful
narrations as an authority ? There is something very

[1] Lib. xii. 9.   [2] Lib. vi. 26.   [3] Lib. xiii. 90.
[4] DIOGENES LAERTIUS (*in vita* EMPEDOCLIS) says, that AGRIGENTUM
contained only 800,000 inhabitants.
[5] Idyll. 17.   [6] Lib. i. 18.   [7] Id. ibid.

rational, I own, in LYSIAS's [1] argument upon this subject. Had not XERXES's army been incredibly numerous, says he, he had never made a bridge over the HELLESPONT : It had been much easier to have transported his men over so short a passage, with the numerous shipping of which he was master.

POLYBIUS [2] says, that the ROMANS, between the first and second PUNIC wars, being threatened with an invasion from the GAULS, mustered all their own forces, and those of their allies, and found them amount to seven hundred thousand men able to bear arms : A great number surely, and which, when joined to the slaves, is *probably not less, if not rather more, than that extent of country affords at present.[3] The enumeration too seems to have been made with some exactness ; and POLYBIUS gives us the detail of the particulars. But might not the number be magnified, in order to encourage the people ?

DIODORUS SICULUS [4] makes the same enumeration amount to near a million. These variations are suspicious. He plainly too supposes, that ITALY in his time was not so populous : Another suspicious circumstance. For who can believe, that the inhabitants of that country diminished from the time of the first PUNIC war to that of the *triumvirates* ?

JULIUS CÆSAR, according to APPIAN,[5] encountered four millions of GAULS, killed one million, and made another million prisoners.[6] Supposing the number of the enemy's army and that of the slain could be exactly assigned, which never is possible ; how could it be known how often the

---

[1] *Orat. funebris*, 193.   [2] Lib. ii. 24.

[3] The country that supplied this number, was not above a third of ITALY, *viz.* the Pope's dominions, TUSCANY, and a part of the kingdom of NAPLES : †But perhaps in those early times there were very few slaves, except in ROME, or the great cities.

[4] Lib. ii. 5.   [5] CELTICA, c. 2.

[6] PLUTARCH (*in vita* CAES. 15) makes the number that CAESAR fought with amount to three millions ; JULIAN (*in* CAESARIBUS) to two.

* probably not less, if not rather more=probably more [*A–C*].

† [*The rest of this sentence not in A–B*].

same man returned into the armies, or how distinguish the new from the old levied soldiers ? No attention ought ever to be given to such loose, exaggerated calculations ; especially where the author does not tell us the mediums, upon which the calculations were founded.

PATERCULUS [1] makes the number of GAULS killed by CÆSAR amount only to 400,000 : A more probable account, and more easily reconciled to the history of these wars given by that conqueror himself in his Commentaries.[2] *The most bloody of his battles were fought against the HELVETII and the GERMANS.

One would imagine, that every circumstance of the life and actions of DIONYSIUS the elder might be regarded as authentic, and free from all fabulous exaggeration ; both because he lived at a time when letters flourished most in GREECE, and because his chief historian was PHILISTUS, a man allowed to be of great genius, and who was a courtier and minister of that prince. But can we admit, that he had a standing army of 100,000 foot, 10,000 horse, and a fleet of 400 gallies ? [3] These, we may observe, were mercenary forces, and subsisted upon pay, like our armies in EUROPE. For the citizens were all disarmed ; and when DION afterwards invaded SICILY, and called on his countrymen to vindicate their liberty, he was obliged to bring arms along with him, which he distributed among those who joined him.[4] In a state where agriculture alone flourishes, there may be many inhabitants ; and if these be all armed and disciplined, a

---

[1] Lib. ii. cap. 47.

[2] †PLINY, lib. vii. cap. 25, says, that CÆSAR used to boast, that there had fallen in battle against him one million one hundred and ninety-two thousand men, besides those who perished in the civil wars. It is not probable, that that conqueror could ever pretend to be so exact in his computation. But allowing the fact, it is likely, that the HELVETII, GERMANS, and BRITONS, whom he slaughtered, would amount to near a half of the number.

[3] DIOD. SIC. lib. ii. 5. [4] PLUTARCH *in vita* DIONYS. 25.

* [*This sentence not in A–H*]. † [*This footnote not in A–H*].

great force may be called out upon occasion : But great bodies of mercenary troops can never be maintained, without either great trade and numerous manufactures, or extensive dominions. The United Provinces never were masters of such a force by sea and land, as that which is said to belong to Dionysius ; yet they possess as large a territory, perfectly well cultivated, and have much more resources from their commerce and industry. Diodorus Siculus allows, that, even in his time, the army of Dionysius appeared incredible ; that is, as I interpret it, was entirely a fiction, and the opinion arose from the exaggerated flattery of the courtiers, and perhaps from the vanity and policy of the tyrant himself.*

It is a usual fallacy, to consider all the ages of antiquity

---

* +The critical art may very justly be suspected of temerity when it pretends to correct or dispute the plain testimony of antient historians by any probable or analogical reasonings : Yet the licence of authors upon all subjects, particularly with regard to numbers, is so great, that we ought still to retain a kind of doubt or reserve, whenever the facts advanc'd depart, in the least, from the common bounds of nature and experience. I shall give an instance with regard to modern history. Sir *William Temple* tells us, in his memoirs, that, having a free conversation with *Charles* the II, he took the opportunity of representing to that monarch the impossibility of introducing into this island the religion and government of *France*, chiefly on account of the great force requisite to subdue the spirit and liberty of so brave a people. "The Romans, says he, were forc'd to keep up twelve legions for that purpose" (a great absurdity [1]) "and *Cromwell* left an army of near eighty thousand men". Must not this last be regarded as unquestion'd by future critics, when they find it asserted by a wise and learned minister of state contemporary to the fact, and who address his discourse, upon an ungrateful subject, to a great monarch who was also contemporary, and who himself broke those very forces about fourteen years before ? Yet by the most undoubted authority, we may insist, that *Cromwell's* army, when he died, did not amount to half the number here mention'd. [2] [A–D].

[1] Strabo, lib. 4, says, that one legion would be sufficient, with a few cavalry ; but the *Romans* commonly kept up somewhat a greater force in this island, which they never took the pains entirely to subdue.

[2] [*Not in A–B*]. It appears that Cromwell's parliament, in 1656, settled but 1,300,000 pounds a year on him for the constant charges of government in all the three kingdoms. See Scobel, chap. 31. This was to supply the fleet, army, and civil list. It appears from Whitelocke, that in the year 1649, the sum of 80,000 pounds a month was the estimate for 40,000 men. We must conclude, therefore, that Cromwell had much less than that number upon pay in 1656. In the very instrument of government, 20,000 foot and 10,000 horse are fixed by Cromwell himself, and afterwards confirmed by the parliament, as the regular standing army of the commonwealth. That number, indeed, seems not to have been much exceeded during the whole time of the protectorship. See farther Thurlo, Vol. ii, pp. 413, 499, 568. We may there see, that though the Protector had more considerable armies in *Ireland* and *Scotland*, he had not sometimes more than 4,000 or 5,000 men in England.

as one period, and to compute the numbers contained in the great cities mentioned by ancient authors, as if these cities had been all cotemporary. The GREEK colonies flourished extremely in SICILY during the age of ALEXANDER : But in AUGUSTUS's time they were so decayed, that almost all the produce of that fertile island was consumed in ITALY.[1]

Let us now examine the numbers of inhabitants assigned to particular cities in antiquity ; and omitting the numbers of NINEVEH, BABYLON, and the EGYPTIAN THEBES, let us confine ourselves to the sphere of real history, to the GRECIAN and ROMAN states. I must own, the more I consider this subject, the more am I inclined to scepticism, with regard to the great populousness ascribed to ancient times.

ATHENS is said by PLATO [2] to be a very great city ; and it was surely the greatest of all the GREEK [3] cities, except SYRACUSE, which was nearly about the same size in THUCYDIDES's [4] time, and afterwards encreased beyond it. For CICERO [5] mentions it as the greatest of all the GREEK cities in his time ; not comprehending, I suppose, either ANTIOCH or ALEXANDRIA under that denomination. ATHENÆUS [6] says, that, by the enumeration of DEMETRIUS PHALEREUS, there were in ATHENS 21,000 citizens, 10,000 strangers, and 400,000 slaves. This number is much insisted on by those whose opinion I call in question, and is esteemed a fundamental fact to their purpose : But, in my opinion, there is no point of criticism more certain, than that ATHENÆUS and CTESICLES, whom he quotes, are here mistaken, and that the number of slaves is, at least,

---

[1] STRABO, lib. vi. 273.   [2] *Apolog.* SOCR. 29 D.

[3] ARGOS seems also to have been a great city ; for LYSIAS contents himself with saying that it did not exceed ATHENS. *Orat.* 34, 922.

[4] Lib. vi. See also PLUTARCH *in vita* NICIAE, 17.

[5] *Orat. contra* VERREM, lib. iv. cap. 52. STRABO, lib. vi. 270, says, it was twenty-two miles in compass. But then we are to consider, that it contained two harbours within it ; one of which was a very large one, and might be regarded as a kind of bay.

[6] Lib. vi. cap. 20.

augmented by a whole cypher, and ought not to be regarded as more than 40,000.

First, When the number of citizens is said to be 21,000 by ATHENÆUS,[1] men of full age are only understood. For, (1.) HERODOTUS says,[2] that ARISTAGORAS, ambassador from the IONIANS, found it harder to deceive one SPARTAN than 30,000 ATHENIANS ; meaning, in a loose way, the whole state, supposed to be met in one popular assembly, excluding the women and children. (2.) THUCYDIDES [3] says, that, making allowance for all the absentees in the fleet, army, garrisons, and for people employed in their private affairs, the ATHENIAN assembly never rose to five thousand. (3.) The forces, enumerated by the same historian,[4] being all citizens, and amounting to 13,000 heavy-armed infantry, prove the same method of calculation ; as also the whole tenor of the GREEK historians, who always understand men of full age when they assign the number of citizens in any republic. Now, these being but the fourth of the inhabitants, the free ATHENIANS were by this account 84,000 ; the strangers 40,000 ; and the slaves, calculating by the smaller number, and allowing that they married and propagated at the same rate with freemen, were 160,000 ; and the whole of the inhabitants 284,000 : A number surely large enough. The other number, 1,720,000, makes ATHENS larger than LONDON and PARIS united.

Secondly, There were but 10,000 houses in ATHENS.[5]

Thirdly, Though the extent of the walls, as given us by THUCYDIDES,[6] be great, (to wit, eighteen miles, beside the sea-coast) : Yet XENOPHON [7] says, there was much waste ground within the walls. They seem indeed to have joined four distinct and separate cities.[8]

---

[1] DEMOSTHENES assigns 20,000 ; *contra* ARISTOG. 785.
[2] Lib. v. 99.   [3] Lib. viii. 72.
[4] Lib. ii. 13. DIODORUS SICULUS's account perfectly agrees, lib. xii. 40.
[5] XENOPHON. *Mem.* lib. iii. 6, 14.
[6] Lib. ii. 13.   [7] *De ratione red.* 2, 6.
[8] We are to observe, that when DIONYSIUS HALYCARNASSAEUS says,

Fourthly, No insurrection of the slaves, or suspicion of insurrection, is ever mentioned by historians ; except one commotion of the miners.[1]

Fifthly, The treatment of slaves by the ATHENIANS is said by XENOPHON,[2] and DEMOSTHENES,[3] and PLAUTUS,[4] to have been extremely gentle and indulgent : Which could never have been the case, had the disproportion been twenty to one. The disproportion is not so great in any of our colonies ; yet are we obliged to exercise a rigorous military government over the negroes.

Sixthly, No man is ever esteemed rich for possessing what may be reckoned an equal distribution of property in any country, or even triple or quadruple that wealth. Thus every person in ENGLAND is computed by some to spend sixpence a day : Yet is he esteemed but poor who has five times that sum. Now TIMARCHUS is said by ÆSCHINES [5] to have been left in easy circumstances ; but he was master only of ten slaves employed in manufactures. LYSIAS and his brother, two strangers, were proscribed by the thirty for their great riches ; though they had but sixty a-piece.[6] DEMOSTHENES was left very rich by his father ; yet he had no more than fifty-two slaves.[7] His work-house, of twenty cabinet-makers, is said to be a very considerable manufactory.[8]

Seventhly, During the DECELIAN war, as the GREEK historians call it, 20,000 slaves deserted, and brought the

[1] ATHEN. lib. vi. 104.
[2] *De rep.* ATHEN. 1.
[3] PHILIP. 3, 31.
[4] STICHO. 3, 1, 39.
[5] *Contra* TIMARCH. 42.
[6] *Orat.* xii.
[7] *Contra* APHOB. 816.
[8] Ibid.

that if we regard the ancient walls of ROME, the extent of that city will not appear greater than that of ATHENS ; he must mean the ACROPOLIS and high town only. No ancient author ever speaks of the PYRAEUM, PHALERUS, and MUNYCHIA, as the same with ATHENS. Much less can it be supposed, that DIONYSIUS would consider the matter in that light, after the walls of CIMON and PERICLES were destroyed, and ATHENS was entirely separated from these other towns. This observation destroys all VOSSIUS's reasonings, and introduces common sense into these calculations.

ATHENIANS to great distress, as we learn from THUCYDIDES.[1] This could not have happened, had they been only the twentieth part. The best slaves would not desert.

Eighthly, XENOPHON [2] proposes a scheme for maintaining by the public 10,000 slaves : And that so great a number may possibly be supported, any one will be convinced, says he, who considers the numbers we possessed before the DECELIAN war. A way of speaking altogether incompatible with the larger number of ATHENÆUS.

Ninthly, The whole *census* of the state of ATHENS was less than 6000 talents. And though numbers in ancient manuscripts be often suspected by critics, yet this is unexceptionable ; both because DEMOSTHENES,[3] who gives it, gives also the detail, which checks him ; and because POLYBIUS [4] assigns the same number, and reasons upon it. Now, the most vulgar slave could yield by his labour an *obolus* a day, over and above his maintenance, as we learn from XENOPHON,[5] who says, that NICIAS's overseer paid his master so much for slaves, whom he employed *in mines. If you will take the pains to estimate an *obolus* a day, and the slaves at 400,000, computing only at four years purchase, you will find the sum above 12,000 talents ; even though allowance be made for the great number of holidays in ATHENS. Besides, many of the slaves would have a much greater value from their art. The lowest that DEMOSTHENES estimates any of his [6] father's slaves is two minas a head. And upon this supposition, it is a little difficult, I confess, to reconcile even the number of 40,000 slaves with the *census* of 6000 talents.

Tenthly, CHIOS is said by THUCYDIDES,[7] to contain more slaves than any GREEK city, except SPARTA. SPARTA then

[1] Lib. vii. 27.
[2] *De rat. red.* 4, 25.
[3] *De classibus,* 183.
[4] Lib. ii. cap. 62.
[5] *De rat. red.* 4, 14.
[6] *Contra* APHOBUM, 816.
[7] Lib. viii. 40.

* in mines = in digging of mines, and also kept up the number of slaves [*A–B*] ; in digging of mines [*C–H*].

had more than ATHENS, in proportion to the number of citizens. The SPARTANS were 9000 in the town, 30,000 in the country.[1] The male slaves, therefore, of full age, must have been more than 780,000 ; the whole more than 3,120,000. A number impossible to be maintained in a narrow barren country, such as LACONIA, which has no trade. Had the HELOTES been so very numerous, the murder of 2000 mentioned by THUCYDIDES,[2] would have irritated them, without weakening them.

Besides, we are to consider, that the number assigned by ATHENÆUS,[3] whatever it is, comprehends all the inhabitants of ATTICA, as well as those of ATHENS. The ATHENIANS affected much a country life, as we learn from THUCYDIDES[4] ; and when they were all chased into town, by the invasion of their territory during the PELOPON-NESIAN war, the city was not able to contain them ; and they were obliged to lie in the porticoes, temples, and even streets, for want of lodging.[5]

The same remark is to be extended to all the other GREEK cities ; and when the number of citizens is assigned, we must always understand it to comprehend the inhabitants of the neighbouring country, as well as of the city. Yet, even with this allowance, it must be confessed, that GREECE was a populous country, and exceeded what we could imagine concerning so narrow a territory, naturally not very fertile, and which drew no supplies of corn from other places. For, excepting ATHENS, which traded to PONTUS for that commodity, the other cities seem to have subsisted chiefly from their neighbouring territory.[6]

---

[1] PLUTARCH, *in vita* LYCURG. 8.   [2] Lib. iv. 80.

[3] The same author affirms, that CORINTH had once 460,000 slaves, ÆGINA 470,000. But the foregoing arguments hold stronger against these facts, which are indeed entirely absurd and impossible. It is however remarkable, that ATHENÆUS cites so great an authority as ARISTOTLE for this last fact : And the scholiast on PINDAR mentions the same number of slaves in ÆGINA.

[4] Lib. ii. 14.   [5] Id. lib. ii. 17.

[6] DEMOST. *contra* LEPT. 466. The Athenians brought yearly from PONTUS 400,000 medimni or bushels of corn, as appeared from the custom-

RHODES is well known to have been a city of extensive commerce, and of great fame and splendor ; yet it contained only 6,000 citizens able to bear arms, when it was besieged by DEMETRIUS.[1]

THEBES was always one of the capital cities of GREECE[2]: But the number of its citizens exceeded not those of RHODES.[3] PHLIASIA is said to be a small city by XENOPHON,[4] yet we find that it contained 6,000 citizens.[5] I pretend not to reconcile these two facts. *Perhaps,

[1] DIOD. SIC. lib. xx. 84.   [2] ISOCR. *paneg.*

[3] DIOD. SIC. lib. xvii. 14.† When Alexander attacked Thebes, we may safely conclude that almost all the inhabitants were present. Whoever is acquainted with the spirit of the Greeks, especially of the Thebans, will never suspect that any of them would desert their country when it was reduced to such extreme peril and distress. As Alexander took the town by storm, all those who bore arms were put to the sword without mercy, and they amounted only to 6,000 men. Among these were some strangers and manumitted slaves. The captives, consisting of old men, women, children, and slaves, were sold, and they amounted to 30,000. We may therefore conclude, that the free citizens in Thebes, of both sexes and all ages, were near 24,000, the strangers and slaves about 12,000. These last, we may observe, were somewhat fewer in proportion than at Athens, as is reasonable to imagine from this circumstance, that Athens was a town of more trade to support slaves, and of more entertainment to allure strangers. It is also to be remarked, that 36,000 was the whole number of people, both in the city of Thebes and the neighbouring territory. A very moderate number, it must be confessed ; and this computation, being founded on facts which appear indisputable, must have great weight in the present controversy. The above-mentioned number of Rhodians, too, were all the inhabitants of the island who were free, and able to bear arms.

[4] *Hist.* GRAEC. lib. vii. 2, 1.   [5] Id. lib. vii.

* [*The rest of this paragraph not in A–B*].
† lib. xvii. 14=lib. 15 and 17 [*A–B, omitting rest of footnote*].

---

house books. And this was the greater part of their importation of corn. This, by the by, is a strong proof that there is some great mistake in the foregoing passage of Athenæus. For Attica itself was so barren of corn, that it produced not enough even to maintain the peasants. Tit. Liv. lib. xliii, cap. 6. ‡And 400,000 medimni would scarcely feed 100,000 men during a twelvemonth. Lucian, in his *navigium sive vota*, says, that a ship, which, by the dimensions he gives, seems to have been about the size of our third rates, carried as much corn as would maintain Attica for a twelvemonth. But perhaps Athens was decayed at that time ; and, besides, it is not safe to trust to such loose rhetorical calculations.

‡ [*This sentence not in A–G ; the next not in A–F*].

XENOPHON calls PHLIASIA a small town, because it made
but a small figure in GREECE, and maintained only a
subordinate alliance with SPARTA ; or perhaps the
country, belonging to it, was extensive, and most of the
citizens were employed in the cultivation of it, and dwelt
in the neighbouring villages.

MANTINEA was equal to any city in ARCADIA [1] :
Consequently it was equal to MEGALOPOLIS, which was
fifty stadia, or six miles and a quarter in circumference.[2]
But MANTINEA had only 3,000 citizens.[3] The GREEK
cities, therefore, contained often fields and gardens,
together with the houses ; and we cannot judge of them
by the extent of their walls. ATHENS contained no more
than 10,000 houses ; yet its walls, with the sea-coast,
were above twenty miles in extent. SYRACUSE was twenty-
two miles in circumference ; yet was scarcely ever spoken
of by the ancients as more populous than ATHENS. BABY-
LON was a square of fifteen miles, or sixty miles in circuit ;
but it contained large cultivated fields and inclosures, as
we learn from PLINY. Though AURELIAN's wall was fifty
miles in circumference [4] ; the circuit of all the thirteen
divisions of ROME, taken apart, according to PUBLIUS
VICTOR, was only about forty-three miles. When an
enemy invaded the country, all the inhabitants retired
within the walls of the ancient cities, with their cattle and
furniture, and instruments of husbandry : and the great
height, to which the walls were raised, enabled a small
number to defend them with facility.

SPARTA, says XENOPHON,[5] is one of the cities of GREECE
that has the fewest inhabitants. Yet POLYBIUS [6] says
that it was forty-eight stadia in circumference, and was
round.

All the ÆTOLIANS able to bear arms in ANTIPATER's

---

[1] POLYB. lib. ii. 56. [2] POLYB. lib. ix. cap. 20.
[3] LYSIAS, *orat.* 34, 92. [4] VOPISCUS *in vita* AUREL. 222 B.
[5] *De rep.* LACED. I, I. This passage is not easily reconciled with that
of PLUTARCH above, who says, that SPARTA had 9,000 citizens.
[6] POLYB. lib. ix. cap. 20.

time, deducting some few garrisons, were but ten thousand men.[1]

POLYBIUS [2] tells us, that the ACHÆAN league might, without any inconvenience, march 30 or 40,000 men : And this account seems probable : For that league comprehended the greater part of PELOPONNESUS. Yet PAUSANIAS,[3] speaking of the same period, says, that all the ACHÆANS able to bear arms, even when several manumitted slaves were joined to them, did not amount to fifteen thousand.

The THESSALIANS, till their final conquest by the ROMANS, were, in all ages, turbulent, factious, seditious, disorderly.[4] It is not therefore natural to suppose, that this part of GREECE abounded much in people.

*We are told by THUCYDIDES,[5] that the part of PELOPONNESUS, adjoining to PYLOS, was desart and uncultivated. HERODOTUS says,[6] that MACEDONIA was full of lions and wild bulls ; animals which can only inhabit vast unpeopled forests. These were the two extremities of GREECE.

†All the inhabitants of EPIRUS, of all ages, sexes, and conditions, who were sold by PAULUS ÆMILIUS, amounted only to 150,000.[7] Yet EPIRUS might be double the extent of YORKSHIRE. ‡

---

[1] DIOD. SIC. lib. xviii, 24.   [2] LEGAT.
[3] *In* ACHAICIS, 7. 15, 7.
[4] TIT. LIV. lib. xxxiv. cap. 51. PLATO *in* CRITONE, 53 D.
[5] Lib. iv. 3.   [6] Lib. vii. 126.
[7] TIT. LIV. lib. xlv. cap. 34.

---

* [*This paragraph not in A–B*].   † All the=The whole [*A–B*].
‡ +A late *French* writer, in his *observations on the Greeks*, has remark'd that *Philip of Macedon*, being declar'd captain-general of the *Greeks*, wou'd have been back'd by the force of 230,000 of that nation in his intended expedition against *Persia*. This number comprehends, I suppose, all the free citizens, throughout all the cities ; but the authority, on which that computation is founded, has, I own, escap'd either my memory or reading ; and that writer, tho' otherwise very ingenious, has given into a bad practice, of delivering a great deal of erudition, without one citation. But supposing, that that enumeration cou'd be justify'd by good authority from antiquity, we may establish the following computation. The free *Greeks* of all ages

*Justin [1] tells us, that, when Philip of Macedon was declared head of the Greek confederacy, he called a congress of all the states, except the Lacedemonians, who refused to concur ; and he found the force of the whole, upon computation, to amount to 200,000 infantry, and 15,000 cavalry. This must be understood to be all the citizens capable of bearing arms. For as the Greek republics maintained no mercenary forces, and had no militia distinct from the whole body of the citizens, it is not conceivable what other medium there could be of computation. That such an army could ever, by Greece, be brought into the field, and be maintained there, is contrary to all history. Upon this supposition, therefore, we may thus reason. The free Greeks of all ages and sexes were 860,000. The slaves, estimating them by the number of Athenian slaves as above, who seldom married or had families, were double the male citizens of full age, to wit, 430,000. And all the inhabitants of ancient Greece, excepting Laconia, were about one million two hundred and ninety thousand : No mighty number, nor exceeding what may be found at present in Scotland, a country of not much greater extent, and very indifferently peopled.

We may now consider the numbers of people in Rome and Italy, and collect all the lights afforded us by scattered passages in ancient authors. We shall find, upon the whole, a great difficulty in fixing any opinion on that head ; and no reason to support those exaggerated calculations, so much insisted on by modern writers.

[1] Lib. ix. cap. 5.

* [*This paragraph not in A–B*].

---

and sexes were 920,000 : The slaves, computing them by the number of *Athenian* slaves as above, who seldom marry'd or had families, were double the male citizens of full age, viz. 460,000. And the whole inhabitants of antient *Greece* about one million, three hundred and eighty thousand. No mighty number nor much exceeding what may be found at present in *Scotland*, a country of nearly the same extent, and which is very indifferently peopl'd [*A–B, as footnote*].

DIONYSIUS HALICARNASSÆUS [1] says, that the ancient walls of ROME were nearly of the same compass with those of ATHENS, but that the suburbs ran out to a great extent ; and it was difficult to tell, where the town ended or the country began. In some places of ROME, it appears, from the same author,[2] from JUVENAL,[3] and from other ancient writers,[4] that the houses were high, and families lived in separate storeys, one above another : But it is probable, that these were only the poorer citizens, and only in some few streets. If we may judge from the younger PLINY's [5] account of his own house, and from BARTOLI's plans of ancient buildings, the men of quality had very spacious palaces ; and their buildings were like the CHINESE houses at this day, where each apartment is separated from the rest and rises no higher than a single storey. To which if we add, that the ROMAN nobility much affected extensive porticoes, and even woods [6] in town ; we may perhaps allow VOSSIUS (though there is no manner of

---

[1] Lib. iv. 13. [2] Lib. x. 32.

[3] *Satyr.* iii. 1. 269, 270.

[4] STRABO, liv. v. says, that the emperor AUGUSTUS prohibited the raising houses higher than seventy feet. In another passage, lib. xvi. he speaks of the houses of ROME as remarkably high. See also to the same purpose VITRUVIUS, lib. ii. cap. 8. ARISTIDES the sophist, in his oration εἰς Ῥώμην, says, that ROME consisted of cities on the top of cities ; and that if one were to spread it out, and unfold it, it would cover the whole surface of ITALY. Where an author indulges himself in such extravagant declamations, and gives so much into the hyperbolical style, one knows not how far he must be reduced. But this reasoning seems natural : If ROME was built in so scattered a manner as DIONYSIUS says, and ran so much into the country, there must have been very few streets where the houses were raised so high. It is only for want of room, that any body builds in that inconvenient manner.

[5] LIB. ii. epist. 16. lib. v. epist. 6. It is true, PLINY there describes a country-house : But since that was the idea which the ancients formed of a magnificent and convenient building, the great men would certainly build the same way in town. "In laxitatem ruris excurrunt", says SENECA of the rich and voluptuous, epist. 114. VALERIUS MAXIMUS, lib. iv. cap. 4. speaking of CINCINNATUS's field of four acres, says, "Anguste se habitare nunc putat, cujus domus tantum patet quantum CINCINNATI rura patuerant". To the same purpose see lib. xxxvi. cap. 15, also lib. xviii. cap. 2.

[6] VITRUV. lih. v. cap. 11. TACIT. annal. lib. xi. cap. 3. SUETON. *in vita* OCTAV. cap. 72, &c.

reason for it) to read the famous passage of the elder PLINY [1] his own way, without admitting the extravagant consequences which he draws from it.

[1] "MOENIA ejus (ROMAE) collegere ambitu imperatoribus, censoribusque VESPASIANIS, A.U.C. 828. pass. xiii. MCC. complex a montesseptem, ipsa dividitur in regiones quatuordecim, compita earum 265. Ejusdem spatii mensura, currente a milliario in capite ROM. Fori statuto, ad singulas portas, quae sunt hodie numero 37, ita ut duodecim portae semel numerentur, praetereanturque ex veteribus septem, quae esse desierunt, efficit passuum per directum 30,775. Ad extrema vero tectorum cum castris praetoriis ab codem Milliario, per vicos omnium viarum, mensura collegit paulo amplius septuaginta millia passuum. Quo si quis altitudinem tectorum addat, dignam profecto, aestimationem concipiat, fateaturque nullius urbis magnitudinem in toto orbe potuisse ei comparari". PLIN. lib. iii. cap. 5.

All the best manuscripts of PLINY read the passage as here cited, and fix the compass of the walls of ROME to be thirteen miles. The question is, What PLINY means by 30,775 paces, and how that number was formed? The manner in which I conceive it, is this. ROME was a semicircular area of thirteen miles circumference. The Forum, and consequently the Milliarium, we know, was situated on the banks of the TYBER, and near the center of the circle, or upon the diameter of the semicircular area. Though there were thirty-seven gates to ROME, yet only twelve of them had straight streets, leading from them to the Milliarium. PLINY, therefore, having assigned the circumference of ROME, and knowing that that alone was not sufficient to give us a just notion of its surface, uses this farther method. He supposes all the streets, leading from the Milliarium to the twelve gates, to be laid together into one straight line, and supposes we run along that line, so as to count each gate once : In which case, he says, that the whole line is 30,775 paces : Or, in other words, that each street or radius of the semi-circular area is upon an average two miles and a half ; and the whole length of ROME is five miles, and its breadth about half as much, besides the scattered suburbs.

PERE HARDOUIN understands this passage in the same manner ; with regard to the laying together the several streets of ROME into one line, in order to compose 30,775 paces : But then he supposes, that streets led from the Milliarium to every gate, and that no street exceeded 800 paces in length. But (1.) a semicircular area, whose radius was only 800 paces, could never have a circumference near thirteen miles, the compass of ROME as assigned by PLINY. A radius of two miles and a half forms very nearly that circumference. (2.) There is an absurdity in supposing a city so built as to have streets running to its center from every gate in its circumference. These streets must interfere as they approach. (3.) This diminishes too much from the greatness of ancient ROME, and reduces that city below even BRISTOL or ROTTERDAM.

The sense which VOSSIUS in his *Observationes variae* puts on this passage of PLINY, errs widely in the other extreme. One manuscript of no authority, instead of thirteen miles, has assigned thirty miles for the compass of the walls of ROME. And VOSSIUS understands this only of the curvilinear part of the circumference ; supposing, that as the TYBER formed the

The number of citizens who received corn by the public distribution in the time of Augustus, were two hundred thousand.[1] This one would esteem a pretty certain ground of calculation : Yet is it attended with such circumstances as throw us back into doubt and uncertainty.

Did the poorer citizens only receive the distribution ? It was calculated, to be sure, chiefly for their benefit. But it appears from a passage in Cicero [2] that the rich might

---

[1] *Ex monument. Ancyr.*   [2] *Tusc.* *Quaest.* lib. iii. cap. 48.

---

diameter, there were no walls built on that side. But (1.) this reading is allowed to be contrary to almost all the manuscripts. (2.) Why should Pliny, a concise writer, repeat the compass of the walls of Rome in two successive sentences ? (3.) Why repeat it with so sensible a variation ? (4.) What is the meaning of Pliny's mentioning twice the Milliarium, if a line was measured that had no dependence on the Milliarium ? (5.) Aurelian's wall is said by Vopiscus to have been drawn *laxiore ambitu*, and to have comprehended all the buildings and suburbs on the north side of the Tyber ; yet its compass was only fifty miles ; and even here critics suspect some mistake or corruption in the text ; since the walls, which remain, and which are supposed to be the same with Aurelian's, exceed not twelve miles. It is not probable, that Rome would diminish from Augustus to Aurelian. It remained still the capital of the same empire ; and none of the civil wars in that long period, except the tumults on the death of Maximus and Balbinus, ever affected the city. Caracalla is said by Aurelius Victor to have encreased Rome. (6.) There are no remains of ancient buildings, which mark any such greatness of Rome. Vossius's reply to this objection seems absurd. That the rubbish would sink sixty or seventy feet under ground. It appears from Spartian (*in vita Severi*) that the five-mile stone *in via Lavicana* was out of the city. (7.) Olympiodorus and Publius Victor fix the number of houses in Rome to be betwixt forty and fifty thousand. (8.) The very extravagance of the consequences drawn by this critic, as well as Lipsius, if they be necessary, destroys the foundation on which they are grounded : That Rome contained fourteen millions of inhabitants ; while the whole kingdom of France contains only five, according to his computation, &c.

The only objection to the sense which we have affixed above to the passage of Pliny, seems to lie in this, That Pliny, after mentioning the thirty-seven gates of Rome, assigns only a reason for suppressing the seven old ones, and says nothing of the eighteen gates, the streets leading from which terminated, according to my opinion, before they reached the Forum. But as Pliny was writing to the Romans, who perfectly knew the disposition of the streets, it is not strange he should take a circumstance for granted, which was so familiar to every body. Perhaps too, many of these gates led to wharfs upon the river.

also take their portion, and that it was esteemed no reproach in them to apply for it.

To whom was the corn given ; whether only to heads of families, or to every man, woman, and child ? The portion every month was five *modii* to each [1] (about ⅚ of a bushel). This was too little for a family, and too much for an individual. A very accurate antiquary,[2] therefore, infers, that it was given to every man of full age : But he allows the matter to be uncertain.

Was it strictly enquired, whether the claimant lived within the precincts of Rome ; or was it sufficient, that he presented himself at the monthly distribution ? This last seems more probable.[3]

Were there no false claimants ? We are told,[4] that CÆSAR struck off at once 170,000, who had creeped in without a just title ; and it is very little probable, that he remedied all abuses.

But, lastly, what proportion of slaves must we assign to these citizens ? This is the most material question ; and the most uncertain. It is very doubtful, whether ATHENS can be established as a rule for ROME. Perhaps the ATHENIANS had more slaves, because they employed them in manufactures, for which a capital city, like ROME, seems not so proper. Perhaps, on the other hand, the ROMANS had more slaves, on account of their superior luxury and riches.

There were exact bills of mortality kept at ROME ; but no ancient author has given us the number of burials, except SUETONIUS,[5] who tells us, that in one season, there were 30,000 names carried to the temple of LIBITINA :

---

[1] *Licinius apud Sallust. hist. frag. lib.* iii.

[2] *Nicolaus Hortensius de re frumentaria Roman.*

[3] Not to take the people too much from their business, AUGUSTUS ordained the distribution of corn to be made only thrice a-year : But the people finding the monthly distributions more convenient, (as preserving, I suppose, a more regular œconomy in their family) desired to have them restored, SUETON. AUGUST. cap. 40. Had not some of the people come from some distance for their corn, AUGUSTUS's precaution seems superfluous.

[4] *Sueton. in Jul.* cap. 41. [5] *In vita Neronis,* 39.

But this was during a plague ; which can afford no certain foundation for any inference.

The public corn, though distributed only to 20,000 citizens, affected very considerably the whole agriculture of ITALY [1] : a fact no wise reconcileable to some modern exaggerations with regard to the inhabitants of that country.

The best ground of conjecture I can find concerning the greatness of ancient Rome is this : We are told by HERODIAN,[2] that ANTIOCH and ALEXANDRIA were very little inferior to ROME. It appears from DIODORUS SICULUS,[3] that one straight street of ALEXANDRIA reaching from gate to gate, was five miles long ; and as ALEXANDRIA was much more extended in length than breadth, it seems to have been a city nearly of the bulk of PARIS [4] ; and ROME might be about the size of LONDON.

---

[1] *Sueton. Aug.* cap. 42. [2] Lib. iv. cap. 5.
[3] Lib. xvii. 52.

[4] Quintus Curtius says, its walls were ten miles in circumference, when founded by Alexander, lib. iv. cap. 8. Strabo, who had travelled to Alexandria, as well as Diodorus Siculus, says it was scarce four miles long, and in most places about a mile broad, lib. xvii. Pliny says it resembled a Macedonian cassock, stretching out in the corners, lib. v. cap. 10. Notwithstanding this bulk of Alexandria, which seems but moderate, Diodorus Siculus, speaking of its circuit as drawn by Alexander (which it never exceeded, as we learn from Ammianus Marcellinus, lib. xxii. cap. 16.) says it was μεγέθει διαφέροντα, *extremely great*, ibid. The reason which he assigns for its surpassing all cities in the world (for he excepts not Rome) is, that it contained 300,000 free inhabitants. He also mentions the revenues of the kings, to wit, 6,000 talents, as another circumstance to the same purpose ; no such mighty sum in our eyes, even though we make allowance for the different value of money. What Strabo says of the neighbouring country, means only that it was peopled, οἰκούμενα καλῶς. Might not one affirm, without any great hyperbole, that the whole banks of the river, from Gravesend to Windsor, are one city ? This is even more than Strabo says of the banks of the lake Mareotis, and of the canal to Canopus. It is a vulgar saying in Italy, that the king of Sardinia has but one town in Piedmont, for it is all a town. Agrippa, *in Josephus de bello Judiac.* lib. ii. cap. 16, to make his audience comprehend the excessive greatness of Alexandria, which he endeavours to magnify, describes only the compass of the city as drawn by Alexander ; a clear proof that the bulk of the inhabitants were lodged there, and that the neighbouring country was no more than what might be expected about all great towns, very well cultivated, and well peopled.

There lived in ALEXANDRIA, in DIODORUS SICULUS's time,[1] 300,000 free people, comprehending, I suppose, women and children.[2] But what number of slaves? Had we any just ground to fix these at an equal number with the free inhabitants, it would favour the foregoing computation.

There is a passage in HERODIAN, which is a little surprising. He says positively, that the palace of the Emperor was as large as all the rest of the city.[3] This was NERO's golden house, which is indeed represented by SUETONIUS [4] and PLINY as of an enormous extent [5]; but no power of imagination can make us conceive it to bear any proportion to such a city as LONDON.

We may observe, had the historian been relating NERO's extravagance, and had he made use of such an expression, it would have had much less weight; these rhetorical exaggerations being so apt to creep into an author's style, even when the most chaste and correct. But it is mentioned by HERODIAN only by the by, in relating the quarrels between GETA and CARACALLA.

It appears from the same historian,[6] that there was then much land uncultivated, and put to no manner of

---

[1] Lib. xvii. 52.

[2] He says ἐλεύθεροι, not πολῖται, which last expression must have been understood of citizens alone, and grown men.

[3] Lib. iv. cap. 1. πάσης πόλεως. POLITIAN interprets it "aedibus majoribus etiam reliqua urbe".

[4] He says (in NERONE cap. 30) that a portico or piazza of it was 3000 feet long; "tanta laxitas ut porticus triplices milliarias haberet". He cannot mean three miles. For the whole extent of the house from the PALATINE to the ESQUILINE was not near so great. So when VOPISC. *in* AURELIANO mentions a portico in SALLUST's gardens, which he calls *porticus milliarensis*, it must be understood of a thousand feet. So also HORACE;
> "Nulla decempedis
>   Metata privatis opacam
> Porticus excipiebat Arcton". Lib. 2. ode 15.

So also in lib. 1. *satyr.* 8.
> "Mille pedes in fronte, trecentos cippus in agrum
>   Hic dabat".

[5] PLINIUS, lib. xxxvi. cap. 15. "Bis vidimus urbem totam cingi domibus principum, CAII ac NERONIS".

[6] Lib. ii. cap. 15.

use ; and he ascribes it as a great praise to PERTINAX, that he allowed every one to take such land either in ITALY or elsewhere, and cultivate it as he pleased, without paying any taxes. *Lands uncultivated, and put to no manner of use !* This is not heard of in any part of CHRISTENDOM ; except in some remote parts of HUNGARY ; as I have been informed. And it surely corresponds very ill with that idea of the extreme populousness of antiquity, so much insisted on.

We learn from VOPISCUS,[1] that there was even in ETRURIA much fertile land uncultivated, which the Emperor AURELIAN intended to convert into vineyards, in order to furnish the ROMAN people with a gratuitous distribution of wine ; a very proper expedient for depopulating still farther that capital and all the neighbouring territories.

It may not be amiss to take notice of the account which POLYBIUS [2] gives of the great herds of swine to be met with in TUSCANY and LOMBARDY, as well as in GREECE, and of the method of feeding them which was then practised. "There are great herds of swine", says he, "throughout all "ITALY, particularly in former times, through ETRURIA "and CISALPINE GAUL. And a herd frequently consists of "a thousand or more swine. When one of these herds in "feeding meets with another, they mix together ; and the "swine-herds have no other expedient for separating them "than to go to different quarters, where they sound their "horn ; and these animals, being accustomed to that "signal, run immediately each to the horn of his own "keeper. Whereas in GREECE, if the herds of swine happen "to mix in the forests, he who has the greater flock, takes "cunningly the opportunity of driving all away. And "thieves are very apt to purloin the straggling hogs, which "have wandered to a great distance from their keeper in "search of food".

May we not infer from this account, that the north of

---

[1] *In* AURELIAN, cap. 48.   [2] Lib. xii. cap. 2.

ITALY, as well as GREECE, was then much less peopled,
and worse cultivated, than at present? How could these
vast herds be fed in a country so full of inclosures, so
improved by agriculture, so divided by farms, so planted
with vines and corn intermingled together? I must
confess, that POLYBIUS's relation has more the air of that
œconomy which is to be met with in our AMERICAN
colonies, than the management of a EUROPEAN country.

We meet with a reflection in ARISTOTLE's [1] Ethics,
which seems unaccountable on any supposition, and by
proving too much in favour of our present reasoning, may
be thought really to prove nothing. That philosopher,
treating of friendship, and observing, that this relation
ought neither to be contracted to a very few, nor extended
over a great multitude, illustrates his opinion by the
following argument. "In like manner", says he, "as a
"city cannot subsist, if it either have so few inhabitants
"as ten, or so many as a hundred thousand; so is there a
"mediocrity required in the number of friends; and you
"destroy the essence of friendship by running into either
"extreme". What! impossible that a city can contain a
hundred thousand inhabitants! Had ARISTOTLE never
seen nor heard of a city so populous? This, I must own,
passes my comprehension.

PLINY [2] tells us that SELEUCIA, the seat of the GREEK
empire in the East, was reported to contain 600,000 people.
CARTHAGE is said by STRABO [3] to have contained 700,000.
The inhabitants of PEKIN are not much more numerous.
LONDON, PARIS, and CONSTANTINOPLE, may admit of nearly
the same computation; at least, the two latter cities do
not exceed it. ROME, ALEXANDRIA, ANTIOCH, we have
already spoken of. From the experience of past and
present ages, one might conjecture that there is a kind of
impossibility, that any city could ever rise much beyond

[1] Lib. ix. cap. 10. His expression is ἄνθρωπος, not πολίτης;
inhabitant, not citizen.
[2] Lib. vi. cap. 28.   [3] Lib. xvii. 833.

this proportion. Whether the grandeur of a city be founded on commerce or on empire, there seem to be invincible obstacles, which prevent its farther progress. The seats of vast monarchies, by introducing extravagant luxury, irregular expence, idleness, dependence, and false ideas of rank and superiority, are improper for commerce. Extensive commerce checks itself, by raising the price of all labour and commodities. When a great court engages the attendance of a numerous nobility, possessed of overgrown fortunes, the middling gentry remain in their provincial towns, where they can make a figure on a moderate income. And if the dominions of a state arrive at an enormous size, there necessarily arise many capitals, in the remoter provinces, whither all the inhabitants, except a few courtiers, repair for education, fortune, and amusement.[1] LONDON, by uniting extensive commerce and middling empire, has, perhaps, arrived at a greatness, which no city will ever be able to exceed.

Chuse DOVER or CALAIS for a center : Draw a circle of two hundred miles radius : You comprehend LONDON, PARIS, the NETHERLANDS, the UNITED PROVINCES, and some of the best cultivated parts of FRANCE and ENGLAND. It may safely, I think, be affirmed, that no spot of ground can be found, in antiquity, of equal extent, which contained near so many great and populous cities, and was so stocked with riches and inhabitants. To balance, in both periods, the states, which possessed most art, knowledge, civility, and the best police, seems the truest method of comparison.

It is an observation of L'ABBE DU BOS,[2] that ITALY is warmer at present than it was in ancient times. "The "annals of ROME tell us", says he, "that in the year 480 "*ab U.C.* the winter was so severe that it destroyed the

---

[1] Such were ALEXANDRIA, ANTIOCH, CARTHAGE, EPHESUS, LYONS, &c. in the ROMAN empire. Such are even BOURDEAUX, THOLOUSE, DIJON, RENNES, ROUEN, AIX, &c. in FRANCE ; DUBLIN, EDINBURGH, YORK, in the BRITISH dominions.

[2] Vol. 2. Sect. 16.

"trees. The Tyber froze in Rome, and the ground was
"covered with snow for forty days. When Juvenal [1]
"describes a superstitious woman, he represents her as
"breaking the ice of the Tyber, that she might perform
"her ablutions :

Hybernum fracta glacie descendet in amnem,
Ter matutino Tyberi mergetur.

"He speaks of that river's freezing as a common event.
"Many passages of Horace suppose the streets of Rome
"full of snow and ice. We should have more certainty
"with regard to this point, had the ancients known the use
"of thermometers : But their writers, without intending
"it, give us information, sufficient to convince us, that the
"winters are now much more temperate at Rome than
"formerly. At present the Tyber no more freezes at
"Rome than the Nile at Cairo. The Romans esteem the
"winters very rigorous, if the snow lie two days, and if one
"see for eight and forty hours a few icicles hang from a
"fountain that has a north exposure".

The observation of this ingenious critic may be
extended to other European climates. Who could discover the mild climate of France in Diodorus Siculus's [2]
description of that of Gaul ? "As it is a northern climate",
says he, "it is infested with cold to an extreme degree. In
"cloudy weather, instead of rain there fall great snows ;
"and in clear weather it there freezes so excessive hard,
"that the rivers acquire bridges of their own substance,
"over which, not only single travellers may pass, but large
"armies, accompanied with all their baggage and loaded
"waggons. And there being many rivers in Gaul, the
"Rhone, the Rhine, &c., almost all of them are frozen
"over ; and it is usual, in order to prevent falling, to
"cover the ice with chaff and straw at the places where
"the road passes". *Colder than a Gallic Winter*, is used

[1] *Sat.* 6. 522.   [2] *Lib.* iv. 25.

* [*This sentence not in A–C ; the next not in A–H*].

by PETRONIUS as a proverbial expression. ARISTOTLE says, that GAUL is so cold a climate that an ass could not live in it.[1]

North of the CEVENNES, says STRABO,[2] GAUL produces not figs and olives : And the vines, which have been planted, bear not grapes, that will ripen.

OVID positively maintains, with all the serious affirmation of prose, that the EUXINE sea was frozen over every winter in his time ; and he appeals to ROMAN governours, whom he names, for the truth of his assertion.[3] This seldom or never happens at present in the latitude of TOMI, whither OVID was banished. All the complaints of the same poet seem to mark a rigour of the seasons, which is scarcely experienced at present in PETERSBURGH or STOCKHOLM.

TOURNEFORT, a *Provençal*, who had travelled into the same country, observes that there is not a finer climate in the world : And he asserts that nothing but OVID's melancholy could have given him such dismal ideas of it. But the facts, mentioned by that poet, are too circumstantial to bear any such interpretation.

POLYBIUS [4] says that the climate in ARCADIA was very cold, and the air moist.

"ITALY", says VARRO,[5] "is the most temperate climate in EUROPE. The inland parts" (GAUL, GERMANY, and PANNONIA, no doubt) "have almost perpetual winter".

The northern parts of SPAIN, according to STRABO,[6] are but ill inhabited, because of the great cold.

Allowing, therefore, this remark to be just, that EUROPE is becoming warmer than formerly ; how can we account for it ? Plainly, by no other method, than by supposing that the land is at present much better cultivated, and that the woods are cleared, which formerly threw a shade

[1] *De generat, anim.* lib. ii. 8, 14.   [2] Lib. iv. 178.
[3] *Trist.* lib. iii. eleg. 10.   *De Ponto,* lib. iv. eleg. 7, 9, 10.
[4] Lib. iv. cap. 21.   [5] Lib. i. cap. 2.
[6] Lib. iii. 137.

upon the earth, and kept the rays of the sun from penetrating to it. Our northern colonies in AMERICA become more temperate, in proportion as the woods are felled ; [1] but in general, every one may remark that cold is still much more severely felt, both in North and South AMERICA, than in places under the same latitude in EUROPE.

SASERNA, quoted by COLUMELLA,[2] affirmed that the disposition of the heavens was altered before his time, and that the air had become much milder and warmer ; as appears hence, says he, that many places now abound with vineyards and olive plantations, which formerly, by reason of the rigour of the climate, could raise none of these productions. Such a change, if real, will be allowed an evident sign of the better cultivation and peopling of countries before the age of SASERNA [3] ; and if it be continued to the present times, is a proof, that these advantages have been continually encreasing throughout this part of the world.

Let us now cast our eye over all the countries which are the scene of ancient and modern history, and compare their past and present situation : We shall not, perhaps, find such foundation for the complaint of the present emptiness and desolation of the world. ÆGYPT is represented by MAILLET, to whom we owe the best account of it, as extremely populous ; though he esteems the number of its inhabitants to be diminished. SYRIA, and the Lesser ASIA, as well as the coast of BARBARY, I can readily own, to be desart in comparison of their ancient condition. The depopulation of GREECE is also obvious. But whether

---

[1] The warm southern colonies also become more healthful : And it is remarkable, that in the SPANISH histories of the first discovery and conquest of these countries, they appear to have been very healthful ; being then well peopled and cultivated. No account of the sickness or decay of CORTES's or PIZARRO's small armies.

[2] Lib. i. cap. 1 .

[3] He seems to have lived about the time of the younger AFRICANUS ; lib. i. cap. 1.

the country now called TURKEY in EUROPE may not, in general, contain more inhabitants than during the flourishing period of GREECE, may be a little doubtful. The THRACIANS seem then to have lived like the TARTARS at present, by pasturage and plunder [1] : The GETES were still more uncivilized [2] : And the ILLYRIANS were no better.[3] These occupy nine-tenths of that country : And though the government of the TURKS be not very favourable to industry and propagation ; yet it preserves at least peace and order among the inhabitants ; and is preferable to that barbarous, unsettled condition, in which they anciently lived.

POLAND and MUSCOVY in EUROPE are not populous ; but are certainly much more so than the ancient SARMATIA and SCYTHIA ; where no husbandry or tillage was ever heard of, and pasturage was the sole art by which the people were maintained. The like observation may be extended to DENMARK and SWEDEN. No one ought to esteem the immense swarms of people, which formerly came from the North, and over-ran all EUROPE, to be any objection to this opinion. Where a whole nation, or even half of it remove their seat, it is easy to imagine, what a prodigious multitude they must form ; with what desperate valour they must make their attacks ; and how the terror they strike into the invaded nations will make these magnify, in their imagination, both the courage and multitude of the invaders. SCOTLAND is neither extensive nor populous ; but were the half of its inhabitants to seek new seats, they would form a colony as numerous as the TEUTONS and CIMBRI ; and would shake all EUROPE, supposing it in no better condition for defence than formerly.

GERMANY has surely at present twenty times more inhabitants than in ancient times, when they cultivated

---

[1] *Xenoph. Exp.* lib. vii. *Polyb.* lib. iv. cap. 45.
[2] *Ovid. passim. &c. Strabo,* lib. vii.
[3] *Polyb.* lib. ii. cap. 12.

no ground, and each tribe valued itself on the extensive desolation which it spread around ; as we learn from CÆSAR,[1] and TACITUS,[2] and STRABO.[3] A proof, that the division into small republics will not alone render a nation populous, unless attended with the spirit of peace, order, and industry.

The barbarous condition of BRITAIN in former times is well known, and the thinness of its inhabitants may easily be conjectured, both from their barbarity, and from a circumstance mentioned by HERODIAN,[4] that all BRITAIN was marshy, even in SEVERUS's time, after the ROMANS had been fully settled in it above a century.

It is not easily imagined, that the GAULS were anciently much more advanced in the arts of life than their northern neighbours ; since they travelled to this island for their education in the mysteries of the religion and philosophy of the DRUIDS.[5] I cannot, therefore, think, that GAUL was then near so populous as FRANCE is at present.

Were we to believe, indeed, and join together the testimony of APPIAN, and that of DIODORUS SICULUS, we must admit of an incredible populousness in GAUL. The former historian [6] says, that there were 400 nations in that country ; the latter [7] affirms, that the largest of the GALLIC nations consisted of 200,000 men, besides women and children, and the least of 50,000. Calculating, therefore, at a medium, we must admit of near 200 millions of people, in a country, which we esteem populous at present, though supposed to contain little more than twenty.[8] Such calculations, therefore, by their extravagance, lose all manner of authority. We may observe, that the equality of property, to which the populousness of antiquity may be ascribed, had no place among the

---

[1] *De Bello Gallico*, lib. vi. 23.   [2] *De Moribus Germ.*
[3] Lib. vii.   [4] Lib. iii. cap. 47.
[5] CÆSAR *de Bello Gallico*, lib. vi. 13. STRABO, lib. vii. 290 says, the GAULS were not much more improved than the GERMANS.
[6] Celt. pars 1. lib. iv. 2.   [7] Lib. v. 25.
[8] Ancient GAUL was much more extensive than modern FRANCE.

GAULS.[1] Their intestine wars also, before CÆSAR's time, were almost perpetual.[2] And STRABO [3] observes, that, though all GAUL was cultivated, yet was it not cultivated with any skill or care ; the genius of the inhabitants leading them less to arts than arms, till their slavery under ROME produced peace among themselves.

CÆSAR [4] enumerates very particularly the great forces which were levied in BELGIUM to oppose his conquest, and makes them amount to 208,000. These were not the whole people able to bear arms : For the same historian tells us, that the BELLOVACI could have brought a hundred thousand men into the field, though they engaged only for sixty. Taking the whole, therefore, in this proportion of ten to six, *the sum of fighting men in all the states of BELGIUM was about 350,000 ; all the inhabitants a million and a half. And BELGIUM being about a fourth of GAUL, that country might contain six millions, which is not near the third of its present inhabitants.[5] †We are informed by CÆSAR, that the GAULS had no fixed property in land ; but that the chieftains, when any death happened in a family, made a new division of all the lands among the

---

[1] CÆSAR *de Bello Gallico*, lib. vi. 13.
[2] *Id. ibid.* 15.   [3] Lib. iv. 178.
[4] *De Bello Gallico*, lib. ii. 4.
[5] It appears from CÆSAR's account, that the GAULS had no domestic slaves, ‡(who formed a different order from the *Plebes*.) The whole common people were indeed a kind of slaves to the nobility, as the people of POLAND are at this day : And a nobleman of GAUL had sometimes ten thousand dependants of this kind. Nor can we doubt, that the armies were composed of the people as well as of the nobility : An army of 100,000 noblemen from a very small state is incredible. The fighting men amongst the HELVETII were the fourth part of the whole inhabitants ; a clear proof that all the males of miltary age bore arms. See CÆSAR *de bello Gall.* lib. 1.
We may remark, that the numbers in CÆSAR's commentaries can be more depended on than those of any other antient author, because of the GREEK translation, which still remains, and which checks the LATIN original.

* about 350,000 = above half a million ; all the = the whole ; a fourth = the fourth ; six millions = eight millions ; not near = scarce above [*A–B*].
† [*The rest of this paragraph not in A–D*].
‡ (who . . . *Plebes*) [*not in A–C*].

several members of the family. This is the custom of *Tanistry*, which so long prevailed in IRELAND, and which retained that country in a state of misery, barbarism and desolation.

The ancient HELVETIA was 250 miles in length, and 180 in breadth, according to the same author [1] ; yet contained only 360,000 inhabitants. The canton of BERNE alone has, at present, as many people.

After this computation of APPIAN and DIODORUS SICULUS, I know not, whether I dare affirm, that the modern DUTCH are more numerous than the ancient BATAVI.

SPAIN is, perhaps, decayed from what it was three centuries ago ; but if we step backward two thousand years, and consider the restless, turbulent, unsettled condition of its inhabitants, we may probably be inclined to think that it is now much more populous. Many SPANIARDS killed themselves, when deprived of their arms by the ROMANS.[2] It appears from PLUTARCH,[3] that robbery and plunder were esteemed honourable among the SPANIARDS. HIRTIUS [4] represents in the same light the situation of that country in CÆSAR's time ; and he says, that every man was obliged to live in castles and walled towns for his security. It was not till its final conquest under AUGUSTUS, that these disorders were repressed.[5] The account which STRABO [6] and JUSTIN [7] give of SPAIN, corresponds exactly with those above mentioned. How much, therefore, must it diminish from our idea of the populousness of antiquity, when we find that TULLY, comparing ITALY, AFRIC, GAUL, GREECE, and SPAIN, mentions the great number of inhabitants, as the peculiar circumstance, which rendered this latter country formidable ? [8]

---

[1] *De Bello Gallico*, lib. i. 2.　　[2] *Titi Livii*, lib. xxxiv. cap. 17.
[3] *In vita Marii*. 6.　　[4] *De Bello Hisp*. 8.
[5] *Vell. Paterc.* lib. ii. §90.　　[6] Lib. iii.　　[7] Lib. xliv.
[8] "Nec numero Hispanos, nec robore Gallos, nec calliditate Poenos, nec artibus Graecos, nec denique hoc ipso jus gentis, ac terrae domestico

ITALY, however, it is probable, has decayed : But how many great cities does it still contain ? VENICE, GENOA, PAVIA, TURIN, MILAN, NAPLES, FLORENCE, LEGHORN, which either subsisted not in ancient times, or were then very inconsiderable ? If we reflect on this, we shall not be apt to carry matters to so great an extreme as is usual, with regard to this subject.

When the ROMAN authors complain, that ITALY, which formerly exported corn, became dependent on all the provinces for its daily bread, they never ascribe this alteration to the encrease of its inhabitants, but to the neglect of tillage and agriculture.[1] A natural effect of that pernicious practice of importing corn, in order to distribute it *gratis* among the ROMAN citizens, and a very bad means of multiplying the inhabitants of any country.[2] The *sportula*, so much talked of by MARTIAL and JUVENAL, being presents regularly made by the great lords to their smaller clients, must have had a like tendency to produce idleness, debauchery, and a continual decay among the people. *The parish-rates have at present the same bad consequences in ENGLAND.

Were I to assign a period, when I imagine this part of the world might possibly contain more inhabitants than at present, I should pitch upon the age of TRAJAN and the ANTONINES ; the great extent of the ROMAN empire being then civilized and cultivated, settled almost in a profound

---

[1] VARRO *de re rustica*, lib. ii. praef. COLUMELLA praef. SUETON. AUGUST. cap. 42.

[2] Though the observations of L'Abbé du Bos should be admitted, that ITALY is now warmer than in former times, the consequence may not be necessary, that it is more populous or better cultivated. If the other countries of EUROPE were more savage and woody, the cold winds that blew from them, might affect the climate of Italy.

* [*This sentence not in A*].

---

nativoque sensu, Italos ipsos ac Latinos—superavimus". *De harusp. resp.* cap. 9. The disorders of SPAIN seem to have been almost proverbial : "Nec impacatos a tergo horrebis Iberos". *Virg. Georg.* lib. iii. 408. The IBERI are here plainly taken, by a poetical figure, for robbers in general.

peace both foreign and domestic, and living under the same regular police and government.[1] But we are told that all extensive governments, especially absolute monarchies, are pernicious to population, and contain a

[1] The inhabitants of MARSEILLES lost not their superiority over the GAULS in commerce and the mechanic arts, till the ROMAN dominion turned the latter from arms to agriculture and civil life. See STRABO, lib. iv. 180-1. That author, in several places, repeats the observation concerning the improvement arising from the ROMAN arts and civility : And he lived at the time when the change was new, and would be more sensible. So also PLINY : "Quis enim non, communicato orbe terrarum, majestate ROMANI imperii, profecisse vitam putet, commercio rerum ac societate festæ pacis, omniaque etiam, quæ occulta antea fuerant, in promiscuo usu facta. Lib. xiv. proem. Numine deûm electa (speaking of ITALY) quae cœlum ipsum clarius faceret, sparsa congregaret imperia, ritusque molliret, & tot populorum discordes, ferasque linguas sermonis commercio contraheret ad colloquia, & humanitatem homini daret ; breviterque, una cunctarum gentium in toto orbe patria fieret" ; lib. ii. cap. 5. Nothing can be stronger to this purpose than the following passage from TERTULLIAN, who lived about the age of SEVERUS. "Certe quidem ipse orbis in promptu est, cultior de die & instructior pristino. Omnia jam pervia, omnia nota, omnia negotiosa. Solitudines famosas retro fundi amoenissimi, obliteraverunt, silvas arva domuerunt, feras pecora fugaverunt ; arenae scruntur, saxa panguntur, paludes eliquantur, tantae urbes, quantae non casae quondam. Jam nec insulae horrent, nec scopuli terrent ; ubique domus, ubique populus, ubique respublica, ubique vita. Summum testimonium frequentiae humanae, onerosi sumus mundo, vix nobis elementa sufficiunt ; & necessitates arctiores, et querelae apud omnes, dum jam nos natura non sustinet". *De anima*, cap. 30. The air of rhetoric and declamation which appears in this passage, diminishes somewhat from its authority, but does not entirely destroy it.* The same remark may be extended to the following passage of ARISTIDES the sophist, who lived in the age of ADRIAN. "The whole world", says he, addressing himself to the ROMANS, "seems to keep one holiday ; and mankind, laying aside the sword which they formerly wore, now betake themselves to feasting and to joy. The cities, forgetting their ancient animosities, preserve only one emulation, which shall embellish itself most by every art and ornament ; Theatres every where arise, amphitheatres, porticoes, aqueducts, temples, schools, academies ; and one may safely pronounce, that the sinking world has been again raised by your auspicious empire. Nor have cities alone received an encrease of ornament and beauty ; but the whole earth, like a garden or paradise, is cultivated and adorned : Insomuch, that such of mankind as are placed out of the limits of your empire (who are but few) seem to merit our sympathy and compassion".

It is remarkable, that though DIODORUS SICULUS makes the inhabitants of ÆGYPT, when conquered by the ROMANS, amount only to three millions ;

* +A man of violent imagination, such as *Tertullian*, augments everything equally ; and for that reason his comparative judgments are the most to be depended on [*A-B*].

secret vice and poison, which destroy the effect of all these promising appearances.[1] To confirm this, there is a passage cited from PLUTARCH,[2] which being somewhat singular, we shall here examine it.

That author, endeavouring to account for the silence of many of the oracles, says, that it may be ascribed to the present desolation of the world, proceeding from former wars and factions ; which common calamity, he adds, has fallen heavier upon GREECE than on any other country ; insomuch, that the whole could scarcely at present furnish three thousand warriors ; a number which, in the time of the MEDIAN war, were supplied by the single city of MEGARA. The gods, therefore, who affect works of dignity and importance, have suppressed many of their oracles, and deign not to use so many interpreters of their will to so diminutive a people.

I must confess, that this passage contains so many difficulties, that I know not what to make of it. You may observe, that PLUTARCH assigns, for a cause of the decay of mankind, not the extensive dominion of the ROMANS, but the former wars and factions of the several states ; all which were quieted by the ROMAN arms.

---

[1] *L'Esprit de Loix*, liv. xxiii. chap. 19.   [2] *De Orac. Defectu.*

---

yet JOSEPH. *de bello Jud.* lib. ii. cap. 16. says, that its inhabitants, excluding those of ALEXANDRIA, were seven millions and a half, in the reign of NERO : And he expressly says, that he drew this account from the books of the ROMAN publicans, who levied the poll-tax. STRABO, lib. xvii. 797, praises the superior police of the ROMANS with regard to the finances of ÆGYPT, above that of its former monarchs : and no part of administration is more essential to the happiness of a people. Yet we read in ATHENÆUS, (lib. i. cap. 25.) who flourished during the reign of the ANTONINES, that the town MAREIA, near ALEXANDRIA, which was formerly a large city, had dwindled into a village. This is not, properly speaking, a contradiction. SUIDAS (AUGUST.) says, that the Emperor AUGUSTUS, having numbered the whole ROMAN empire, found it contained only 4,101,017 men (ἄνδρες). There is here surely some great mistake, either in the author or transcriber. But this authority, feeble as it is, may be sufficient to counterbalance the exaggerated accounts of HERODOTUS and DIODORUS SICULUS with regard to more early times.

PLUTARCH'S reasoning, therefore, is directly contrary to the inference, which is drawn from the fact he advances.

POLYBIUS supposes, that GREECE had become more prosperous and flourishing after the establishment of the ROMAN yoke [1]; and though that historian wrote before these conquerors had degenerated, from being the patrons, to be the plunderers of mankind ; yet, as we find from TACITUS,[2] that the severity of the emperors afterwards corrected the licence of the governors, we have no reason to think that extensive monarchy so destructive as it is often represented.

We learn from STRABO,[3] that the ROMANS, from their regard to the GREEKS, maintained, to his time, most of the privileges and liberties of that celebrated nation ; and NERO afterwards rather encreased them.[4] How therefore can we imagine, that the ROMAN yoke was so burdensome over that part of the world ? The oppression of the proconsuls was checked ; and the magistracies in GREECE being all bestowed, in the several cities, by the free votes of the people, there was no necessity for the competitors to attend the emperor's court. If great numbers went to seek their fortunes in ROME, and advance themselves by learning or eloquence, the commodities of their native country, many of them would return with the fortunes which they had acquired, and thereby enrich the GRECIAN commonwealths.

But PLUTARCH says, that the general depopulation had been more sensibly felt in GREECE than in any other

---

[1] LIB. ii. cap. 62. It may perhaps be imagined, that POLYBIUS, being dependent on ROME, would naturally extol the ROMAN dominion. But, in the *first* place, POLYBIUS, though one sees sometimes instances of his caution, discovers no symptoms of flattery. *Secondly*, This opinion is only delivered in a single stroke, by the by, while he is intent upon another subject ; and it is allowed, if there be any suspicion of an author's insincerity, that these oblique propositions discover his real opinion better than his more formal and direct assertions.

[2] *Annal.* lib. i. cap. 2. [3] Lib. viii. and ix.

[4] PLUTARCH. *De his qui sero a Numine puniuntur.*

country. How is this reconcileable to its superior privileges and advantages?

Besides, this passage, by proving too much, really proves nothing. *Only three thousand men able to bear arms in all* GREECE ! Who can admit so strange a proposition, especially if we consider the great number of GREEK cities, whose names still remain in history, and which are mentioned by writers long after the age of PLUTARCH ? There are there surely ten times more people at present, when there scarcely remains a city in all the bounds of ancient GREECE. That country is still tolerably cultivated, and furnishes a sure supply of corn, in case of any scarcity in SPAIN, ITALY, or the south of FRANCE.

We may observe, that the ancient frugality of the GREEKS, and their equality of property, still subsisted during the age of PLUTARCH ; as appears from LUCIAN.[1] Nor is there any ground to imagine, that that country was possessed by a few masters, and a great number of slaves.

It is probable, indeed, that military discipline, being entirely useless, was extremely neglected in GREECE after the establishment of the ROMAN empire ; and if these commonwealths, formerly so warlike and ambitious, maintained each of them a small city-guard, to prevent mobbish disorders, it is all they had occasion for : And these, perhaps, did not amount to 3,000 men, throughout all GREECE. I own, that, if PLUTARCH had this fact in his eye, he is here guilty of a gross paralogism, and assigns causes no wise proportioned to the effects. But is it so great a prodigy, that an author should fall into a mistake of this nature ? [2]

---

[1] *De mercede conductis.*

[2] I must confess that that discourse of PLUTARCH, concerning the silence of the oracles, is in general of so odd a texture, and so unlike his other productions, that one is at a loss what judgment to form of it. 'Tis wrote in dialogue, which is a method of composition that PLUTARCH commonly little affects. The personages he introduces advance very wild, absurd, and contradictory opinions, more like the visionary system

Of the Populousness of Ancient Nations

But whatever force may remain in this passage of PLUTARCH, we shall endeavour to counterbalance it by as remarkable a passage in DIODORUS SICULUS, where the historian, after mentioning NINUS's army of 1,700,000 foot and 200,000 horse, endeavours to support the credibility of this account by some posterior facts ; and adds, that we must not form a notion of the ancient populousness of mankind from the present emptiness and depopulation which is spread over the world.[1] Thus an author, who lived at that very period of antiquity which is represented as most populous,[2] complains of the desolation which then prevailed, gives the preference to former times, and has recourse to ancient fables as a foundation for his opinion. The humour of blaming the present, and admiring the past, is strongly rooted in human nature, and has an influence even on persons endued with the profoundest judgment and most extensive learning.

[1] Lib. ii. 5.
[2] He was contemporary with CÆSAR and AUGUSTUS.

---

or ravings of PLATO than the solid sense of PLUTARCH. There runs also thro' the whole an air of superstition and credulity, which resembles very little the spirit that appears in other philosophical compositions of that author. For 'tis remarkable, that tho' PLUTARCH be an historian as superstitious as HERODOTUS or LIVY, yet there is scarcely, in all antiquity, a philosopher less superstitious, excepting CICERO and LUCIAN. I must therefore confess, that a passage of PLUTARCH, cited from this discourse, has much less authority with me, than if it had been found in most of his other compositions.

There is only one other discourse of PLUTARCH liable to like objections, *viz.* that *concerning those whose punishment is delayed by the Deity.* It is also wrote in dialogue, contains like superstitious, wild visions, and seems to have been chiefly composed in rivalship to PLATO, particularly his last book *de republica.*

And here I cannot but observe, that Mons. FONTENELLE, a writer eminent for candor, seems to have departed a little from his usual character, when he endeavours to throw a ridicule upon PLUTARCH on account of passages to be met with in this dialogue concerning oracles. The absurdities here put into the mouths of the several personages are not to be ascribed to PLUTARCH. He makes them refute each other ; and, in general, he seems to intend the ridiculing of those very opinions, which FONTENELLE would ridicule him for maintaining. See *Histoire des oracles.*

183

Essays on Economics

ADDITIONAL NOTE
(See above, p. 108*n*.)

In a letter to Montesquieu (June 1753) Hume makes essentially the same comment concerning Wallace's work, and adds : "I believe the chief merit of my performance was my forcing Mr. Wallace, by a kind of challenge, to publish the learned *Dissertation* which he had, for some time, kept by him." Calling attention to an enclosure containing corrections of errors in his own essay, he adds : "I could have made many more amendments, by correcting the errors remarked by my antagonist ; but as that would have injured his work, I shall abstain at present, in hopes that a new edition will give me an opportunity." *Correspondance de Montesquieu*, ed. F. Gebelin and M. Morize, Paris 1914, ii, pp. 467–9. In his reply, Montesquieu praises both Hume and Wallace for the spirit in which they have conducted the debate. *Op. cit.*, ii, p. 480. For a discussion of Hume's relations with Wallace, see E. C. Mossner, *The Forgotten Hume*, N.Y. 1943, pp. 105 ff.—ED.

RELEVANT EXTRACTS
FROM
HUME'S CORRESPONDENCE
1749-1776

HUME TO MONTESQUIEU

10 April 1749 [1]

. . . It is impossible to make any reasonable objection to what you say, on p. 357, of the advantages of having taxes levied by the state [*par régie*] rather than by delegated private collectors [*fermiers*].[2] I shall relate to you, however, an observation which I heard made recently on this subject : If a nation does not begin in the first place with *fermiers*, it will never derive the full advantage which it can derive from taxation ; there are a hundred thousand tricks and devices for dealing with fraud on the part of individuals, which are suggested to the *fermiers* by self-interest, and which the government collectors would never have dreamed of ; however, the government collectors can put these devices into practice when they have been taught them by the private collectors. In England, the excise was levied at first by *fermiers*, and the whole system of this branch of our taxes, which are very well administered, was borrowed from them.

---

[1] [Taken from J. Y. T. Greig, *The Letters of David Hume*, I, 136–8, and translated from the French. Hume is here discussing various points in Montesquieu's *L'Esprit des lois*. Other matters of a non-economic nature are considered in the earlier portion of the letter. Montesquieu's reply to this letter is of a general nature and contains no technical discussion of Hume's points. Cf. *Correspondance de Montesquieu*, ed. F. Gebelin and M. Morize (Paris 1914), II, 188. Two other (non-technical) letters of Montesquieu to Hume are on record : *Corr.*, II, pp. 222, 479. On the above letter of Hume's itself, however, there appears the following general comment by Montesquieu : "Letter of David Hume which should be copied in the Collection. It is full of insight and good sense. There are some remarks which may be used for my last edition of *L'Esprit des lois*, and I can say that, of a host of papers which have been written on this subject, it is perhaps the only one which makes so much sense. I will be able to omit some worthless points". Cf. *op. cit.*, p. 169n. Translated from the French. For a general comment on the relation between the economics of Hume and Montesquieu cf. above, p. lvi n.—ED.]

[2] [BOOK XX, chap. 19.—ED.]

VOL. II, p. 10, ch. ix.[1] Banks are convenient, but it may be questioned whether they are of very much value. Before 1706, there was a sufficient quantity of gold and silver in all our colonies for ordinary purposes ; paper credit or current paper was introduced in them, which caused all the silver to depart and had such pernicious consequences that Parliament is resolved to abolish it at this session. The same thing was undertaken, at about the same time, in your colony of Canada, but it was wisely given up in the very · beginning. These banks were, indeed, very different from the banks in Europe : they issued paper without ⟨the⟩ silver to make it circulate. Here are the main lines of my reasoning, which I submit for your judgment : The abundance of gold and silver in a state is very advantageous to it, if one considers the neighbouring states, because those foreigners will exchange for it their goods and labour ; but, in respect to domestic commerce, this abundance of gold and silver is of no advantage whatever ; on the contrary, it raises the cost of labour and hinders exportation ; paper has the same inconveniences as coined money, and none of its advantages.

Page 12, ch. xi.[2] It appears that we are, in England, too much concerned about the balance of trade. It is difficult for a loss of balance to reach the point where it will do considerable harm to a nation. If half the money in England were suddenly destroyed, labour and goods would suddenly become so cheap that there would suddenly follow a great quantity of exports which would attract to us the money of all our neighbours. If half the money which is in England were suddenly doubled, goods would suddenly become more expensive, imports would rise to the disadvantage of exports and our money would be

---

[1] [BOOK XX, chap. 10. Concerning this and the main thesis of the following paragraph, cf. Hume's essays "Of Money" and "Of the Balance of Trade", above, pp. 33, 60 ff.—ED.]

[2] [BOOK XX, chap. 11.—[ED.

spread among all our neighbours. It does not seem that money, any more than water, can be raised or lowered anywhere much beyond the level it has in places where communication is open, but that it must rise and fall in proportion to the goods and labour contained in each state.

Page 116, ch. xvii.[1] The enumeration which you make of the disadvantages of public debts is quite correct. But have they no advantage ? The merchants who have capital in the public funds keep but little money in their coffers for the needs of their business ; they can dispose of this capital whenever they please to meet any demand. Consequently, this capital serves two ends : first, to yield them a fixed revenue : secondly, to advance their business ; consequently the merchant is able to conduct his business with smaller profits on his goods, which is advantageous for trade. When I spoke of this to a man who is extremely well-informed, Lord Lonsdale, he pointed out to me another advantage, which however appears to me more dubious : capital which is held in the public funds, he said to me, is in constant circulation and forms a kind of money ; the abundance of money lowers the interest rate and encourages trade.[2]

Your opinion on public debts has already been quoted in the House of Lords by Lord Bath, formerly Mr Pulteney,

[1] [BOOK XXII, chap. 17. Cf. Hume's essay "Of Public Credit", above, pp. 93-6, where the following point as well as some of Montesquieu's own points are incorporated in the analysis.—ED.]

[2] [For a discussion of Hume's views on the relation between money, the rate of interest, and the level of employment, cf. above, p. lxxii. With regard to the points made in this paragraph, Montesquieu inscribed the following note : "What Mr Hume says concerning public debts and the remark of Milord Lonsdale do not require that I change anything, because I have distinguished the circulating paper which represents the currency or that which represents a commercial firm, from that which only represents a debt. The first two can have all the advantages of the third and produce all the good effects we attribute to the third, such as the convenience of traders. As for the currency of the colonies, he [Hume] himself offers the reason for the pernicious effects which have resulted from it : it was not redeemable and there was no money at all to pay it". Cf. *Correspondance de Montesquieu*, II, 179n. Translated from the French.—ED.]

a peer of great distinction ; now a member of the opposition party ; you know that these distinctions are with us not of long duration and are very casual.

OSWALD TO HUME

10 October 1749 [1]

. . . You observe, with great justice, the groundlessness of all such jealousy in any countrey while its people and industry remain ; and had you concluded with the necessity there was therefore of taking these circumstances into consideration, along with the state of the trade and the gold and silver of any countrey, before any judgement was formed on the balance of its trade—before any jealousys were entertained on that head, or any remedys applied to a supposed wrong, &c. —I should have expected with the greatest pleasure, from so good a hand, some of the justest observations on the reciprocal effects which these produce on each other. . . .

But you attempt in the Essay to cure this jealousy in a different manner, and endeavour to dispel all fear, with respect to the balance of trade, by proving that this balance, as it exists in different countreys, simply depends on the greater or less plenty of money in each, and that on either side it naturally and necessarily corrects itself. People and industry, tho' mentioned in your first proposition, enter for nothing into the argument which is adduced to prove it. They are not all along supposed to

[1] [Taken from *Selections from the Family Papers Preserved at Caldwell* (Glasgow 1854), VOL. I, 93–107. The bulk of this letter concerns Hume's argument in the essay "Of the Balance of Trade", which, apparently together with other of the economic essays, Oswald had seen in manuscript. The letter is very long and as much of it appears to be rather repetitious and deals in detail with some points which Hume's reply gives only brief attention, it has been substantially abridged. Omitted portions appearing to require attention are noted below.—ED.]

be affected by the greater plenty or scarcity of money, which circumstances alone are respectively supposed to direct the different states of the balance, in the same infallible manner as gravity directs all communicating fluids to their level. . . .

Your argument seems to be this : The price of all things, depending necessarily on their quantity and the quantity of money to purchase them, alters the quantity of money, whether by increasing or diminishing it, and the price of all things is altered in the same proportion. An overbalance in trade is only acquired, and can only be preserved, by the low price of labour and commoditys. Whenever, therefore, the overbalance creates a greater quantity of money in any one countrey than is in the neighbouring countreys, and consequently raises the price of labour and commoditys, the balance will turn in favour of the others. . . . Now this proposition is so far from being universally true, that in any countrey which has a free communication with its neighbours, it is, I think evidently false. For, in such a countrey, suppose the quantity of money to be annihilated in any given proportion, it will not necessarily follow that the price of all labour and commoditys will sink in the same proportion ; because these objects, not being confined to the mere quantity of money in that countrey, may, and, unless obstructions of a foreign nation interfered, necessarily would be purchased by money of other neighbouring countreys with which there is a supposed communication, and where a like diminution of money had not taken place.

The same consequence will plainly follow on a miraculous augmentation of the quantity of money in any countrey, under the like circumstances of communication : . . . The increased quantity of money would not necessarily increase the price of all labour and commoditys ; because the increased quantity, not being confined to the home labour and commoditys, might, and certainly would, be sent to purchase both from foreign countreys, which importation, unless obstructed by arbitrary and absurd laws, would keep down the price of commoditys to the level of foreign countreys [1] ; and if the price of labour still continued for a short time at a higher rate than that level, it would only serve, by attracting foreigners, to increase the number of useful inhabitants in proportion to the increased quantity of money. . . .

. . . it does not therefore follow that the quantity of money either is the same, or naturally will become the same, in all such countreys [2] ; because the cultivation and population of the one may increase, and naturally will increase, while the cultivation and population of the other may diminish.

When effects are considered in the order as they happen, this, I think will appear plain, and be further confirmed from universal experience, where unnatural or artificial obstructions are not interposed, and even receive an additional confirmation in those cases where such obstructions are interposed. Let your own supposition be taken for a moment : "That the money of Gt. Britain was multiply'd fourfold in one night" ; let it be further supposed, as the first effect, that all labour "and commoditys should rise four times in their price" ; what would be the further consequence ? 'Tis evident, on the one hand, while this situation lasted, that no commoditys or labour could be exported from Britain, and consequently none of its necessarys of life, materials of manufacture, or even manufacturers, labourers, or other such people. But, say you, all things would be imported from the neighbour countreys, notwithstanding the severest laws to the contrary, which is certainly true. But would not the necessarys of life and materials of manufacture imported at low prices necessarily reduce the price of labour and

---

[1] [Cf. above, p. lvi *n*.—ED.]

[2] [It was probably this which prompted Hume's footnote in the essay "Of the Balance of Trade". Cf. above, p. 66*n*.—ED.]

commodities ? Would not a very small proportion, and consequently, a very small quantity of the increased money exported suffice for this purpose ? Would there not in this interval be the greatest possible encouragement for cultivation at home, and a flowing in of inhabitants from abroad, to enjoy the high price of labour while it lasted—and even the level price, after it was reduced to it—amidst such a constant demand and such plenty of necessarys, as plenty of money, which, in other words, is nothing but a representative of plenty, would constantly preserve ? And might not such a countrcy, (preserving even a greater quantity of money than its neighbours,) by such superabundant quantity of necessarys and materials produced or imported, be enabled still to preserve the level price of labour and commoditys, and consequently be not only the manufacturer but the storehouse of the world ? There seem to me to be no natural causes whatever, no more than a plenty of money, which could prevent this. . . .[1]

But to return to the question you ask : how is the balance kept in the provinces of every kingdom, but by the force of this principle, which makes it impossible for money to lose its level, and either to rise or sink beyond the proportion of the labour and commoditys that is in each province ? But if the balance was kept in the manner you suppose, would it not necessarily occasion a constant

---

[1] [Cf. above, p. lxvi. Following the above passage there appears a discussion of several pages which deals with the manner in which "artificial causes" (such as internal taxes, and prohibitions both on the import of goods and the export of specie) undermine the beneficial effects of an influx of specie on home industry. Several pages are also devoted to the cases of Spain and China (which Hume had cited in his essay) to illustrate the point, made above, that it is primarily the relation of the quantity of money to the level of industry, and not the former alone, which is important in explaining international specie flows. In passing it is said that Spain developed its industry "in a much greater degree than is generally imagined". With regard to China it is argued that if distances were diminished "China . . . instead of draining the nations of Europe of their specie [as Hume had argued] would soon find itself drained of its cheap necessarys of life and materials of manufacture . . ." These seem to be the points which occasioned Hume's references to the cases of China and Spain in his reply presented below.—Ed.]

reciprocal drain betwixt the Capital and the distant provinces, and a constant fluctuation of price in all labour and commoditys ? Is any such thing observed to happen ? The Capital has a constant balance in its favour. There, most kinds of labour and commoditys are constantly dearer than in the provinces, and a plenty of money always greater. But these effects continue constant and without variation. The only difference observable is that the Capital goes on constantly increasing in its number of inhabitants, its buildings, arts, industry, and cultivation, notwithstanding this difference in the price of labour and commoditys ; for a difference there is, tho' not so great as is generally imagined.

The case, I presume, would be precisely the same with a countrey which should have a constant balance in its favour against the neighbouring nations of Europe, and with a rich trading Capital and its own provinces. . . . The advantages of a rich countrey in this respect, compared with the disadvantages of a poor one, are almost infinite, and all infallibly take place, after a free communication of the necessarys of life and materials of manufacture, and an easy settlement of new inhabitants, are established.[1] A countrey in this situation would, in some measure, be the capital of the world, while all neighbour countreys would, in respect of its advantages, tho' not of their own, be as its provinces. Neighbour countreys could not throw in such obstructions in its way, unless it co-operated with them, as to prevent it from having all the necessarys of life, materials of manufacture, labourers, and, consequently, labour, as cheap as with them, together with a balance of treasure arising in its favour ; and, notwithstanding this last circumstance, it would soon appear, that, under favour of the others, it could make up manufactures cheaper than in any other

---

[1] [Here and in the remarks of the following two paragraphs Oswald may have had in mind Hume's treatment of the relations between rich and poor countries in the essay "Of Money", above, pp. 34–5.—ED.]

part of the world. Poor countreys, with cheap necessarys,
some cheap materials, and even cheap labour in some
things, do not always, nay, seldom do, and but in a few
cases, work up manufactures so cheaply as in the provinces
of a rich countrey, and, what is most surprising, as even
in its capital. The reasons are obvious : the materials
of all manufactures are various, and poor countreys, while
they have some cheap, have frequently most part dearer
than in wealthy countreys ; which have or may have all
(witness Holland), att the constant lowest level of their
neighbours.

Poor countreys have no greater constancy in the
demand for their manufactures than in the price of their
materials. They have rich foreign stores only for a
market, while wealthy countreys have their own consumption besides ; and though this quick demand, in the
first instance, tends to raise the rate of wages, yet, as it is
corrected by the attraction of new inhabitants, it only
produces permanently that good effect, while the want of
it in poor countreys destroys the manufactures themselves,
and sends out the manufacturers. Poor countreys are
ever at a great loss in the article of cheap necessarys, by
means of their little cultivation, which every now and
then renders the price of them dearer than in rich
countreys—a circumstance which the manufacturers of
such poor countreys cannot long support ; while rich
countreys, on the other hand, by the variety of their
cultivation, are rarely subject to such accidents, and are
easily supplied att the level rate. . . .

As to the paper money of Britain consisting in its debts,
it is certainly attended with a very bad consequence, viz.
the necessity of raising, by taxes, such a quantity of
money as to satisfy the stipulated annuity attending it.
But I am not of opinion that it has any of the bad consequences you further ascribe to it.[1] Such papers, like all

---

[1] [It would appear that in this paragraph Oswald is referring to Hume's
argument in the essay "Of Public Credit", above, pp. 95 ff.—ED.]

other mortgages whatever, are only marks that such a quantity of money of a countrey, distributed into different hands, does really belong to the holders of the paper in the manner therein expressed ; and in no sense is paper made equivalent to money, but as it represents it with a perfect reality and full effect. . . . Such paper money will be found, I fancy, upon examination, neither to raise nor diminish the price of labour and commoditys, but in proportion as the taxes which are raised to pay the annuity raise the price of labour and commoditys, which they certainly do most perniciously. Such paper money will be found to have as good effect in foreign transactions as any gold and silver whatever . . . while its annuity is pay'd or obligations comply'd with ; . . . and those who are possessed of it . . . may, every day, if they chuse it, have as great quantitys of goods from abroad in return for it as the quantity of money it represents. . . .

I am at a loss to understand how you can ascribe the great quantity of bullion in France to the want of proper credit. Surely the government securitys of France consist of a much larger capital, and are attended with a much greater annuity than those of Britain. They are not so circulating or not so easily transfered ; they are therefore not so saleable, and do not so truly represent what they are intended for. This is all the difference I can see : for saleable and transferable they still are, tho' with greater difficulty ; and consequently are so far paper credit still. . . . As to the paper money of the colonys, 'tis all a cheat, and, like all other cheats, has been attended with very bad consequences . . . those nominal pounds have altered in their value, and diminished in proportion as the paper increased. According as such nominal pounds procure labour and commoditys in the countrey, and according as the state of their trade is with the mother countrey, the relation betwixt them and sterling alters— the rate of exchange against them increases ; as it always will do in proportion to this uncertainty.

HUME TO OSWALD

1 November 1750 [1]

. . . I confess I was a little displeased with you for neglecting me so long ; but you have made ample compensation. This commerce, I find, is of advantage to both of us ; to me, by the new lights you communicate, and to you, by giving you occasion to examine these subjects more accurately. I shall here deliver my opinion of your reasonings with the freedom which you deserve.

I never meant to say that money, in all countries which communicate, must necessarily be on a level, but only on a level proportioned to their people, industry, and commodities. That is, where there is double people, &c. there will be double money, and so on ; and that the only way of keeping or increasing money is, by keeping and increasing the people and industry ; not by prohibitions of exporting money, or by taxes on commodities, the methods commonly thought of. I believe we differ little on this head. You allow, that if all the money in England were increased four-fold in one night, there would be a sudden rise of prices ; but then, say you, the importation of foreign commodities would soon lower the prices. Here, then, is the flowing out of the money already begun. But, say you, a small part of this stock of money would suffice to buy foreign commodities, and lower the prices. I grant it would for one year, till the imported commodities be consumed. But must not the same thing be renewed next year ? No, say you ; the additional stock of money may, in this interval, so increase the people and industry, as to enable them to retain their money. Here I am extremely pleased with your reasoning. I agree with you, that the increase of money, if not too sudden,

[1] [Taken from Greig, *op. cit.*, I, 142-4.—Ed.]

naturally increases people and industry, and by that means may retain itself ; but if it do not produce such an increase, nothing will retain it except hoarding. Suppose twenty millions brought into Scotland ; suppose that, by some fatality, we take no advantage of this to augment our industry or people, how much would remain in the quarter of a century ? Not a shilling more than we have at present. My expression in the Essay needs correction, which has occasioned you to mistake it.

Your enumeration of the advantages of rich countries above poor, in point of trade, is very just and curious ; but I cannot agree with you that, barring ill policy or accidents, the former might proceed gaining upon the latter for ever. The growth of every thing, both in arts and nature, at last checks itself. The rich country would acquire and retain all the manufactures, that require great stock or great skill ; but the poor country would gain from it all the simpler and more laborious. The manufactures of London, you know, are steel, lace, silk, books, coaches, watches, furniture, fashions. But the outlying provinces have the linen and woollen trades.

The distance of China is a physical impediment to the communication, by reducing our commerce to a few commodities ; and by heightening the price of these commodities, on account of the long voyage, the monopolies and the taxes. A Chinese works for three-halfpence a day, and is very industrious. Were he as near us as France or Spain, every thing we use would be Chinese, till money and prices came to a level ; that is, to such a level as is proportioned to the numbers of people, industry, and commodities of both countries.

A part of our public funds serve in places of money ; for our merchants, but still more our bankers, keep less cash by them when they have stock, because they can dispose of that upon any sudden demand. This is not the case with the French funds. The *rentes* of the Hotel de Ville are not transferable, but are most of them entailed in the families. At least, I know there is a great difference in this respect betwixt them and the *actions* of the Indian company.

That the industry and people of Spain, after the discovery of the West Indies, at first increased more than is commonly imagined, is a very curious fact; and I doubt not but you say so upon good authority, though I have not met with that observation in any author.

Besides the bad effect of the paper credit in our Colonies, as it was a cheat, it must also be allowed that it banished gold and silver, by supplying their place. On the whole, my intention in the Essay was both to remove people's errors, who are apt, from chimerical calculations, to imagine they are losing their specie, though they can show in no instance that either their people or industry diminish; and also to expose the absurdity of guarding money otherwise than by watching over the people and their industry, and preserving or increasing them. To prohibit the exportation of money, or the importation of commodities, is mistaken policy; and I have the pleasure of seeing you agree with me.

I have no more to say but compliments; and therefore shall conclude.

HUME TO LORD KAMES

4 March 1758 [1]

. . . I am very much obliged to you for allowing me a reading of Mr. Tucker's [2] papers; in all that gentleman's

[1] [Taken from Greig, *op. cit.*, 1, 270-2.—Ed.]

[2] [This and the following letters contain Hume's discussion with Josiah Tucker (1712-99). This letter deals with Tucker's criticism of Hume's position on the relation between poor and rich countries which had appeared in the essay "Of Money". Cf. above, pp. 33-46. For some reason Lord Kames acted as the intermediary in the discussion. Tucker's earlier correspondence does not seem to be on record (and one is also left to speculate on the full scope of the subjects covered by the "papers" referred to by Hume). However, in his later *Four Tracts on Political and*

productions, which have come to my hand, I can perceive a profound knowledge of the theory of commerce, joined to an enlarged acquaintance with its practice ; and I own I have received both pleasure and instruction from the perusal of them. The papers which your Lordship has been pleased to communicate to me, do not belie this character. All the advantages which the author insists upon as belonging to a nation of extensive commerce, are undoubtedly real : great capital, extensive correspondence, skilful expedients of facilitating labour, dexterity, industry, &c., these circumstances give them an undisputed superiority over poor nations, who are ignorant and unexperienced.[1] The question is, whether these advantages can go on, increasing trade *in infinitum*, or whether they do not at last come to a *ne plus ultra*, and check themselves, by begetting disadvantages, which at first retard, and at last finally stop their progress. Among these disadvantages, we may reckon the dear price of provisions and labour, which enables the poorer country to rival them, first in the coarser manufactures, and then in those which are more elaborate. Were it otherwise, commerce, if not dissipated by violent conquests, would go on perpetually increasing, and one spot of the globe would engross the art and industry of the whole. I am

---

[1] [In the excellence of its analysis, Tucker's final statement of this portion of his position is worthy of attention in its own right. Cf. his *Four Tracts*, pp. 30 ff. It should also be noted that in this connexion Tucker proposes a plan of assistance which England might undertake with regard to relatively underdeveloped Scotland, which, in essential particulars, resembles the current programmes of assistance to underdeveloped areas. Cf. *ibid.*, p. 42.—ED.]

Commercial Subjects (Gloucester 1774) Tucker presented his version of the entire argument with Hume. From this it is clear that he had been led to question Hume's position because, as it implied that the rich country could preserve its gains only by conquering the poor, it rendered the "Rule of national self-preservation . . . inconsistent with the Principle of universal Benevolence" (p. 20). However, Tucker's first statement seemed to have been devoted entirely to supporting the equally unbenevolent view that the wealthy country could expand indefinitely at the expense of the poor. It is mainly to this that Hume's letter is addressed.

pleased when I find the author insist on the advantages of England, and prognosticate thence the continuance and even further progress of the opulence of that country ; but I still indulge myself in the hopes that we in Scotland possess also some advantages, which may enable us to share with them in wealth and industry. It is certain that the simpler kind of industry ought first to be attempted in a country like ours. The finest arts will flourish best in the capital : those of next value in the more opulent provinces · the coarser in the remote countries. The carriage of provisions to the capital is a tax upon them ; and a great many of them are of such a nature as cannot at all be transported. It is then great encouragement to settle in the countries where they are produced ; and tho a rich country, by its other advantages, may long maintain its ground against a poorer, which makes attempts towards commerce, it will not be able entirely to annihilate or oppress it.

The author, conformable to the character both of a divine and a philosopher, draws an argument from the goodness of Providence ; but I think it may be turned against him. It was never surely the intention of Providence, that any one nation should be a monopolizer of wealth : and the growth of all bodies, artificial as well as natural, is stopped by internal causes, derived from their enormous size and greatness. Great empires, great cities, great commerce, all of them receive a check, not from accidental events, but necessary principles.

There is a hint thrown out in the papers, which gave me great satisfaction, because it concurs with a principle which I have thrown out to your Lordship, and which you seemed not to disapprove of. I was indeed so pleased with it, that, as I told you, I intended to make it the subject of a political discourse, as soon as I should have occasion to give a new edition of that work.[1] My principle

[1] [Later in 1758 Hume published his essay "Of the Jealousy of Trade", which treated the said "principle". Cf. above, pp. 78–82.—Ed.]

is levelled against the narrow malignity and envy of nations, which can never bear to see their neighbours thriving, but continually repine at any new efforts towards industry made by any other nation. We desire, and seem by our absurd politics to endeavour to repress trade in all our neighbours, and would be glad that all Europe were reduced to the same state of desolation as Turkey : the consequence of which must be, that we would have little more than domestic trade, and would have nobody either to sell or buy from us. I remember, that in a conversation on this head with your Lordship, I asked whether a man who opened a shop in Tartary was likely to meet with many customers. This narrow spirit of nations, as well as individuals, ought carefully to be repressed ; and I am glad to find that Mr. Tucker is likely to employ his talents and abilities in so useful a manner.

TUCKER TO LORD KAMES

6 July 1758 [1]

. . . I beg my respectful compliments to Mr David Hume, with thanks for his ingenious animadversions. They are very plausible and well urged ; but fall short of conviction : And I must observe in general upon this argument, both to your Lordship and Mr Hume, That as you allow all the matter of fact, viz. That the rich industrious country doth sell all manner of *complete* manufactures cheaper than the poor industrious country, it is of little consequence to the main of the argument, whether I can rightly account for this phænomenon or not. Be it, that I am mistaken, yet the matter of fact is the same : and while that holds good—and no one

---

[1] [Taken from A. F. T. Woodhouselee, *Memoirs of the Life and Writings of the Honourable Henry Home of Kames* (Edinburgh 1807), II, App. 4–6.—ED.]

exception can be brought against it in all history—my
general position must be right, though my method of
accounting for it may be judged unsatisfactory. If such
is the effect, a cause there must be ; though I may have
assigned a wrong one.

As to the phrase of a country increasing in commerce
and manufactures *ad infinitum* ; I except against the term ;
and would not choose that my poor *finite* understanding
should be involved in disquisitions about *infinites*. It is
sufficient for this purpose to say, That the progress would
be indefinite : for I apprehend, no man can mark out
the limits, or reasonably affirm, "*Hitherto* shall an industrious and moral nation increase in the quantity of their
manufactures, the numbers of their people, and stock of
wealth, and *no farther*".[1]

In regard to the monopoly which the rich country
would thus acquire over a poor one, in the sale of its
manufactures, the fact must be acknowledged ; but the
consequences supposed to result from it, may be obviated
to such a degree, as to prevent any dangers arising from
it. True it is, that *caeteris paribus*, the rich industrious
country would always undersell the poor one ; and by
that means attract the trade of all poorer countries to
itself ;—but it is equally true, that if either of these poor
countries hath any *peculiar* produce of its own, it may
prohibit its exportation till it be wrought up into a
complete manufacture. It is true likewise, that all of
them have it in their power to load the manufactures of
the rich country upon entering their territories, with such
high duties as shall turn the scale in favour of their own
manufactures, or of the manufactures of some other
nation, whose progress in trade they have less cause to
fear, or envy. Thus it is, in my poor apprehension, that

[1] [In his *Four Tracts* (p. 56) Tucker rejects Hume's analogical argument
to the effect that "great commerce", as all things in nature, ultimately
undermines itself by growing over-large. Unlike natural bodies, he contends, society is a teleological entity and thus can take steps to correct the
undermining forces.—ED.]

the rich may be prevented from swallowing up the poor ; at the same time, and by the same methods, that the poor are stimulated and excited to emulate the rich.[1]

The last objection of Mr Hume's was, That as the poorer country, by having wages and raw materials cheaper, would certainly undersell the rich one in the coarse and more imperfect manufactures, so likewise it would from thence gradually ascend to others, till at last it equalled, and perhaps exceeded the rich country in every thing. But, with deference to Mr Hume, I would beg him to reconsider this argument. The point he builds upon, is the cheapness of wages and of raw materials : But will the wages and raw materials remain still at the same low price, after the country is become so much the richer than it was before ? Surely not : Surely they will advance in price, in proportion to the advancement of every thing else. And therefore the grand advantage which he supposes the poor country to have over the rich, in point of cheapness of wages, and of raw materials, will

---

[1] [In his *Four Tracts* Tucker argues more fully that the growth of the rich country need not occur at the expense of the poor and (though he again incongruously counsels the possible desirability of protection), he stresses the mutually self-sustaining nature of international economic growth (pp. 51-2). Among other points he emphasises two arguments which play a key role in Hume's essay "Of the Jealousy of Trade" (where Hume abandons his earlier position on the relations of poor and rich countries) : the relation between the growth of foreign income and the demand for home exports, and the general role of international factor heterogeneity (cf. above, p. 79). Tucker took credit for converting Hume (cf. *Four Tracts*, p. vii). This appears to be justified, within limits. Apparently Tucker enabled Hume to overcome the barrier of his initial thinking on the question of poor country and rich country, and the discussion helped him to see and better organise the implications of other parts of his own position, which already contained much of the basis of his general free-trade argument, including elements paralleling Tucker's. Though in a different way, international factor heterogeneity is stressed in the essay "Of the Balance of Trade" ; and in his letter to Lord Kames, in which early in the discussion he states his intention to publish a full defence of free trade, Hume indicates he had earlier arrived at an understanding of the argument concerning the relation between income and demand. Cf. above, pp. 201-2.—ED.]

grow less and less every day. In short, though both
countries may still go on in their respective improvements,
the poor country, according to my apprehension, can
never overtake the rich, unless it be through the fault and
mismanagement of the latter.

TURGOT TO HUME

23 July 1766 [1]

. . . I am tempted at the same time to send you a trifle
of a very different kind ; it is the programme of an
academic Prize which I have decided to submit on a
subject which we have sometimes argued about.[2] The
best way of solving this problem, like all others, is to
have it discussed in public. I have tried to set forth
clearly the problem and the different aspects under which
one can consider it. I would very much hope that you
will have the time to give us your ideas on it. We should
accept your contributions even though they were in
English. Our liberal philosophers, followers of Quesnay,[3]
strongly support the system of their master. It is a
system from which English writers are quite removed
today ; and it is too difficult to reconcile its principles
with the ambition to monopolise the commerce of the
world, to hope that they will adopt it soon. It would,
therefore, be very desirable that Mr Pitt, and all those
who lead nations, should think like Quesnay on all
points. I am very much afraid that your famous dema-

---

[1] [Taken from *Oeuvres de Turgot*, ed. Gustave Schelle (Paris 1914), II,
495–6, and translated from the French.—ED.]

[2] [The shifting and incidence of taxes. There does not appear to be
any earlier recorded correspondence on the question, and possibly earlier
discussion took place during personal meetings between the two. When
this was sent Hume had already published his essay "Of Taxes" dealing
with this subject. Cf. above, pp. 83–9.—ED.]

[3] [Now known as the "physiocrats".—ED.]

gogue follows very different principles and believes himself interested in preserving in your nation the prejudices that you have called *Jealousy of Trade*. It would be a great misfortune for the two nations. I think, however, that there is an equal tiring on both parts for this madness to last much longer. One must hope that this [madness] will not develop and that peace will permit you to carry out the promises that you have made to your friends in this country, to come back to see them.

HUME TO TURGOT

5 August 1766 [1]

. . . I approve . . . very much of your Premium ; but why limit so much the Discourse of the Memorialists by taking it for granted as a certain Truth, that all Taxes fall upon the Proprietors of Land ? You know, that no Government in any Age or any Country of the World, ever went upon that Supposition : Taxes have always been supposed to rest upon those who pay them by consuming the Commodity ; and this universal Practice joined to the obvious Appearances of things leaves at least room for Doubt. Perhaps it would not have been amiss to have proposed the Question itself as an Object of Dispute.

TURGOT TO HUME

7 September 1766 [2]

. . . I do not know why you thought that those who would maintain that indirect taxation is favourable to landowners would be excluded from participating in my

[1] Taken from Greig, *op cit.*, II, 76.
[2] [Taken from *Oeuvres de Turgot*, II, 502–3 and translated from the French.—ED.]

contest. I assure you that if you wish to give us an essay in which the question is treated from this point of view, it will be very well received. It is true that the explanations seem to direct authors to view it in a different light. But as a matter of fact I have set up this competition rather in order to encourage working on an appreciation of the effects of indirect taxation, an evaluation which is still uncertain for me with regard to the quota, than to have the general question treated, upon which I have complete convictions.

I have said that it is agreed that indirect taxation fell entirely on landowners, because in effect I thought that the largest part of those who defend indirect taxation for other reasons, would agree, especially for the last fifteen to twenty years, and because the majority of people with whom I had occasion to converse on this matter agreed. I know very well that the practice of all governments does not at all conform to this principle ; but you know as well as I that the principles practiced by all governments do not change as easily as speculative principles. The financial system of all peoples was formed at times when there was little reflection on such matters ; and even if one were convinced that such a system was established on ruinous foundations, one would still have much trouble and it would take much time to upset a completely established system, and to substitute another for it. You also know as well as I do what is the great end of all governments on earth : submission and money. The object is, as they say, to pluck the bird without making it squeal ; now it is the proprietors who are squealing, and one has always preferred to attack them indirectly, because then they notice the harm only when the thing has become an accepted fact, and besides, there is not enough information, nor have the principles been quite clearly demonstrated, for them to attribute the harm which they suffer to its true cause.

HUME TO TURGOT

[Late September 1766 [1]]

. . . Tho' you must be tired too of my Letter, I am tempted to say a Word to the political Question, which has been often agitated between us, viz the Method of laying on Taxes, Whether it is better to impose them on landed Possessions or on Consumptions. You will own, that, as the public Revenue is employ'd for the Defence of the whole Community, it is more equitable to levy it from the whole ; but you say, that this is impracticable : It will fall on the Land at last ; and it is better to lay it on there directly. You suppose then that the Labourers always raise the Price of their Labour in proportion to the Taxes. But this is contrary to Experience. Labour is dearer in Neuf-chatel and other parts of Swisserland, where there are no Taxes, than in the neighbouring Provinces of France, where there are a great many. There are almost no Taxes on the English Colonies ; yet Labour is three times dearer there than in any Country of Europe. There are great Taxes on Consumptions in Holland, but the Republic possesses no Land, on which they can fall. The Price of Labour will always depend on the Quantity of Labour and the Quantity of Demand ; not on the Taxes.[2] The Tradesmen who work in Cloath, that is exported, cannot raise the Price of their Labour ; because in that Case the Price of the Cloath wou'd become too dear to be sold in foreign Markets : Neither can the Tradesmen who work in Cloath for home Consumption raise their Prices ; since there cannot be two Prices for the same Species of Labour. This extends to

---

[1] [Taken from Greig, *op. cit.*, II, 93–5.—ED.]

[2] [The arguments following represent a restatement and further elaboration of points which appear in the essay "Of Taxes". Cf. above, pp. 86–8.—ED.]

all Commodities of which there is any part exported, that is, to almost every Commodity. Even were there some Commodities of which no part is exported, the Price of Labour employ'd in them, cou'd not rise ; for this high Price wou'd tempt so many hands to go into that Species of Industry as must immediatly [*sic*] bring down the Prices.   It appears to me that where a Tax is laid on Consumption, the immediate Consequence is that either the Tradesmen consume less or work more.   No Man is so industrious but he may add some Hours more in the Week to his Labour : And scarce any one is so poor but he can retrench something of his Expence.   What happens when the Corn rises in its Prices ?   Do not the poor both live worse and labour more ?   A Tax has the same effect. I beg you also to consider, that, besides the Proprietors of Land and the labouring Poor, there is in every civilised Community a very large and a very opulent Body who employ their Stocks in Commerce and who enjoy a great Revenue from their giving Labour to the poorer sort.   I am perswaded that in France and England the Revenue of this kind is much greater than that which arises from Land :   For besides Merchants, properly speaking, I comprehend in this Class all Shop-Keepers and Master-Tradesmen of every Species.   Now it is very just, that these shoud pay for the Support of the Community, which can only be where Taxes are lay'd on Consumptions.   There seems to me no Pretence for saying that this order of Men are necessitated to throw their Taxes on the Proprietors of Land, since their Profits and Income can surely bear Retrenchment. . . .

TURGOT TO HUME

25 March 1767 [1]

. . . I would very much have liked to enter into some
detail on the question of the tax ; but to answer your
objections, I would have, so to speak, to write a book
and deserve my own prize. I only want to indicate to
you the position from which I start and which I think
is incontestable ; that is there is no other revenue possible
in a state but the annual production of the earth ; that the
total production is divided into two parts : the first,
connected with the reproduction of the following year
and which consists not only of the part of the fruits which
the growers consume in kind, but in addition all that they
use to pay workers of all kinds who work for them : black-
smiths, wheelrights, barrelmakers, weavers, woodcutters,
etc. ; it also includes their profits and interest on their
loans. The other part is the net profit which the farmer
turns over to the proprietor, whenever the latter is a
different person, which is not always the case ; the
proprietor uses it to pay all who work for him. This
understood, the tax which is not borne by the proprietor
directly must necessarily fall, either upon the wage-
earners who live on the net product, or upon those whose
labour is paid out of the farmer's share. If the wage has
been reduced by competition to its precise level, it must
be raised ; and, since it cannot be raised except at the
expense of those who pay, a part falls back on the proprietor
for the expenditures which he makes from his net product ;
the other part increases the espenditure of the farmers,
who are thereby compelled to give less to the proprietor.
In any case, it is the proprietor who pays.

---

[1] [Taken from *Oeuvres de Turgot*, II, 662-5 and translated from the
French.—Ed.]

You say that I assume that wages increase in proportion to taxes, and that experience proves the falseness of this principle ; and you observe correctly that it is not higher or lower taxes that determine the wage-level, but solely the relationship of supply and demand.

Certainly this principle has never been contested ; it is the only principle which immediately sets the price level of everything which has value in trade. But we must distinguish two kinds of price level : the *current price*, which is established by the relationship of supply and demand, and the *fundamental price*, which for a piece of merchandise is what the item costs the artisan. For the wage of the artisan, the fundamental price is the cost of his subsistence. We cannot tax the wage-earner without increasing the cost of his subsistence, since the tax must be added to his former expenses. We therefore are increasing the fundamental price of labour. Now, although the fundamental price is not the immediate basis of the current value, it is nevertheless a minimum beneath which the latter cannot sink. For, if a merchant suffers loss on his merchandise, he stops selling or manufacturing ; if an artisan is unable to live from his labour, he becomes a beggar or leaves the country. That is not all : the artisan must make a certain profit, to take care of contingencies, to bring up his family. In a country where trade and industry are free and active, competition sets this profit at the lowest rate possible. There is established a kind of balance between the value of all the products of the land, the consumption of different kinds of supplies, different kinds of manufactured goods, the number of men employed and their wage-scale.

Wages cannot even be fixed and remain constantly at a certain level, except by virtue of this balance and the influence that all parts of society, all branches of production and trade have on each other. That established, if we increase one of the weights, it is inevitable that there will result a movement in the entire machine which will tend to re-establish the former balance. The ratio of the current value of wages to their fundamental value was established by the laws of this balance, and by the combination of all the circumstances in which all parts of society found themselves.

You increase the fundamental value : the circumstances which previously fixed the ratio of the current value to this fundamental value must bring up the current value to the point where the ratio is re-established. I know that this effect will not be sudden, and that in every complicated machine there is friction which slows up the effects which are theoretically demonstrated to be most infallible. Even a perfectly homogeneous fluid reaches its level only after a certain time, but it always does reach its level in time. The same is true of the balance of the values that we are examining. The artisan, as you say, endeavours to work harder or consume less ; but all that is only temporary. There is doubtless no man who works as hard as he could work. But it is not natural, either, for men to work as hard as they could, just as it is not natural for a rope to be as taut as it can be. A degree of relaxation is necessary in every machine, or otherwise it would be in danger of breaking at every instant. This degree of relaxation in labour is fixed by a thousand causes which remain after taxation and, consequently, if by a first effort the tension did augment, things would soon resume their natural condition.

What I have said of increased labour, I also say of reduced consumption. The needs are always the same. That kind of superfluity, which one can if need be reduce, is still a necessary element in the normal subsistence of artisans and their families. Molière's miser said that, when there is enough dinner for five, a sixth can always find something to eat : but this reasoning, if carried a bit further, would soon arrive at absurdity. I shall add that reduction of consumption has another and a terrible effect on the proprietor's revenue, caused by the reduction in the value of foodstuffs and of the products of his land.[1]

I shall not go into detail about the objection concerning foreign commerce, which I cannot consider a very important subject in any country, except in so far as it contributes to the increase in land revenue, and which, moreover, cannot be taxed without causing it to diminish. But I am pressed for time, and I am obliged to conclude, although I should have much to say on the disadvantages of consumer taxes, the collection of which is a constant infringement on the citizens' freedom : it means searching them at the customs, entering their homes for subsidy claims [*les droits d'aides*] and excises, not to mention the horrors of smuggling and the lives of men sacrificed to the pecuniary interests of the tax authority : that is a fine lesson that legislation gives to highway robbers. . . .[2]

---

[1] [It is evident that this exchange did little to join, much less resolve, the issue, and this is reflected in Hume's exasperation with the physiocrats (cf. below, p. 215). Turgot ignores Hume's contention that surpluses are to be found in entrepreneurial returns and does not seem to recognise that the subsistence theory of wages involved a commitment to a particular theory of population growth which required justification.—ED.]

[2] [In a later letter to Hume (8 March 1768) Turgot writes concerning the outcome of his competition for an essay on taxation. He reports that he is not entirely satisfied with the one that received the prize, that another essay took much the same position as Hume did, and that while he is satisfied in "having stirred up the disputants, and thereby served the public", he would like to continue the debate with Hume. Cf. *Letters of Eminent Persons Addressed to David Hume*, ed. J. H. Burton (Edinburgh 1849), pp. 162–3. Hume apparently never did resume the argument, at least in writing. His last recorded communication to Turgot containing a reference to it calls attention to the position taken by Tucker whose works he was then sending Turgot. "You will see, that Dr. Tucker is no friend to the new Theory of Finances, which has made so many respectable Proselytes in France". Cf. Greig, *op. cit.*, II, 183.—ED.]

HUME TO MORELLET

10 July 1769 [1]

. . . That part of your prospectus,[2] in which you endeavour to prove that there enters nothing of human convention in the establishment of money, is certainly very
curious, and very elaborately cómposed ; and yet I cannot
forbear thinking that the common opinion has some
foundation. It is true, money must always be made of
some materials, which have intrinsic value, otherwise
it would be multiplied without end, and would sink to
nothing. But, when I take a shilling, I consider it not as
a useful metal, but as something which another will take
from me ; and the person who shall convert it into metal
is, probably, several millions of removes distant. You
know that all states have made it criminal to melt their
coin ; and, tho this is a law which cannot well be executed,
it is not to be supposed that, if it could, it would entirely
destroy the value of the money, according to your hypoth-
esis. You have a base coin, called billon, in France,
composed of silver and copper, which has a ready currency,
tho the separation of the two metals, and the reduction
of them to their primitive state, would, I am told, be
both expensive and troublesome. Our shillings and
sixpences, which are almost our only silver coin, are so
much worn by use, that they are twenty, thirty, or forty
per cent below their original value ; yet they pass currency
which can arise only from a tacit convention. Our

---

[1] [Taken from Greig, *op. cit.*, II, 204-5.—ED.]
[2] [Hume is referring to Morellet's prospectus of his *Dictionnaire du
commerce*. In a letter of 16 May 1769 Morellet had enclosed copies of this.
He had asked Hume to send these to several others (General Conway,
Adam Smith, William Robertson, Dean Tucker and Benjamin Franklin),
and to comment on the work. Cf. *Letters of Eminent Persons Addressed to
David Hume*, pp. 310–11.—ED.]

colonies in America, for want of specie, used to coin a
paper currency ; which were not bank notes, because
there was no place appointed to give money in exchange ;
yet this paper currency passed in all payments, by convention ; and might have gone on, had it not been
abused by the several assemblies, who issued paper without
end, and thereby discredited the currency.

You mention several kinds of money, sheep, oxen, fish,
employed as measures of exchange, or as money, in
different parts of the world You have overlooked that,
in our colony of Pennsylvania, the land itself, which is the
chief commodity, is coined, and passes in circulation.
The manner of conducting this affair is as follows :—A
planter, immediately after he purchases any land, can go
to a public office and receive notes to the amount of half
the value of his land ; which notes he employs in all
payments, and they circulate through the whole colony,
by convention. To prevent the public from being over-
whelmed by this fictitious money, there are two means
employed—first, the notes issued to any one planter, must
not exceed a certain sum, whatever may be the value of
his land : secondly, every planter is obliged to pay back
into the public office every year one tenth part of his
notes ; the whole, of course, is annihilated in ten years ;
after which, it is again allowed him to take out new notes
to half the value of his land. An account of this curious
operation would enrich your dictionary ; and you may
have a more particular detail of it, if you please, from
Dr Franklin, who will be in Paris about this time, and will
be glad to see you. I conveyed to him your prospectus,
and he expressed to me a great esteem of it.

I see that, in your prospectus, you take care not to
disoblige your economists,[1] by any declaration of your
sentiments ; in which I commend your prudence. But I
hope that in your work you will thunder them, and crush
them, and pound them, and reduce them to dust and

[1] [The eighteenth-century term for the physiocrats.—Ed.]

ashes ! They are, indeed, the set of men the most chimerical and most arrogant that now exist, since the annihilation of the Sorbonne. I ask your pardon for saying so, as I know you belong to that venerable body. I wonder what could engage our friend, M. Turgot, to herd among them ; I mean, among the economists ; tho I believe he was also a Sorbonnist. . . .

HUME TO ADAM SMITH

1 April 1776 [1]

. . . I am much pleas'd with your Performance [2] ; and the Perusal of it has taken me from a State of great Anxiety. It was a Work of so much Expectation, by yourself, by your Friends, and by the Public, that I trembled for its Appearance ; but am now much relieved. Not but that the Reading of it necessarily requires so much

---

[1] [Taken from Greig, *op. cit.*, II, 311–12.—ED.]

[2] [Smith's *Wealth of Nations*, which had been published on 9 March. There are many other letters between Hume and Smith on record. but—surprisingly, in view of their close friendship, and the many discussions they may be presumed to have had—these contain virtually no pointed reference to matters of an economic nature. In a mock-serious comment appearing in an earlier letter to Smith (dated 10 April 1767), it is possible that Hume is referring to economic among other matters when he says : "I am positive you are in the wrong in many of your Speculations, especially where you have the misfortune to differ from me". Greig, *op. cit.*, II, 207.

In another letter to Smith (dated 27 June 1772), after discussing the failure of several banks in Scotland and stating that "even the Bank of England is not entirely free from suspicion", Hume asks : "Do these Events anywise affect your Theory ? Or will it occasion the Revisal of any Chapters ? " He then concludes : "On the whole, I believe, that the Check given to our exorbitant and ill grounded Credit will prove of Advantage in the long run, as it will reduce people to more solid and less sanguine Projects, and at the same time introduce Frugality among the Merchants and Manufacturers : What say you ? Here is Food for your Speculation." *Op. cit.*, pp. 263–4. Cf. above, pp. 35, 68*n*. The failure of the banks is referred to in another letter to Smith, *op. cit.*, pp. 265–6. Hume further refers to *The Wealth of Nations*, in passing, *op. cit.*, pp. 214, 266, 308.—ED.]

Attention, and the Public is disposed to give so little, that I shall still doubt for some time of its being at first very popular. But it has Depth and Solidity and Acuteness, and is so much illustrated by curious Facts, that it must at last take the public Attention. It is probably much improved by your last Abode in London. If you were here at my Fireside, I shoud dispute some of your Principles. I cannot think, that the Rent of Farms makes any part of the Price of the Produce,[1] but that the Price is determined altogether by the Quantity and the Demand. It appears to me impossible, that the King of France can take a Seigniorage of 8 per cent upon the Coinage. No body would bring Bullion to the mint : It woud be all sent to Holland or England, where it might be coined and sent back to France for less than two per cent. Accordingly Neckre[2] says, that the French King takes only two per cent of Seigniorage. But these and a hundred other Points are fit only to be discussed in Conversation ; which, till you tell me the contrary, I shall still flatter myself with soon. I hope it will be soon : For I am in a very bad state of Health and cannot afford a long Delay. . . .

[1] [Hume is referring to Smith's contention that "the rent of land . . . makes a third component part" of the price of commodities. Cf. *Wealth of Nations*, BK. I, chap. vi, p. 49. As Greig observes, Hume's comment is notable for its anticipation of the Ricardian theory of rent.—ED.]

[2] [Jacques Neckre (1742–1804), minister of finance to Louis XVI and author of *Essai sur la législation et le commerce des grains* (1775).—ED.]

NOTE ON THE TEXT

HITHERTO the only critical edition of Hume's essays on economics has been that contained in the third volume of *The Philosophical Works of David Hume*, edited by T. H. Green and T. H. Grose. Published in 1875, this excellent edition has been out of print since 1918. It reproduces the text of the edition of 1777, which "though posthumously published was Hume's own definitive edition of his works" (Jessop). It also reports all substantive divergences from the final text occurring in the many editions published in Hume's lifetime.

The text of the essays printed in this volume is based on that of Green and Grose ; but theirs has been checked independently against the edition of 1777, and against those which preceded it. Like them, I have also indicated all apparently substantive changes in the successive editions. This I do partly by explicit statements and partly by means of two symbols : namely +, which indicates that the words that follow it are found in the editions cited, but not in subsequent editions ; and =, which indicates that the words following it are found in the editions cited, but are subsequently replaced by those printed at the beginning of that entry (and of course in the text itself).

In general, the spellings used in reporting variants are those found in the two earliest editions (*A*, *B*). Apart from this, however, I have followed Green and Grose, and have not tried to record such comparatively minor details as changes of spelling and punctuation in subsequent editions.

All the passages from Hume's own letters will be found in *The Letters of David Hume* (2 vols., Oxford 1932), edited by J. Y. T. Greig. All the translations are my own.

E. R.

INDEX

Action, desire for : and happiness, 21-2, xcv-xcix ; affects rate of interest, 50, 53-4, lxxix ; in Hume's economic psychology, xxxv-xliv, lii-liii ; and taxes, lxxxii.

agriculture : in economic growth, 5-6, 10-12, 49-52.

art and industry : see COMMERCE ; LUXURY.

association, principle of : xxvi, xlv-xlvi and n. See also SYMPATHY.

avarice : see GAIN, DESIRE FOR.

Bacon, Francis : 16.

balance of trade : between poor and rich countries, 34-5, 191-5, lviii-lx ; affected by hoarding, 36, 75 ; between trading nations generally, 56, 60-77, 188-9, lvi n ; affected by exchange rates, 64n ; Hume's discussion with Oswald on, 190-9 ; Hume's discussion with Tucker on, 199-205 ; in mercantilist doctrine, xiii-xiv, xxxii n ; historical perspective in Hume's treatment of, lv-lx. See also TARIFFS.

banks : development of, 70-1. See also CREDIT, BANK.

barter : see MONEY.

belief, Hume's doctrine of : xxvi-xxvii. See also EMPIRICISM.

Bentham, Jeremy : xlix.

Cantillon, Richard : lix n, lxiii n.

capital : see INTEREST RATES.

causality : see EMPIRICISM.

classical doctrines before Hume : summary of, xv-xvi.

commerce : generally enhances power of the state, 4-14, 23-4 ; contributes to happiness, 5-6, 10-14, 21-2, xcv-xcix ; motives underlying the growth of, 9-14 passim, 21-2, Introduction, chap. 2 ; and functions of the

merchant, 51-2 ; accompanied by growth of public debt, 93-4 ; stimulates population growth, 143-6. See also ECONOMIC GROWTH ; LUXURY.

consumption : promotes economic growth, 10-14, 93-4 ; stimulates employment, 30-1. See also PLEASURE, DESIRE FOR.

credit, bank · raises prices and induces specie-outflow, 35-6, 67-70, 72-3, 75, 95n, 199 ; jeopardises monetary solvency, 35, 68n ; promotes trade and economic growth, 70-1, lxvi n ; Montesquieu's views on, considered by Hume, 188-9 ; and Hume's interest theory, lxxi-lxxii. See also MONEY.

difficulty, effects of, on labour. See HARDSHIP.

economic growth : emphasis on, before Hume, xiii-xiv ; general place of, in Hume's economic thought, xvi-xxv, cv-cvi ; Hume's and Smith's treatment of, compared, cvi-cx. For Hume's treatment of, in specific major contexts, see BALANCE OF TRADE ; COMMERCE , FOREIGN TRADE ; FREE TRADE ; INTEREST RATES ; LUXURY ; MONEY ; POPULATION ; PUBLIC DEBT ; TAXES.

economic motives : self-interested nature of, 8-14, xxxiii ; and ingredients of happiness, 21-2, xcv-xcix ; effect of, on rate of interest, 49-54, lxix ; determine incidence of taxes, 83-5, lxxxii-lxxxiii ; and Hume's emphasis on psychology, xix-xxv ; as the basis for a science of economics, xxv-xxx ; and instincts, xlix-li ; for general analysis of Hume's treatment of, see Introduction,

Index

chap. 2; Hume's and Smith's treatment of, compared, cvi–cx. *See also* LABOUR.

economics, the scientific elements in : 3–4, xxvi–xxxi.

empiricism : in Hume's philosophical and economic thought, xxvi–xxxi.

employment : and expenditures on luxury, 30–1; stimulated by the quantity of money, 37–40, lxiii–lxv; effect of free trade on, 78–82, lxxvii–lxxviii; fluctuations of, affected by taxes, 99.

exchange rates : 64n.

exports : xxxiv. *See also* BALANCE OF TRADE; FOREIGN TRADE; FREE TRADE.

fiscal policy : *see* PUBLIC DEBT.

foreign trade : important in economic growth, 13–15, cvii, 34–5, xxxiv; unimportant in rich economies, 15–16. *See also* BALANCE OF TRADE; FREE TRADE.

free trade : desirable because of international factor heterogeneity, 66–7, 75–6, 79–80; Hume's modifications of his doctrine on, 76, lxxvi–lxxvii; effect of, on employment and economic growth, 78–82; and Hume's discussion with Tucker 199–205; Turgot's support of, 205–206; support of, before Hume, xv; the historical emphasis in Hume's treatment of, lxxii–lxxviii; in domestic markets, and the price mechanism, lxxviii–lxxxi.

frugality : enhanced by economic growth, 31n; reduces interest rates, 49–54, lxviii–lxix; and taxes, 85–7.

gain, desire for : importance of, in the growth of commerce, 13–14, xxx–xxxi; effect of, on expenditure patterns and interest rates, 53–4; in Hume's economic psychology, xliv–xlvii, li–liii.

Gee, Joshua : 61–2.

gold and silver : *see* MONEY.

government : improved by growth of industry, 17–18, 24–5, 28–9;

undermined by public debt, 95, 98–106 *passim*. *See also* COMMERCE; LIBERTY.

Greig, J. Y. T. : xix.

habit : 10–12, 21, xxviii, xliii, lii.

happiness : compatible with powerful state, 5–13 *passim*; enhanced by equality of income, 15, 128; ingredients of, 21–2; enhanced by economic growth, 21–2; contributes to population growth, 112; greater in small states, 128; Hume's views on, how related to classical philosophies, xcv–xcviii.

hardship : effect of, on labour, 17–18, 83–4, xli–xlii.

hedonism : and Hume's economic psychology, xlix–li.

history : general place of, in Hume's economic and philosophical thought, xxi–xxv; and Hume's methodology, xxvi–xxix; as a basis for a science of "politics" (economics), xxix–xxxi; and psychology, in Hume and Smith, cvi–cx. *See also* ECONOMIC GROWTH.

History of England : xxii, xxiii n.

hoarding : *see* BALANCE OF TRADE; MONEY.

Hobbes, Thomas : xix, xlvii n.

human behaviour, variability of : 5, xxviii–xxxi, xcii.

human nature, principles of : place of, in Hume's philosophical and economic thought, xix–xxv; reliability of, in a science of human experience, xxviii. *See also* ECONOMIC MOTIVES.

Hutcheson, Francis : on luxury, xii, ciii.

Hutchinson, Archibald : 102.

imitation : contributes to economic growth, 14, 78–9.

imports : xxxiv. *See also* BALANCE OF TRADE; FOREIGN TRADE; FREE TRADE.

incentives : *see* ECONOMIC MOTIVES.

income, equality of : promotes population growth, 9, 128–31; conducive to happiness, 15; increases tax revenues and state power, 15.

220

indolence : and happiness, 21–2, xcv–xcviii ; and dissipation, 50, 53, 85*n*, xiv–xv, xlviii–xlix.

Industrial Revolution : developments leading to, ix–xi.

industry. *See* ART AND INDUSTRY ; COMMERCE.

instinct : relation of, to Hume's economic psychology, xlix–li.

interest rates : monetary interpretations of, criticised, 47–9, 56–9 ; determined by supply and demand for savings, 49–54 ; a barometer of economic development, 55 ; related to rate of profit, 54 5 ; doctrines on, before Hume, xiv–xvi ; role of history and psychology in Hume's treatment of, lxvii–lxxii ; Hume's criticism of mercantilist view on, considered, lxx–lxxii.

international trade : *see* BALANCE OF TRADE ; FREE TRADE ; FOREIGN TRADE.

Johnson, E. A. J. : xvii *n*.

Kames, Henry Home, Lord : 199 and *n*.

labour : Hume's view of the effect of hardship on, 17–18, xli ; doctrines of mercantilists, xiv–xv ; doctrines of mercantilists and classical economists on, compared with Hume's, xlii–xliv. *See also* ECONOMIC MOTIVES ; WAGES.

liberal arts : encouraged by growth of commerce, 22, 24–5.

liberty : promotes public spirit, 8–9 ; not always found in wealthy economies, 16 ; enhanced by growth of commerce, 28–9 ; and equality of income and small political units, 28–9 ; undermined by public debt, 98–101 ; conducive to population growth, 128–31 ; must be balanced by authority, cii *n*. *See also* GOVERNMENT.

liveliness, desire for : and happiness, 21–2, xcv–xcix ; and rate of interest, 49–54 *passim*, lxviii–lxix ; in Hume's economic psychology, xlvii–xlix.

Locke, John : xix.

luxury : compatible with strong state, 4–14, 23–4 ; lack of in ancient republics, 7–8 ; British moralists' views on, 20, 31, xii, xciii, ciii–civ ; innocent, distinguished from vicious, 19–20 ; expenditures on, and employment, 30–1 ; contributes to happiness, 21–2, xcv–xcix ; promotes growth of liberal arts, 22 ; deepens sense of morality, 22–3, xcix–c ; conducive to improvement of government, 24–5, 27–8 ; does not undermine patriotism, 25–6 ; does not lead to venality, 26–7 ; and commerce, the foundation of liberty, 26–9 ; libertine view on, criticised, 30–2 ; Hume's treatment of, how related to his moral theory, xci–xciii ; role of psychology and history in Hume's treatment of, xciii–cii ; inadequacies in Hume's treatment of, cii–civ. *See also* COMMERCE.

Mandeville, Bernard : on luxury, 31, xii, xciii and *n*, civ.

manufactures : *see* COMMERCE ; ECONOMIC GROWTH.

Marshall, Alfred . xliv.

mercantilism, policies and doctrines of : summary of, xi, xiii–xv ; as related to Hume's (a) emphasis on economic growth, xvi–xvii, cv–cvi, (b) treatment of luxury, xxxii *n*, (c) treatment of effect of hardship on labour, xlii–xliii, (d) monetary theory, lv–lxvii *passim*, (e) interest theory, lxvii–lxxii *passim*, (f) free-trade doctrine, lxxii–lxxxi *passim*, (g) tax theory, lxxxi–lxxxiii ; internal inadequacies in Hume's criticisms of, lix, lxiv–lxvii, lxx–lxxii.

merchants : *see* COMMERCE.

money : and the power of the state, 33, 40–6 ; effect of quantity of, on prices (quantity theory), 33–7, 39, 41–2, 47–9, 68 ; effects of absolute quantity and changes in quantity of, distinguished, 37–40, 48, 68*n*, lxv *n* ; stimulates employment, 37–8, 40 ; stimu-